You Should Read This Book

◆ If you write fundraising letters for a hospital, a college or university, a museum, a health agency, a social service organization, or any nonprofit that needs funds.

◆ If you want to write letters that raise more money for your organization.

◆ If you serve in a leadership role in a nonprofit organization as executive director, development director, or marketing director.

◆ If you are a member of a nonprofit's board of directors and you want to measure the effectiveness of your fundraising appeals.

◆ If you're involved in public relations, advertising, or marketing for a nonprofit organization or institution.

◆ If you want to understand better how fundraising works.

◆ If you want to learn how to write to get results.

◆ If you want to be a more effective writer.

Also by Mal Warwick

Available from Strathmoor Press:

Technology and the Future of Fundraising (1994)

999 Tips, Trends and Guidelines for Successful Direct Mail and Telephone Fundraising (1993)

You Don't Always Get What You Ask For: Using Direct Mail Tests to Raise More Money for Your Organization (1992)

Revolution in the Mailbox: How Direct Mail Fundraising Is Changing the Face of American Society – And How Your Organization Can Benefit (1990)

How to Write Successful Fundraising Letters

MAL WARWICK

STRATHMOOR
PRESS

Berkeley, California

Printed in the United States of America.

ISBN 0-9624891-4-X

First printing March 1994. Second printing September 1994.

Published by Strathmoor Press, 2550 Ninth Street, Suite 1040, Berkeley, California 94710-2516, (510) 843-8888. Strathmoor Press is a subsidiary of Changing America, Inc.

Chapter 2, "The Cardinal Rules of Writing Fundraising Letters," is a much-expanded version of an article that previously appeared under a similar title in a number of publications, including *Fund Raising Management* magazine (January 1993) and my earlier book, *999 Tips, Trends and Guidelines for Successful Direct Mail and Telephone Fundraising* (Strathmoor Press, 1993).

An abbreviated version of Chapter 5, "Twenty-Three Reasons People Respond to Your Fundraising Appeals," appeared as a checklist of "18 Reasons" in *999 Tips, Trends and Guidelines*. A shorter version of the checklist in Chapter 16 was also published in *999 Tips, Trends & Guidelines for Successful Direct Mail & Telephone Fundraising*.

This book is dedicated to the thousands of fundraisers who labor day after day to raise the money that keeps good causes alive – and to the millions who respond to their appeals with generosity and goodwill.

CONTENTS

CONTENTS

PART TWO: CASE STUDIES

CONTENTS

INTRODUCTION

How This Book Came to Be, and What You'll Find Inside

If fundraising by mail is a science (a dubious proposition at best), its fuzziest, most inexact, *least* scientific aspect is writing the letters. There are those in the field who claim fundraising letters can be written by formula, but I'm not one of them. Writing this stuff is tough work, because what's effective for one charity may actually prove counter-productive for another. And what worked *last* year, or *last* time, may not work today.

The reality is that, for most of us mortals, writing of any sort is a royal pain in the neck.

But there are ways to reduce the fuzziness and the pain — and to raise the odds that your letters will bring in every nickel you need, and more. Talent helps, but experience counts for a lot, too.

Over the years I've read thousands of fundraising appeals. No, better make that *tens* of thousands! I've written or edited hundreds of those letters myself. And I've shared in the creative process as a manager or consultant in hundreds, perhaps thousands, of other mailings. All this has given me a front-row seat in a never-ending "copy clinic" — a close-up view of what works and what doesn't (and sometimes even why). This book is my attempt to convey what I've learned about writing fundraising letters.

In three of my previous books, I've explored other elements of fundraising by mail — from choosing mailing lists to working with consultants, from measuring results to designing and producing packages, from strategizing to scheduling. This book isn't about any of those things. It's about *writing*. My topic here is the effective use of written English in the pursuit of charitable gifts.

By an odd mix of circumstances, I seem to have pursued a career that's already varied enough for at least two people, probably three. I've written newspaper stories, magazine articles, science fiction stories, and comic book scripts; ads for newspapers, magazines, radio, and television; sales letters, brochures, and pamphlets; technical manuals; speeches for others and speeches for myself— not to mention all those fundraising letters, plus four previous books about the craft of raising money by mail and phone. I've written fiction and nonfiction, eulogies and humor, short pieces and long. I've written in three languages, and translated from one to another.

Yet, despite all this writing, I don't consider myself a particularly gifted writer. I'm no poet; my prose doesn't sing. I've written no unforgettable passage, contributed no timeless witticism to the language.

But through long practice and painful trial and error, I've learned to do one thing moderately well with my writing: *get results*. And there's just *one* result I want from this book: to help *you* write successful fundraising letters.

I want this book to be *useful* to you. It's intended as a guide to the techniques and approaches that have proved successful for me – a tool-chest of ideas and examples that will help you sharpen your own writing. If you prefer, look on it as a comprehensive review to help you gain perspective on the challenges you face as a writer of fundraising letters.

Oh, there's one more result I hope to achieve with this book: I want you to *enjoy* reading it. I've found I do best what I enjoy the most — while those things I approach with deadly seriousness are least likely to turn out well. I suspect you, too, will find that the more fun you have when you write your fundraising letters, the more money you'll raise.

How this book is organized

I've structured this book in three parts:

◆ Part One ("How to Write Successful Fundraising Letters") contains all the how-to material in ten chapters and can stand on its own. This part will teach you which rules of style and grammar to follow (and which ones to break) when you're writing to raise money. You'll learn a lot, too, about how people actually react when they read fundraising letters. And you'll become acquainted with the eight-step process I pursue when I set out to write a fundraising appeal.

◆ In Part Two ("Case Studies"), you'll find real-world examples of fundraising letters written to achieve seven different goals, with one chapter devoted to each. Some of the case studies include two versions of a letter — "Before" and "After" I edited it — and most of the examples include detailed comments.

◆ Part Three ("The Letter-Writer's Toolbox"), comprising three chapters, wraps up the story with a discussion about outer envelope "teasers" and a set of checklists to help you overcome writer's block. There's also a reading list, an index, and some other stuff publishers typically stick in the back of their books.

If you're looking for a general discussion about writing fundraising letters, you'll find most of it in the first ten chapters. Read Part One — about a hundred pages — plus the first few pages of each subsequent chapter, and you'll understand the approach I recommend. The rest is for the more serious student of fundraising letters.

About the case studies

If you've read my earlier books, you're aware I view fundraising by mail as a three-stage process. First, donors are *acquired* (what a bloodless term!). Then, they are *converted* into repeat donors (another unfortunate but unavoidable choice of words). Finally, donors may be *upgraded* into higher levels of generosity and commitment. In this book I've arranged the case studies roughly along the lines of this three-stage process. (I recognize that those lines blur and converge in the real world of fundraising, but let's not quibble.)

Five of the seven case studies in Chapters 11 through 17 are drawn from the files of EditEXPRESS™, a letter-editing service I've offered since 1990. To judge their value as illustrations, you need to understand how that service works.

I operate EditEXPRESS as an *editor* of fundraising appeals, not as a writer of them. I take pains to make as few changes as possible in the letters I'm

SENT BY:A   :11-13-90 10:19AM :   2022235821→   4158430142:# 5

~~An attitude of energy conservation fits right into the vision of living more lightly on the earth and trying to do better with less.~~

you can

~~We can do it in the obvious areas: home, transportation, and appliances.~~ We've put together a handy chart to show you how much energy ~~could be~~ saved ~~by taking action in various areas.~~ **I've enclosed a copy for you**
to ~~Please~~ post **it** and share **it** with your friends.

But
You may think that changing a ~~single~~ light bulb ~~won't~~ **won't**
make much of a difference. **A** single compact florescent light
bulb uses 1/4 the energy and lasts 10 times as long as an
incandescent bulb giving off the same amount of light!

Compact fluorescent
According **to** the Rocky Mountain Institute, if everyone in   **shut down**
the U.S. switched to ~~these~~ light bulbs, we could close
75 large power plants. ~~That means we could~~ ~~close~~ **half**   **¶ As you can tell**
our nuclear plants -- ~~that's~~ **can** without touching anything   **from the enclosed**
but our lightbulbs! ~~We~~ could make an even bigger   **chart, we**
difference by using the most energy efficient electric
appliances.

Our society squanders immense amounts of energy on
Yet much of the energy used in the US is hidden from the
consumer. Processed food; packaging; ~~food grow using~~ pesticides
and fertilizers made from petroleum products; ~~the energy used to~~ **and on**
transport **,** products across the nation and from around the world.
~~all these energy uses add up.~~

So,
We must pressure businesses and **other large institutions** institutions to become
energy efficient, not only in their direct use of energy, but in   **power to force such**
the less obvious areas, too. **A** It will take a lot of consumer   **a big change in**
                                                                       attitude!
That's why
A Implementing ~~our 8 Point Energy Efficient Economy Project~~ **Co-op America's 3E Program** will
require more staff, time, and money.

to this historic new program
~~Once again we must ask for your help in this important~~
~~project.~~ Your contribution will help lay the foundation for an   **] Note: don't underline**
energy efficient and environmentally healthy economy.   **here.**

We can and we must take control of the future of our
environment by changing the way we spend our money.

We need to **buy** energy efficient and recyclable products,   **← Speech again.**
invest in technology that reduces our need for fossil fuels, and
boycott companies that continue to produce energy wasting
products. We also need to educate businesses on how they can
improve the energy efficiency of their industries and demand that
they do it.

Program
Through your individual actions and your support ~~of~~ Co-op   **for**
America's Energy Efficient Economy ~~Project~~, you ~~must~~ can ~~best~~ **play an**
integral part ~~in~~ ~~the shift~~ from a dirty, fossil fuel-based economy **shifting the US**
to a clean, efficient, renewable energy-based economy.

As a gesture of thanks for your
Please give as generously as you can. ~~Your~~ **a** contribution of

sent to revise. My primary responsibility, as I see it, is to increase the readability of the appeals, taking the word "readability" in the sense that Rudolf Flesch made popular half a century ago. Although the writer or the fundraiser in me might yearn to introduce new information — or even to take an entirely fresh approach — I usually content myself by reshaping and rearranging the material I'm given. (To get a sense of what I mean by this, take a look at the edited copy reproduced on page 12. That's the sort of thing I often do when I take on an editing job.) Most of the time, I'm told, that sort of copyediting has been good enough to achieve a significant improvement in results.

I'm indebted to the following EditEXPRESS clients for their gracious permission to reproduce here the work I performed for them:

◆ *Co-op America*, Washington, DC (Alisa Gravitz, Nancy Miller, Alex Levin)

◆ *Family Service Agency* of San Mateo County, Burlingame, CA (Margaret Ann Niven)

◆ *Food for the Poor*, Deerfield Beach, FL (Janet Copland)

◆ *Peace Action*, Washington, DC (Peter Deccy, Monica Green, Carole Watson)

Two of my clients insisted on anonymity, so I've sanitized the case studies and examples of my work for them, removing any evidence of their identity.

The central theme of this book is that there are different *types* of fundraising letters and that each type presents unique challenges to the writer. To dramatize the unique aspects of each type of fundraising letter, I chose to lead off the seven chapters in Part Two with illustrations from *one* nonprofit organization with an extensive and well organized direct mail fundraising program. I wanted to make clear that a single charity may, indeed, need to write letters of all the types described in this book. To fill that bill, I turned to *Bread for the World* (Washington, DC), a client of Mal Warwick & Associates, Inc. A special word of thanks to Joel Underwood and his colleagues for their generosity and cooperativeness in granting permission for their materials to be reproduced in this volume.

Why you can learn from the case studies — even though your organization is different

The causes and charities represented in this book cover a wide range — from human services to the environment to lobbying against hunger. But what if your organization doesn't happen to fit into one of those categories? Or if it does fit, but you're convinced it's really *different*?

Well, *of course* your group is different! If you're not serving a unique purpose, meeting an unfilled need, or helping a neglected constituency, your organization ought to close its doors without delay. Anyway, you can learn a lot from fundraising letters written by other nonprofit organizations. There are three reasons I strongly believe this:

1. You can learn how the *fundamental rules of writing* apply (or don't apply) to the craft of writing fundraising letters. The fundamentals have nothing to do with your cause or your constituency.

2. By studying examples from other organizations, you can learn how the *special techniques of fundraising* and direct marketing can be put to work in fundraising letters. Those techniques change very little from one cause or constituency to another.

3. You can learn how to improve your fundraising letters if you *distance yourself* from the everyday needs and details of your organization's work. Often, it's much easier to see the forest rather than the trees if you're looking into someone else's forest.

Why a fundraising letter is always more than just a letter

Yes, yes, I know the title of this book refers to fundraising "letters." Yet as you go on a quick run through the following pages, you'll see examples that aren't just letters. Don't sue me.

The reasons for this discrepancy are (a) most people refer to fundraising appeals as "letters" and (b) the letter is almost always the single most important component of an appeal. But the letter is never — repeat, *never* — the only component of a fundraising package. Many other components of the package are important, too.

There once was a time when letters were routinely folded, addressed, stamped, and mailed (they called it "posted" then) without using envelopes. But that doesn't work well in twentieth-century America. So, until we've all converted to E-mail and the letter carrier has been replaced by an electronic equivalent on the Information Superhighway, you'll need an envelope for your fundraising letter.

Almost all the time, you'll need at least two other items as well: a "reply device" (sometimes called a "response device," "coupon," "card," "form," or whatever), plus an envelope to mail it back in. Without such a device and an easy way to return it, most fundraising letters would generate precious few gifts.

Beginners at the craft of writing fundraising letters commonly treat these other components as afterthoughts. I hope after reading this book you won't do so. In fact, you may find you need to devote just as much thought to the reply device and the envelopes — *both* envelopes — as you do to the letter itself.

About some of the people who helped make this book possible

The conventions of the publishing industry conspire to give the impression that one person alone "writes" a book. While there may be circumstances in which that's true, it's certainly not the case with this book.

Consider for a moment how many people played roles in the conception, preparation, and distribution of this volume.

◆ It was Stephen Hitchcock who suggested I build a book around my EditEXPRESS work. This book has become far more than that. Nonetheless, Steve's imprint is visible on every page. His decade-old list of "reasons people give" was the starting point for my work on Chapter 5. More important, however, Steve has been my writing mentor for more than half a dozen years. Much of what he's taught me about writing for results is reflected in the following pages. He reviewed every chapter, page by page, painstakingly editing the most challenging parts. Also, as president of Mal Warwick & Associates, Steve has played a major role in freeing me from the burdens of day-to-day management, so that I'm able to undertake such time-consuming projects as writing books like this.

◆ With one exception, every letter included as an example in Chapters 11 through 17 was drafted by someone else. In many cases I don't know the identity of the author. I urge you to recognize that it was not I. Most of the time, my contribution was limited to playing the critic. (That's the easy part.)

◆ The freelance copywriting team of Deborah Block and Paul Karps generously took time out from a particularly busy season of their work on bread-and-butter fundraising projects to review the first draft of the manuscript. They paid particular attention to the case studies. Because of their sharp eyes and extensive knowledge of fundraising letters, they uncovered a great many inconsistencies. Their detailed critique helped me enormously in transforming a bunch of unrelated assignments performed over a three-year period into the book you hold in your hands. I'm greatly indebted to them, and as a reader of this book, you are, too.

◆ Before putting this book to bed, I sent copies of the second draft to some of the most knowledgeable and experienced people in direct mail fundraising. Their assignment: to tell me — before it was too late — what I'd overlooked, what I'd distorted, and where I'd simply gone wrong. Each of them took the time during the last two weeks of December, 1993, to read the 600-page manuscript and send me comments in writing in time for the New Year (and my printer's deadline). Their comments moved me to cut, pare, and reshape the original text into a form that some of them may no longer recognize. A round of applause, please, for: Lorraine Kupper (American Bible Society), Max Hart (Disabled American Veterans), Hank Rosso (Fund Raising School), Angela McArdell (Greenpeace U.S.A.), and Jerry Panas (Jerold Panas, Linzy & Partners). Jerry Panas — one of the few gifted writers in our field — was especially insightful and thorough.

◆ This book would not have seen the light of day without the help I received from Ina Cooper and Ramona Allen at Mal Warwick & Associates. Ina served as production coordinator, and Ramona faced almost daily assignments to scan or transcribe text and prepare seemingly endless rounds of photocopies. The hours they invested in this project may have equalled my own, and I'm very grateful.

◆ Ten years ago, I couldn't have produced this book in the time available to me. Desktop publishing made it possible – but technology also drove me round the bend. Because the several microcomputers on which I wrote and formatted this book were constantly malfunctioning, several of my most computer-literate friends and associates became far more involved in this project than any of them would ever have wanted. My desktop publishing guru, Craig Johnson, pulled me through many late-night crises with unfailingly level-headed advice. Dan Suzio also helped meet my deadlines and preserve my sanity.

In a sense, I've been working on this book for more than three years — ever since I launched my EditEXPRESS service. In a larger sense, however, I started the project in 1979 when I founded my direct mail fundraising firm, Mal Warwick & Associates, or even in 1949, almost forty-five years ago — when I wrote my first "fundraising" letter home from summer camp. I've put a lot into this book. I hope you get a lot out of it.

— M.W.
Berkeley, California, January 1994

PART ONE

How to Write Successful Fundraising Letters

YOU'RE WRITING FOR *RESULTS* — NOT FOR A PULITZER PRIZE

My brother has never forgiven me. Art was eighteen and about to enter his first year of college. He has since become a respected psychiatrist and taught at universities that rival any I've ever attended. But back then — to my mind, at least — he was just my snot-nosed younger brother. And Art was absolutely, positively guaranteed to stumble over freshman English — or so everyone else in our family was convinced.

Since I was three years older than my brother and a veteran of hundreds of essays, letters, stories, reviews, and critiques, not to mention a few political speeches, our mother pressed me into service during that summer of 1962. As a former English teacher, she was suffering from acute embarrassment in addition to her maternal fear for Art's future.

"Make yourself useful for a change," she said. "Help your brother. Teach him how to write."

This assignment pleased neither Art nor me, but orders were orders. (Our parents were still paying the bills, after all.) With mutual ill will, we took up our new roles: I as a teacher, he as an obedient younger brother.

Things went from bad to worse after I gave Art his first assignment: a 500-word essay entitled "How to Tie Your Shoelaces."

Art wrote that essay — not once or twice but at least a dozen times, each successive draft a mosaic of notations in red, blue, and black pencil. The essay was finished only after painful daily sessions stretching over several weeks. Along the way, there were countless changes in word order and sentence structure. We discarded adjectives and adverbs, shifted prepositions, changed verbs, and thumbed through *Roget's Thesaurus* for sparkling new nouns. But when the job was complete and we were ready to proceed with the second assignment, it was obvious that what Art learned about writing had little to do with any of the changes we'd made in his labored drafts. The essence of what he learned (and I "taught") was this:

1. To write clearly and effectively, the writer must *think* before setting pen to paper (or, more likely nowadays, fingers to the keyboard). Clearly written communication is nothing more — and nothing less — than a reflection of disciplined, logical thinking.

2. When writing to achieve results, the writer must *make things easy for the reader*. Unless held at gunpoint or facing the loss of a job, the reader has no obligation to the writer, and nothing to fear. The reader is free to abandon what she or he is reading and turn to something more rewarding — like badminton or Beethoven, for example.

3. The *right* word is not necessarily the most colorful, or even the most precise word. The right word is the strongest, the most expressive word — the word that communicates the writer's meaning most effectively.

4. A skillful writer can make any subject interesting, amusing, or at least palatable.

Back to *The Elements of Style*

Perhaps I'm kidding myself.

Art may never have learned those four things at all. Or his freshman English teachers might have forced some discipline into his writing where I'd utterly failed. But I cherish the thought that my brother's subsequent academic success had a least a little to do with my drillmaster's brand of summertime writing instruction.

However, like so many of the other times in my life when I thought I was helping someone else, I was really helping myself a lot more. Because that summer, acting in the belief that a good teacher needed to be thoroughly familiar with his text, I reread Strunk and White.

If you're not familiar with that legendary little volume, I suggest you pick up a copy and devour it. If you already know the book, reread it before you start your next writing job. Its title is *The Elements of Style*, its coauthors William Strunk, Jr., and E. B. White. It's readily available in inexpensive paperback editions throughout North America, and — perhaps best of all — *The Elements of Style* is truly a *little* book. My 1950s-vintage paperback version is all of seventy-one pages long — and it hasn't grown a word longer since the last time I looked.

Some writers claim they can get along quite well without Strunk and White, or any other grounding in the basics of writing. For example, I'm told there are hugely successful advertising and public relations copywriters who learned everything they know on the job. I'm skeptical of this assertion, which I ascribe largely to the self-promotion that's so common among people who traffic in myths. But for the sake of argument let's accept the claim that copywriters can learn their craft even if they're ignorant of the fundamentals of English style. That doesn't mean it's a good idea to violate all the rules! In fact, I believe the copywriter's life will be easier — and probably more successful — if it starts with training in the basics. That brings us to Dr. Rudolf Flesch.

Rudolf Flesch's rules of effective writing

Generations of Americans have turned to Rudolf Flesch for advice on effective writing and speaking, and no wonder! Flesch's books, written decades ago, contain insights as fresh today as when they were newly written. I especially recommend his book, *How to Write, Speak and Think More Effectively* (an inexpensive paperback available from NAL/Signet and described in the reading list in the back of this book). Flesch's "25 Rules of Effective Writing" appear on pages 10-11 in that book. They're well worth reading in full, but here's the gist of them:

◆ Write about people, things, and facts.

◆ Write as you speak.

◆ Use contractions.

◆ Use the first person.

◆ Quote what was said or written.

◆ Put yourself in the reader's place.

- Don't be too brief.
- Plan a beginning, middle, and end.
- Go from the rule to the exception, and from the familiar to the new.
- Use abbreviations and short forms of names.
- Use pronouns rather than repeating nouns.
- Use verbs rather than nouns.
- Use the active voice.
- Use small, round figures.
- Be specific. Use illustrations, cases, and examples.
- Start a new sentence for each new idea.
- Keep your sentences and your paragraphs short.
- Use direct questions.
- Underline for emphasis.
- Make your writing interesting *to look at*.

These aren't arbitrary rules of taste or style. They're the result of Flesch's studies of readers' reactions to written material.

Rudolf Flesch is the all-time master of the study of "readability," readability being the likelihood that what you've written will actually be understood (and possibly remembered!) by your readers. Flesch held sway in an era when numerical measurements inspired more faith than they do in today's skeptical society, but his charts, graphs, and scores are still useful.

Flesch found, for example, that two key indicators of the readability of writing were (1) the number of syllables per 100 words and (2) the average length of a sentence (expressed as the number of words).

I won't go into the precise way Flesch defined these two measurements. You can read it yourself in his book (and I hope you will). But look at how Flesch interprets these measurements:

Description of style	Syllables per 100 words	Average sentence length
Very easy	123	8
Easy	131	11
Fairly easy	139	14
Standard	147	17
Fairly difficult	155	21
Difficult	167	25
Very difficult	192	29

In Flesch's lexicon, "very easy" writing is to be found in comic books. "Standard" writing is the earmark of such magazines as *Time*, and "very difficult" writing is found in scientific and professional journals. Rings true, doesn't it?

This chapter averages eleven words per sentence, according to my word processor — pretty easy reading, Flesch would say. Judge for yourself whether you find my writing readable.

But short words and short sentences alone won't make your writing easy to read. Flesch insists (and I agree) that a factor of equal importance is the "human interest" in what you write. Human interest is a function of the proportion of "personal words" (such as personal pronouns and proper names), the frequency with which quotations are used, and the extent to which you engage the reader by challenging, questioning, or directly addressing her.

Flesch's suggestions about how to increase readability are equally useful. Here are some of them:

- Focus on your reader.
- Focus on your purpose.
- Break up sentences and paragraphs.
- Find simpler words.
- Help your reader read (emphasize, anticipate, repeat, summarize).
- Learn to cut unnecessary words.
- Rearrange for emphasis.
- Write to be read aloud.

◆ Rearrange for emphasis.

◆ Write to be read aloud.

◆ Don't write down to your reader.

If you follow all these suggestions, you'll avoid most of the major errors in writing for results — by *removing the obstacles between yourself and your reader.* Now let's take a closer look at some of those obstacles.

How *not* to get results

I can best approach the rules of copywriting through the back door, by advising you on how to avoid the most common errors I see. There are at least fifteen. They're described below, beginning with the five I believe cause the most trouble:

1. CHAOTIC THINKING

Effective writing begins (and ends) with clear, disciplined thought. As E. B. White puts it so elegantly: "Design informs even the simplest structure, whether of brick and steel or of prose. You raise a pup tent from one sort of vision, a cathedral from another. This does not mean that you must sit with a blueprint always in front of you, merely that you had best anticipate what you are getting into." So, before you lay a finger on the keyboard, or position your pen on paper, *make up your mind what it is you want to communicate.* Decide where you want to go, and how you'll get there. If necessary, outline the steps you'll take along the way. If you don't decide in advance what the point is, it's unlikely you'll get it across.

2. HEMMING AND HAWING

There may still be a place for slow and easy writing that meanders from point to point, but I think that approach went out of style with William Faulkner — and there is *no* room for such sloppiness when you're writing to achieve results. Get to the point — the quicker the better! Unless you can devise a clearly superior lead sentence, I suggest you start a letter with the words, "I'm writing you today because." That approach won't win a prize in a creative writing contest — but it does force you to communicate quickly and directly the result you're hoping to achieve with your letter. Creativity doesn't raise money, but directness does. If your writing doesn't get to the point, your readers' eyes and minds will wander off to more profitable pursuits. Bluntness is usually a wiser and more productive course than subtlety.

3. BORING LEADS

If you're faced with the task of writing a six-page letter or a ten-page memo, you'd better be sure your opening paragraph — and especially the opening sentence — is intriguing enough to pique your readers' interest. And that goes double for a letter intended to secure a gift, or sell a product.

Writing that engages the reader often begins with a question, a challenge, a human-interest story, a bold assertion, a familiar phrase turned on its head — or straightforward, unalloyed directness. The special circumstances and conditions of your writing assignment (or simple inspiration) may suggest that one of these approaches is ideal. But it may be enough simply to sum up the points you're going to make — if you state them dramatically enough, and set the proper tone for the audience you're addressing. For example:

I'm writing today to invite you to join me in launching a historic initiative with vast potential to improve the quality of life in our community.

For a general audience, that pompous lead might guarantee your letter will quickly make its way into the proverbial circular file. But for a highbrow group with a demonstrated commitment to your community, and a connection to the person who signs the memo or the letter, the boldness of your claim may be captivating.

4. RUN-ON SENTENCES

Writing of any type suffers from overlong sentences; a letter to raise money or sell software can die a horrible death from this malady. If a sentence is longer than three typewritten lines, analyze it, looking for a way to break it down into two or three simpler and shorter sentences. Almost always, you'll get your point across more effectively if you do so.

Keep this in mind: a reader dedicated enough to tackle Proust or Joyce may be willing to concentrate hard enough to follow a tortured thought all the way to a long-overdue period. (Understandably, the period is sometimes known as a "full stop.") But *your* readers aren't likely to pay that much attention. Long sentences will test readers' limited attention span, and you'll come up the loser.

5. FAILURE TO USE VISUAL DEVICES TO GUIDE THE READER

A novelist who is highly skilled in moving the reader from one page to the next may be able to do so with the power of words alone. Most of us aren't so lucky — and our readers, who often have far more meager incentives to read on for page after page, are typically far less tolerant. To write effectively for impact, you'll probably need to make liberal use of subheads . . . bulleted or numbered series . . . boldfaced section headings . . . and other devices to break the monotony of gray, unbroken text. Only by providing your readers with clues that are visible at a glance can you make your writing actually *look* easy to read — and you'll substantially reinforce that impression by using short sentences and short paragraphs. Signals such as these send an important message to the reader: that you're writing for *her* benefit, not for your own!

In addition to these five major trouble-makers, there are ten other common writing errors that cause problems.

6. INCONCLUSIVE (AND UNINTERESTING) ENDINGS

A strong appeal requires a forceful ending as well as a thought-provoking lead. It's not enough to sum up and repeat the strongest points made along the way. A letter should end on a high note: affirm the relationship between the signer and the recipient and relate the appeal to the organization's mission and the values that inspire it. End with something people will remember.

7. VAGUE LANGUAGE

Bad writing is full of excuses, qualifications, exceptions, and caveats. For example, a sales letter might begin:

Most people agree, this product is one of the best things since the hula hoop.

Well, is it the best — or isn't it? If "most people" agree, then why not write instead as follows:

This incredible product will knock your socks off! Take it from me – it's the best thing since the hula hoop!

Excuses, qualifications, exceptions, and caveats are the lawyer's stock in trade and suggest competence. But when a writer constantly relies on such evasions, they signify fuzzy thinking. If you can't make your case in clear, unequivocal language, it's time to reexamine the reasoning that led you to conclude the case you're presenting was defensible. Your readers won't become excited about helping you if your writing doesn't clearly convey what you want, and why, and when.

8. OVERWRITING

Inexperienced and insecure writers frequently overuse adjectives and adverbs, robbing their writing of clarity and impact. As E. B. White wrote, "The adjective hasn't been built that can pull a weak or inaccurate noun out of a tight place." If you want to write for results, try doing so without using any adjectives at all. You can go back later and insert an adjective or two for the sake of precision or honesty. To the extent you exercise restraint, your readers will thank you — and they'll reward you with the ultimate gift to a writer: they'll go on reading.

9. TEN-DOLLAR WORDS

Like overwriting, the use of long, obscure, and highly technical language is a form of showing off. It's not necessary to write "cessation" when "end" will do, or use "communicate" when you can get the point across with "say" or "write." Unfortunately, this sort of thing is all too common in writing today, and communication suffers as a result. Board chairmen and chief executive officers are especially susceptible to this malady. Avoid it like any deadly (shall I say "communicable"?) disease.

10. "BUSINESS ENGLISH"

The tendency to use widely accepted but grammatically incorrect — and often abysmally wordy — constructions is one of the afflictions of contemporary writing, and it infects a great deal of advertising and fundraising copy. Stay clear of abominations such as the following; choose their equivalents in acceptable English — or shun them all together:

Offensive usage	What to do about it
"accordingly"	"so"
"along the lines of"	"like"
"and/or"	Leave this one to the lawyers!
"as to whether"	"whether"
"at this point in time"	"now" or "today"
"dialogue"	"talk"
"enclosed herewith"	"I'm sending you"
"etc."	Use *very* sparingly.
"finalize"	"finish"
"for the purpose of"	"for"
"implementation"	Just do it!
"in order to"	"To" will suffice.
"inasmuch as"	"because"
"in the event that"	"if"
"interface"	"work with" or "meet"
"make use of"	"use"
"owing to the fact that"	"because"
"per your request"	"as you asked"
"prioritize"	"set priorities"
"prior to"	"before"
"pursuant to"	"according to"
"quite" or "very"	Lilies sell better without gilt!
"results-wise	"the result is that"
"revert back"	"revert"
"the forseeable future"	How far away is that?
"with a view to"	"to"

Then there are all those words wasted because writers — not just in business or government but throughout American society today — insist on doubling up, presumably out of some deep, hidden fear that they'll otherwise fail to get the point across. For example:

"exact opposites"	"Opposites" will suffice.
"the reason is because"	Which is it: "the reason is" — or "because"? Choose one!
"final conclusion"	If it's the conclusion, isn't it final?
"actual experience"	As opposed to an unauthentic experience?
"continue on"	Is the alternative to "continue off?"
"end result"	Give me a break!

You get the point, I hope. From this time forward, I trust you'll be on guard against these boring and objectionable word-wasters. While you're at it, just to humor me, please put the following words on your list of no-no's, too:

"hopefully"	Do you really hope so? Given the way this word is so frequently misused, I think that's unlikely. But if you really hope so, then *say* it!
"frankly"	This word is commonly used when its opposite is intended. It puts the reader on guard. So does, "To be honest with you."
"irregardless"	The correct word is "regardless."
"very unique"	If something's unique, it's one of a kind. Drop the "very."

Every one of these words and phrases is, in its way, a waste of words and a violation of common sense. (Strunk and White comment, sometimes at greater length, about some of these examples.)

11. STILTED LANGUAGE

Just because a word is grammatically correct and properly spelled and precisely expresses the thought

you want to convey doesn't mean it's the *right* word. When seeking to achieve results it's important to write as you speak, using familiar, everyday words. The best way to guard against problems of this sort is to give your writing a roadtest: read your letter aloud before you let anyone else see it. If you have trouble pronouncing a word or phrase, chances are it will trip up your reader, too. Find another way to say what you've written.

12. LACK OF AGREEMENT

One of the most common violations of the rules of grammar is the writer's failure to decide in advance what point a sentence is to make. This confusion is often reflected in a mismatch between its subject and verb, or between a pronoun and its antecedent. For example:

If members choose not to attend, you may obtain a discount instead.

There's nothing wrong with this sentence that a little forethought would have cured. One possible approach:

Members who choose not to attend are eligible for discounts.

This alternative formulation is less likely to trip up the reader, who could easily do a doubletake on the original wording. Note that the corrected version is also two words shorter, making it that much easier to read.

13. DANGLING MODIFIERS

Closely related to the preceding problem, this oh-so-common error typically arises from the same source: foggy thinking. Unfortunately, I know of no way to describe it other than to use the grating language of the grammarian or to give examples:

An example of the very best the community had to offer, the Mayor awarded her the prize last year.

Loaded with valuable benefits, I thought the product was the best I could buy.

To avoid the confusion caused by mismatches like these, try revising them. Usually, there are numerous acceptable alternatives. Here's one example of each:

The Mayor awarded her the prize last year because she exemplified the very best the community has to offer.

It was simply loaded with valuable benefits – the best product I could buy, I thought.

You don't need to know what a "modifier" is: all you have to do is remember when you near the end of the sentence what you were writing about when you started it!

14. OVERUSE OF THE PASSIVE VOICE

There are times when the passive voice is unavoidable, or at least convenient — in the following, for instance:

The snowfall was unprecedented, but the streets were swept clean in record time.

In this example, which is about streets and snow, not people, it's not important *who* swept the streets (although the members of the street-sweeping crew might have a different opinion!). The point of the sentence is clear. Nothing is lost by the use of the passive voice. Usually, however, the passive voice detracts from the impact of a statement. The passive voice is frequently used to evade straightforward assertions of fact. Thus it rarely helps sell products or obtain charitable gifts. For example:

Voting members of the Museum are required to attend one meeting per year to preserve their status and receive all these discounts.

That sentence reads like a passage from a rule-book, not a promise of benefits that might entice someone to join the museum. Try this instead:

As a voting member of the museum, you'll receive all these discounts if you attend just one meeting per year.

Writing for results requires communicating conviction. The active voice helps the writer to be direct and permits the reader to grasp the point more quickly.

15. ATROCIOUS SPELLING

My mother always said that respect for spelling died in the 1950s when "educators" decided there was a better way to teach reading than by using phonetics. I think she was right. I know few Americans younger than I who can spell worth a damn. Fortunately, today, most of us who live by the word are likely to use one of the popular word-processing programs, all of which feature "spell-checking" utilities. I heartily recommend these devices. Using such a program requires only a few seconds, yet it may rescue you from years of mortification. Perhaps you don't care whether there are spelling errors in your copy, *but I do!*

If you heed the fifteen points just outlined — and if you're faithful to Strunk and White's rules of grammar and vocabulary, and Rudolf Flesch's "25 Rules of Effective Writing" — you'll avoid most of the common mistakes that can prevent you from communicating effectively. You'll also be more likely to achieve the results you intend from your fundraising letters. But to write for results you'll need to do more than polish your writing style. Writing for results is different from writing meant merely to describe or report to the reader. Let's take a look at the differences now.

How writing for results is different

There are at least nine differences, all of which might prove to be crucial elements in your fundraising or sales letters.

1. COLLOQUIALISMS

Writing for results requires you to use everyday language and patterns of speech — because you need to communicate readily, without delay or complication, without forcing the reader to work for understanding. (There are exceptions to this rule, but, like much that can be said about writing for results, the exceptions revolve around the audience, not the writer.) Colloquial speech and even slang aren't just acceptable — they're sometimes essential. Like a chatty personal letter, a masterpiece of copywriting will read much more like a conversation at the supermarket than an article in the *New York Times* or the *Harvard Business Review*.

2. CLICHÉS

Most people think, speak, and write in clichés. That, I believe, is *not* a good thing, but it's important for the copywriter to take it into account when sitting down to write. Clichés, after all, are only one step removed from garden-variety colloquialisms; they offer an easy way to communicate thoughts rapidly — precisely because of their familiarity. For the same reason, many readers also find clichés boring, so a tired and overused turn of speech shouldn't be your first line of defense against the difficulty of explaining a complex set of circumstances or making a subtle argument. But sometimes, when writing for results, an old chestnut can help you fill the understanding gap.

Consider, for example, that revolting old cliché, the "pot of gold at the end of the rainbow." I wouldn't be caught dead using this phrase in everyday speech, even in a defenseless moment. But I can think of no phrase that more readily communicates the concept of fabulous wealth and could better provide an appropriate image for a sweepstakes featuring large cash prizes.

3. FIGURES OF SPEECH

You'll probably remember from high school English that similes and metaphors are among the earmarks of "fine literature." A simile is one of those hardworking little figures of speech that crawls up the hillside *"like a train trailing a hundred cars."* By contrast, a metaphor forces the reader to do much of the work, taking it on faith that an abstraction such as a figure of speech might be a train, a Bengal tiger, or a pot of gold.

I have a simple rule about the use of similes and metaphors in writing for results: *Don't use them.* Metaphors require thought; even similes can slow the reader down, or worse. These figures of speech

help communicate complex thoughts and feelings, but only by indirection; any complexities in your message need to be spelled out more directly, or you'll lose your readers.

4. HUMOR AND IRONY

"Creative" advertising copywriters notwithstanding, humor is rarely advisable in writing for results. And avoid entirely that wry, sophisticated form of humor called irony. It's not that some people have no discernible sense of humor, or even that what's humorous to one person might seem tragic to another. The fundamental problem, I believe, is that the written word is an imperfect medium to convey good humor.

In speaking to an audience, you might get a laugh for an even poorly told joke by communicating the humor through tone of voice, gestures, facial expressions, and even the use of props — aided by the natural tendency in most people to feel sympathy for you when you're standing two feet away. However, you have none of those advantages when writing to that same audience. I suggest you keep the jokes to yourself, or tack them up on your refrigerator or the office bulletin board.

5. SENTENCE STRUCTURE

I'll call her Miss Forsythe because, truth to tell, I can't remember her name. Thirty-seven years ago, she taught me in ninth grade English that every sentence must contain a subject and a predicate. Among a great many other rules, all of them delivered in commanding tones and in language that inhibited questions, Miss Forsythe also insisted that a sentence *must never* begin with "and" or "but" and *must never* end with a preposition.

In some forms of writing, those rules are as true today as they were in the 1950s. But not in writing for results. To convey meaning simply and clearly — to respect the informal practices of natural, spoken language and place emphasis where it's needed — Miss Forsythe's rules sometimes need to be ignored. The result may be writing that fails all the tests of conventional sentence structure, punctuation, and grammar — but yields the results you want.

Try these rules instead of Miss Forsythe's:

(a) A sentence expresses a single thought. Sometimes a thought can be expressed in just one word. One. And one's enough.

(b) It's okay to start a sentence with a conjunction. (But don't overdo it. Two sentences in a row that start with "but" are likely to confuse the reader.)

(c) Don't worry about ending sentences with prepositions. Sometimes a preposition is the very best word to end a sentence with.

(d) If at first you're not convinced by (a), (b), and (c), re-read them carefully. You might change your mind.

6. PUNCTUATION

Semicolons. I like semicolons. My thoughts tend to break up into little pieces that don't quite justify sentences of their own. In writing stories, articles, reports — or this book! — I find it natural to stitch clauses together into long sentences by using semicolons. Miss Forsythe would heartily approve; with few exceptions, I get no complaints from my latter-day readers, either. But when I'm seeking results with my writing — when I want my readers to take action — I edit out the semicolons.

Why? Because it's easier to read without semicolons. The eyes glaze over at the sight of long sentences. Periods provide rest and comfort. The capital letters that begin new sentences heighten interest. Why, then, do I persist in using semicolons? Sheer perversity, no doubt! (Or maybe Miss Forsythe did her job all too well!) Grudgingly, however, I've made an effort to limit my use of semicolons in this book.

Dashes. In writing for results, it's often wise to use a dash — what typesetters call an "em-dash" (about twice the width of a hyphen; technically, the width of a capital M). I use a lot of dashes when writing fundraising letters — and I don't feel guilty in the least, no matter what Miss Forsythe might say.

Dashes lend emphasis to your thoughts by setting them apart and increasing the "white space" that surrounds them. (A German professor you'll meet in Chapter 3 insists that dashes arrest the reader's eye and make writing *less* readable, but I choose to ignore his advice on this one, highly personal matter of style.)

Ellipsis. Miss Forsythe would cringe . . . but I don't care. Ellipsis points (". . .") have much the same effect as a dash, particularly if set off by blank spaces before and after the points. Both help convey meaning by splitting complex or urgent thoughts into their component pieces.

7. CONTRACTIONS

Lawyers, top business executives, and even some journalists advocate the sparing use of contractions. Don't pay any attention to them if you want your readers to take action.

Purists would rather you spell out every word, erring on the side of precision, so there can be absolutely no confusion in the minds of your readers. I'd rather you use fewer words, favoring informality and natural speech patterns, so your readers won't feel you're talking down to them.

Contractions such as "I'm," "you've," "don't," and "can't" are usually preferable in copywriting to the longer expressions they're derived from: "I am," "you have," "do not," and "cannot." The shorter form is more easily taken in by the ear, and the eye quickly comprehends the meaning of contractions. Also, negatives catch the reader's attention, sometimes conveying precisely the wrong impression. The word "not" may lodge in the reader's eye like a cinder, causing him to misread the following sentence — or the point of the whole letter.

8. REPETITION

Grammarians are often repelled by writing intended to persuade because it's likely to be riddled with repetition. The repetition is not accidental. Just as a journalist leads an article with the most important piece of news, the copywriter is likely to emphasize those points of greatest potential interest to the reader — by repeating them.

The English language possesses almost unmatched variety, so a writer can describe any benefit or make any offer in a hundred or a thousand different ways. The demands of writing a letter intended to sell products or secure contributions may force the writer to use precisely the same words, over and over again.

9. UNDERLINING AND ITALICS

Miss Forsythe told us never to italicize words unless they're book titles or they come from a foreign language. In the days when handwriting and typewriters were the writer's only options, she meant not to underline words. Today, some editors follow the same rule: I sometimes find my articles or columns appearing shorn of all their carefully chosen italicized emphasis. I keep submitting articles peppered with italics anyway, in hopes my editors will wake up and see what's obvious to me: *italics enhance the reader's understanding* — when used sparingly. Emphasizing important facts or thoughts makes it easier for the reader to grasp the writer's meaning — and easier to review and remember key points. In writing typewriter-style — as, for example, in most fundraising letters — I generally prefer underlining instead of italics, even though I might have 500 alternative typefaces at hand (and most of them available in italic as well as roman fonts). Often it's important to preserve the illusion that I'm really writing on a typewriter.

When does the fun start?

Some writers can produce readable copy in a first, fluid draft. It seems as though the words just keep streaming out of their fingertips, all neatly arranged in precisely the right order. (God, I *hate* those people!) Within the ranks of the top freelance writers, stories abound about the geniuses who can sit down at the keyboard (a typewriter, often enough) at 9:00 in the morning, and type without interruption for three hours. They knock off for an hour's lunch, return for four more hours of unruffled word processing in the afternoon — and end the day with 5,000 salable words, or even 10,000. But these are people who write hundreds of books, or thousands of stories or articles (or both). They get a lot more practice than you're likely to get. And I don't mind admitting they've got a lot more innate talent for writing than I have.

So if you're like me and are a mere mortal, you're going to have to revise, and rewrite, and revise again. Don't make the mistake of believing you've got it right the first time. Chances are, you don't. Whatever it is you're writing, set it aside for a day or two or a week after you've completed your first rough draft, then take a fresh look at it. And don't forget to read your letter aloud. If you can't find something on every page that cries out for revision, you're either a far better writer than I — or you're blind.

In this chapter I've discussed writing of all sorts that's intended to achieve results. But there are rules that apply specifically to the writing of letters designed to produce contributions. I call these "The Cardinal Rules of Writing Fundraising Letters." They're the subject of the following chapter. ▶

THE CARDINAL RULES OF WRITING FUNDRAISING LETTERS

In the last chapter, I talked about writing that's intended to persuade or otherwise produce results. But there are guidelines that apply specifically to writing *fundraising letters*. I call these axioms "The Cardinal Rules of Writing Fundraising Letters."

To illustrate the eight rules spelled out below, I'll refer to the direct mail package reproduced on pages 31 to 38. It's an appeal mailed by St. Joseph's Indian School of Chamberlain, South Dakota; the letter was one of several efforts to secure an additional gift from one of my newsletter's correspondents in the year after we sent the school an unsolicited $15 check. The appeal isn't without flaws — but it does illustrate the eight rules that follow.

1. Use "I" and "you" (but mostly "you").

In fact, "you" should be the word you use most frequently in your fundraising letters. Your appeal is a letter from one individual to another individual. You aren't writing a press release, a position paper, or a brochure.

Rudolf Flesch's studies on readability supply the fundamental reason the words "you" and "I" are important: they provide "human interest." Stories, anecdotes, and common names (and capitalized words in general) have some of the same effect — but the most powerful way to engage the reader is by appealing directly to her: use the word "you."

For example, in the St. Joseph's Indian School fundraising letter, see how Brother David Nagel uses these powerful personal pronouns to establish intimacy:

You are a dream catcher.

I peeked in on some of the younger kids who were already asleep.

You protect our children from nightmares. You save them from poverty, illiteracy, and despair.

I hope you'll keep this card to bring good dreams to yourself and your family.

St. Joseph's Indian School
Chamberlain, South Dakota 57326

October 30, 1992

Dear Friend,

You are a dream catcher.

The Lakota (Sioux) believe that good dreams and nightmares float in the air, and that a special willow frame strung with sinew can screen out nightmares and let only good dreams pass through.

They call the ornament a dream catcher and put one in every tipi and on the cradle board of every baby.

The other evening I was walking through the William House, one of our childrens' homes. I peeked in on some of the younger kids who were already asleep. I watched the children sleeping and dreaming peacefully.

Sweet dreams are something new for so many of the children. They've come from such troubled homes — and nightmares are far more common on the reservations. I thought about the Lakota (Sioux) dream catcher and my thoughts turned to you.

You protect our children from nightmares. You save them from poverty, illiteracy, and despair — a nightmare fate that befalls so many Native Americans on the reservations.

You bring them good dreams — of a bright future as well-educated, young adults with a purpose and strong values. And you help make those dreams come true. You are a dream catcher!

Because you are a guardian of good dreams for the children of St. Joseph's, we want you to have a special gift. I've enclosed a Thanksgiving Card that features the Lakota dream catcher.

I hope you'll keep this card to bring good dreams to yourself and your family, or pass it on to bring good dreams to a faraway loved one at Thanksgiving.

Because so many of our friends are interested in Lakota traditions, we have ordered a small number of

Lakota dream catchers in antique brass.

If you can send a special gift today of $25 or more, I'd love to send you one of these unique ornaments as a special gift from the children of St. Joseph's.

These highly detailed dream catchers make wonderful gifts for children and new parents, and make unique Christmas Tree decorations.

In any event, please send a gift today of whatever you can afford to bring dreams of hope to the children of St. Joseph's. Without people like you, their lives would be a nightmare.

Thanks!

Yours in Christ,

Bro. David Nagel
Director

P.S. Thanksgiving is a special, happy time around here. It's one of the few times when America remembers all the gifts Native Americans gave to this country — and how little they received in return. Please remember the children of St. Joseph's when you offer thanks over your Thanksgiving dinner. We'll be praying for you.

Dreams of Hope for the Children

2150050. 079

Send a gift today of $25 or more, we'll send you a beautiful antique brass Dream Catcher ornament as a special gift from the children of St. Joseph's.

YES!

I want to be a dream catcher to help bring dreams of hope to the children of St. Joseph's.

2150050. 079

Enclosed is my gift of:

(   ) **$25**   (   ) **$15**   (   ) **$48**   (   ) **$**_____

(   ) I have enclosed a gift of $25 or more, please send an antique brass Lakota dream catcher ornament.

Please make your tax-deductible gift payable to St. Joseph's and mail it with this slip. Use the other side for your prayer requests and intentions. Please be sure the return address on the reverse side shows through the window of the enclosed envelope.

St. Joseph's Indian School Chamberlain, South Dakota 57326

PRAY FOR ME

Dear Brother David, I am in need. Please pray for the following intentions:

☐ For my peace of mind

☐ For the health of my loved ones

☐ For my children

☐ For the strength of my marriage

☐ For my health

☐ Other _____

_____

_____

☐ Please send information about your Charitable Gift Annuity.

Please be sure this address shows through the window of the enclosed envelope:

ST. JOSEPH'S INDIAN SCHOOL
CHAMBERLAIN SD 57326

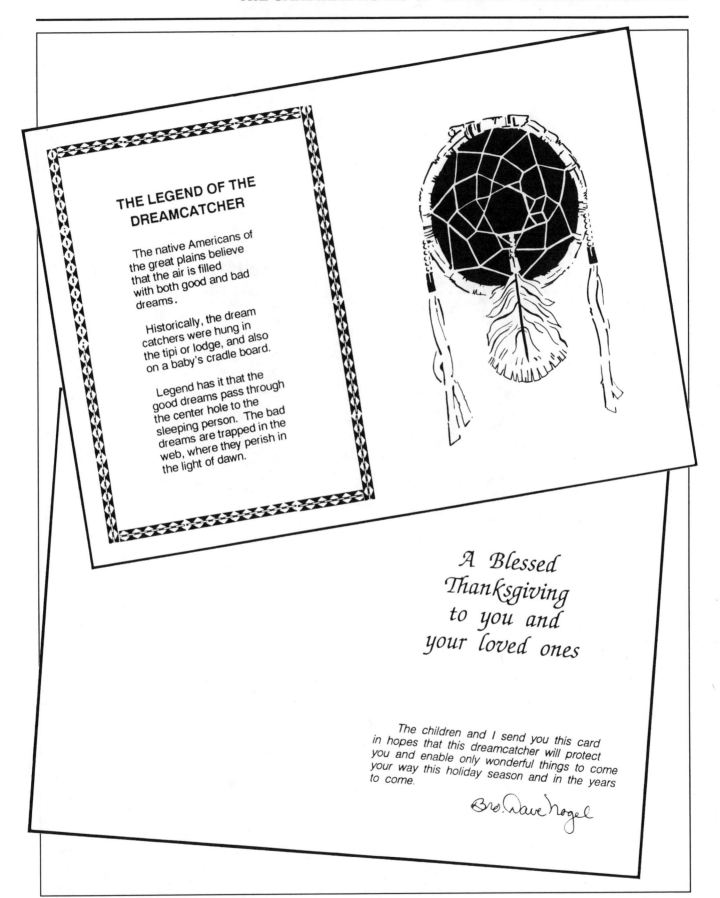

THE LEGEND OF THE DREAMCATCHER

The native Americans of the great plains believe that the air is filled with both good and bad dreams.

Historically, the dream catchers were hung in the tipi or lodge, and also on a baby's cradle board.

Legend has it that the good dreams pass through the center hole to the sleeping person. The bad dreams are trapped in the web, where they perish in the light of dawn.

A Blessed Thanksgiving to you and your loved ones

The children and I send you this card in hopes that this dreamcatcher will protect you and enable only wonderful things to come your way this holiday season and in the years to come.

Bro. Dave Nogel

REMEMBER

1) Donations made to St. Joseph's on or before December 31 are deductible this year if you itemize.

2) A gift that is larger-than-usual might enable you to itemize for your 1992 taxes.

3) Consider a gift of appreciated stocks and avoid capital gains tax or receive a considerable savings if exchanged for a Charitable Gift Annuity.

4) This is a beautiful time of the year to give a memorial gift in honor of a loved one while making a charitable gift to us.

5) The IRS allows a charitable deduction for gifts of property such as antiques, artwork, jewelry, and any type of collection if we can actually use it for the school. The deduction would be for the fair market value of the object given.

6) The joy and satisfaction of making a major type gift to the Lakota boys and girls at St. Joseph's Indian School.

It is always wise to consult your tax advisor before any final contribution is made that may affect your tax outcome.

Special Gifts
St. Joseph's Indian School
P.O. Box 100
Chamberlain, SD 57325-0100

Dear Brother David,

Please use the following information to calculate my Gift Annuity benefits. I understand that I am under no obligation and this personalized proposal is FREE.

☐ Immediate Gift Annuity   ☐ Deferred Gift Annuity (payments to begin year _____)

Amount of Gift Being Considered: $ _____ (Minimum Annuity Amount $1,000.)

Frequency of Payment Desired: ☐ Annual   ☐ 2 Times/Year   ☐ 4 Times/Year   ☐ Monthly
                                                              ($5,000 Min.)   ($10,000 Min.)

☐ We are interested in a Two (Joint) Annuity plan.

Name (Mr., Mrs., Miss) _____

Address _____

City _____ State _____ Zip _____

Telephone _____

Name of Second Annuitant: _____

Birth Date: Month _____ Day _____ Year _____

Birth Date: Month _____ Day _____ Year _____

Relationship of Second Annuitant: _____

Please Note: For proposed annuitant(s) less than 50 years of age, we write only Deferred Payment Annuities—payments typically to start at age 65.
(All information is confidential.)

Note that the *singular* "Dear Friend" is used here — and the same, singular salutation appears even if the letter is addressed to a married couple. (Only one person at a time reads a letter!) Abolish the plural "you" from your vocabulary (as in "Dear Friends," for example). Try to avoid the royal "we," too; it smacks of condescension and will detract from the personal character of your appeal.

Use of the singular will require that you stick to a single letter signer. You'll cause yourself two problems by using more than one signer:

(a) You won't be able to enliven your letter with the personal details and emotional asides that might come naturally in a letter from one person to another.

(b) With multiple signers, you'll sacrifice "suspension of disbelief": your reader's willingness to accept that your letter is actually a personal, one-to-one appeal.

Think about it: how am I to believe that two or three busy people who don't live together or work in the same office have collaborated in writing a fundraising letter to me? Which one of them typed the letter? *(Or was it really someone else?)* Did they both *actually* sign it? These are not questions you want your readers to be asking!

When to break Rule Number 1: You may write a letter in the first-person plural if — but only if — there's a very special reason to do so. For example, if the letter is to be signed by a married couple, or your organization's two venerable cofounders, or a famous Republican and a famous Democrat. Even in such exceptional cases, however, I advise you to craft the letter *as though it were written by only one* of the two signers, in much the same manner as one of those annual family letters that arrive by the bushel every December. Something like this:

Howard and I had a terrific time at the yak farm, but the same can't be said for the yaks. (Yep, you guessed it: the kids were up to their old tricks!)

2. Appeal on the basis of benefits, not needs.

Donors give money because they get something in return (if only good feelings). To tap their generosity, describe what they'll receive in return for their money — such benefits as lives saved, or human dignity gained, or larger causes served. And don't be shy about emphasizing *tangible* benefits. Donors may *tell* you they give money for nobler reasons, but premiums often make a difference. (Remember: most donors read your letters in the privacy of their own homes. They don't have to admit their own mixed motives to anyone — not even themselves.)

Look at how Brother David bases his request for funds to the St. Joseph's Indian School on the benefits to the donor, including both tangible and intangible:

If you can send a special gift today of $25 or more, I'd love to send you one of these unique ornaments as a special gift from the children of St. Joseph's.

These highly detailed dream catchers make wonderful gifts for children and new parents, and make unique Christmas Tree decorations.

In any event, please send a gift today of whatever you can afford to bring dreams of hope to the children of St. Joseph's. Without people like you, their lives would be a nightmare.

When to break Rule Number 2: If you're sending a genuine emergency appeal, you'd be a fool not to write about your organization's needs — and graphically so! But if it isn't a real emergency — and you're *really* in trouble if you habitually cry wolf — then write about benefits, not needs. In the long run, you'll raise a lot more money that way.

3. Ask for money, not for "support."

Almost always, the purpose of a fundraising letter is to ask for *financial* help. Be sure you do so — clearly, explicitly, and repeatedly. The "Ask" (pardon my jargon) shouldn't be an afterthought, tacked onto the end of a letter: it's your *reason* for writing.

Repeat the Ask several times in the body of the letter as well as on the reply device. It may even be appropriate to *lead* your letter with the Ask.

Review the St. Joseph's appeal. Note how the Ask appears twice in the letter and twice again on the reply device. Notice, too, how clear and explicit is the request for funds:

send a special gift today of $25 or more

please send a gift today of whatever you can afford

Send a gift today of $25 or more.

Enclosed is my gift of $25, $15, $48, $____.

When to break Rule Number 3: Many direct mail packages are structured not as appeals for funds but as invitations to join a membership organization. Others feature surveys or other donor involvement devices. In these cases, deemphasize the financial commitment, and highlight membership benefits — or stress the impact of completing the survey or mailing the postcard you've enclosed.

4. Write a package, not a letter.

Your fundraising letter is the single most important element in the mailing package; no fundraising appeal is complete without a letter. But it's only one of several items which must fit smoothly together and work as a *whole*. At a minimum, your package will probably include an outer (or carrier) envelope, a reply envelope, and a reply device in addition to the letter. When you sit down to write, think about how each of these components will help persuade donors to *send money now*. Make sure the same themes, symbols, colors, and typefaces are used on all elements, so the package is as memorable and accessible as possible. And be certain *every* element in the package relates directly to the Big Idea or Marketing Concept that gives the appeal its unity. (We'll be talking about Marketing Concepts in Chapter 9.)

Notice that the St. Joseph's Indian School package on pages 31 to 38 contains seven components:

◆ Two-page letter

◆ Reply device

◆ Photograph of "dreamcatcher" premium (full-color)

◆ "Dreamcatcher" Thanksgiving card

◆ Charitable gift annuity brochure

◆ Reply envelope

◆ Outer (carrier) envelope

Now examine these components carefully. You'll see several earmarks of a successful effort to "package" the contents of this appeal in a unified way:

The "dreamcatcher" theme — the Big Idea in this appeal — is emphasized on every component of the package except for the brochure on gift annuities and the nearly text-free reply envelope.

The "subtext" (or underlying theme) of gift giving is explicit almost everywhere — and implicit everywhere else. There's no mistaking that this is an appeal for funds, but it's couched as an *exchange of gifts.*

Although you can't see it in this book's black-and-white reproduction, the colors used on the outer envelope, on the letter, and on the reply device are identical: black text with bright orange accenting and imagery. (One of the two brochures is printed in dark blue, the other in red and black.)

When to break Rule Number 4: Sometimes it pays to spend a little extra money on a package insert that *doesn't* directly relate to the Marketing Concept. For example, a premium offer might be presented on a "buckslip" — an insert specially designed to highlight the premium — but the offer might not appear anywhere else in the package (with the possible exception of the reply device). Often, in fact, a buckslip works best if it *doesn't* use the same color and design as other package elements. (That way, it stands out more clearly.)

5. Write in American English.

Use compact, powerful words and short, punchy sentences. Favor words that convey emotions over those that communicate thoughts. Avoid foreign phrases or big words. Minimize your use of adjectives and adverbs. Don't use abbreviations or acronyms; spell out names, even if their repetition looks a little silly to you. Repeat (and underline) key words and phrases.

Brother David's simple, unadorned language, free of pretense, helps convey the strength of his appeal:

> *good dreams and nightmares*
>
> *the younger kids*
>
> *You bring them good dreams*
>
> *to bring dreams of hope to the children*

When to break Rule Number 5: A letter that could have been written by a twelve-year-old might not look right bearing the signature of a college president or a U.S. senator, so follow this rule judiciously. (But don't make the mistake of confusing big words, complex sentences, and complicated thoughts with intelligent communication: the most literate fundraising letter needs to be clear and straightforward.)

6. Format your letter for easy reading.

Be conscious of the white space you're leaving around your copy; the eye needs rest. Indent every paragraph. Avoid paragraphs more than seven lines long, but vary the size of your paragraphs. Use bullets and indented paragraphs. In long letters, try subheads that are centered and underlined. Underline sparingly but consistently throughout your letter — enough to call attention to key words and phrases (especially those that highlight the benefits to the reader), but not so much as to distract the eye from your message.

Take another look at the St. Joseph's appeal. Notice that not one paragraph in the body of the letter is longer than five lines (and there's *only* one that long!). Only the P.S. exceeds that limit, with seven lines. Every paragraph is indented the standard five spaces, even though the letter is printed on Monarch-sized paper. There are neither underlining nor bulleted points in Brother David's appeal,

but they aren't needed here; the letter is short enough, and sufficiently appealing. It's easy to read.

When to break Rule Number 6: Don't mechanically follow this rule. Some special formats, such as telegrams or handwritten notes, have formatting rules of their own. Don't ignore them. Remember that you want the reader to believe — or at least to *act* as though she believes — that you've sent her a telegram, a handwritten note, or a personal letter.

7. Give your readers a reason to send money NOW.

Creating a sense of urgency is one of your biggest copywriting challenges. Try to find a genuine reason why gifts are needed right away: for example, a deadline for a matching grant or an approaching election date. Or tie your fund request to a budgetary deadline so you can argue why "gifts are needed within the next 15 days." There is *always* a reason to send a gift now. And the argument for the urgency of your appeal bears repeating — ideally, not just in the text of your letter, but also in a P.S. and on the reply device.

There are several ways Brother David's builds a sense of urgency in his appeal for the children of St. Joseph's Indian School:

◆ The emphasis on Thanksgiving in an appeal dated October 30 provides a natural and easily understood deadline.

◆ The brochure headlining "End of the Year Pre-Planning" sets a fallback date — December 31 — thus laying down a second line of urgency.

◆ Brother David's comment that "we have ordered a small number of Lakota dream catchers" implies that the supply could run out quickly, leaving the donor *without* "wonderful gifts for children and new parents."

◆ The topic of "poverty, illiteracy, and despair" is freighted with urgency all its own.

When to break Rule Number 7: Be very careful about fixed deadlines if you're mailing via bulk rate.

(Instead of giving a date, use a phrase like "within the next two weeks.") Don't overuse the same arguments for urgency, lest your credibility suffer. And try *not* to depend on deadlines based on actual dates in large-scale mailings to acquire new donors: the value of those letters will almost always be greater if you can continue to use the same letter over and over again.

8. Write as long a letter as you need to make the case for your offer.

Not everyone will read every word you write, but some recipients will do so, no matter how long your letter. Others will scan your copy for the information that interests them the most. To be certain you push *their* hot buttons, use every strong argument you can devise for your readers to send you money now. And to spell out every argument may mean writing a *very* long letter; it may also mean repeating what you've written to the same donors many times in the past. But don't worry about boring your readers by restating your case: research repeatedly reveals that even the most active donors remember very little about the organizations they support.

Brother David's appeal for St. Joseph's is only two pages long. But if all the information contained in the two inserts devoted specifically to the "dream-catcher" offer were to be included in the letter rather than printed as separate items, the appeal would run to three pages. (It's much better the way it is!) Still, this letter doesn't convey enough information about St. Joseph's to answer the questions that might occur to a *prospective* donor who's never before heard of the school. (For starters: "How many kids attend the school? Where is Chamberlain? Does all the money come from donors like me, or does the government pay, too?") This appeal was mailed to a previous donor who, presumably, has had those questions answered.

When to break Rule Number 8: Not every organization — and not every appeal — calls for a long letter. A well-known organization with a readily identifiable purpose might be able to make its case with only a sentence or two. The American Red Cross, for example, or a prominent children's hospital; a few words might get the point across, in either case. Similarly, in writing to your proven donors, you can sometimes state the argument for a straightforward membership renewal or special appeal in few words. "It's time to renew your membership" is a good example.

Three more things to keep in mind

If you write for impact — heeding the basics of strong and effective writing outlined in Chapter 1 — and if you follow the eight rules I've just described, you won't go far wrong when you write your next fundraising appeal. But I suggest you also keep in mind the psychology of the position you've placed yourself in as the signer of your letter. You might want to consider the following as three additional rules of writing fundraising letters:

◆ "You" — the signer — are an individual human being, with hopes, fears, convictions, and experiences. Look at how Brother David takes up that challenge, writing about "sweet dreams," "nightmares," "despair," "loved ones," and "wonderful gifts." This is no masterpiece of self-revelation, but it gives a sense of a man who is engaged in his work and feels strongly about the kids at the school.

◆ "You" are writing to one person — the addressee — who has hopes, fears, convictions, and experiences, too. Note how Brother David appeals directly to the donor's feelings: "You bring them good feelings," "to bring good dreams to yourself and your family," "Without people like you, their lives would be a nightmare."

◆ Regardless of its mission, your organization addresses human needs on many levels, intangible as well as concrete, emotional as well as practical. Those are the things people care about. Remember that Brother David doesn't write about budgets, and fiscal years, and funding shortfalls. He writes about *the kids,* their dreams, their night-mares.

Join me now on an excursion into the realm of donor psychology as we examine "How a Fund-raising Letter Is Like a Personal Visit." ▶

3

HOW A FUNDRAISING LETTER IS LIKE A PERSONAL VISIT

Most of us who write letters to raise funds — or to sell products or services, for that matter — have a one-word answer to the question "How do you know whether that will work?" Our answer is "Test."

A German professor of direct marketing named Siegfried Vögele has *two* answers. He's just as firmly committed as any of us to the rigors of head-to-head testing to determine which of two or more variations in copy, design, or content will secure the best response. But Vögele can also cite chapter and verse from a second and different realm of research that uses such devices as eye-motion cameras and machines that measure subtle changes in skin chemistry. This research, conducted over many years, has given him profound and detailed knowledge of the ways human beings actually react when they hold direct mail materials in their hands.

Many of us guess about these things; we have insights or hunches. Siegfried Vögele often *knows*.

Professor Vögele has been practicing and teaching his craft in Germany since the 1970s. In 1980, he caused a sensation at the all-European direct marketing conference (held every year at Montreux, Switzerland) and has taught his Dialogue Method throughout Europe ever since. Thousands of marketers have attended his seminars. Articles based on his eye-motion research have made their way into America (including a lengthy adaptation in my own 1993 book, *999 Tips, Trends and Guidelines for Successful Direct Mail and Telephone Fundraising*). Vögele's *Handbook of Direct Mail*, published in German in 1984, has been translated into Italian, French, and — more recently — English. In other words, the story's getting out. (Please see the reading list at the back of this book for details about both of these books.)

The translation of Vögele's *Handbook* leaves much to be desired, as does the structure and organization of the original material. So I'll do my best to lay out for you in the following pages the essence of Vögele's Dialogue Method as it applies to writing

How to Write Successful Fundraising Letters

direct mail letters — and I'll carry the translation one step further into the realm of fundraising.

What happens in a personal fundraising visit

The doorbell rings. You're not expecting anyone but, good citizen that you are, you trudge to the front door, switch on the porch light, and squint through the peephole.

There she is: nineteen, twenty years old, scruffily dressed, a clipboard tightly gripped in one hand and an eager smile pasted on her face. Now, just between you and me, let's admit it: you're thinking, "Who is this young person? What does she want with me at this hour? Is this another of those annoying canvassers? Do I have to write another check for twenty or twenty-five bucks to get her to leave? What group does she represent, and why are they bothering me? Am I *really* going to let this little pest inside my home?"

Okay: let's assume you actually open the door, say something civil to the kid, and listen to her long enough to hear that the young woman is representing a charity called [fill-in-the-blank]. Not only that, but there's something she says — you're not quite sure what — about how what [fill-in-the-blank] is doing actually relates to things you care about. Besides, she's a beguiling young person who appears to have a bright future. You sigh, open the door a little wider, and (still reluctant) let her into the house.

Now perched on the edge of your living-room couch, the young canvasser launches into her pitch for [fill-in-the-blank]. You're not listening closely, but you get the gist of it. Every so often you nod, smile, or gesture with your hands. Encouraged, she plunges ahead, keeping her eyes on you all the while she speaks, emphasizing this or that or the other thing as you demonstrate more interest (or less) by the way you nod your head, fold or uncross your arms, or even occasionally ask a question or venture a comment. There are lots of questions on your mind — you can't avoid that — but you pose few of them, not wanting to drag out this unwanted conversation. Also, you don't understand or agree with everything the fundraiser says, but when you frown, shrug or lift your eyebrows in a questioning way, she slips in a quick answer or makes a reassuring statement, then quickly rushes on to the next point. All this goes on for a few minutes, until the fundraiser says . . . *something* . . . that really catches your attention.

Fully engaged for the moment, you make a casual reference to an experience related to what she's just said and — just to be polite — you ask her a pointed question. With a rush, she launches into a detailed answer. It's interesting for a few seconds, but then your eyes start glazing over (don't deny it, you know it happens!). Noticing your discomfort, the young woman makes some comment about the lateness of the hour and immediately makes her pitch: "So, can I count on you for a gift of fifty dollars tonight to help [fill-in-the-blank]?"

Fifty dollars is far too much, so you demur, settling for $25 instead. (Truth to tell, you're just as interested in getting the kid to leave you alone as you are in helping [fill-in-the-blank].) The canvasser gratefully volunteers to wait while you retrieve your checkbook. She accepts your gift with effusive thanks and departs, leaving behind a thin sheaf of papers with the latest developments at [fill-in-the-blank] and a promise that soon you'll be hearing from them again so you'll know how your gift has been used.

Now, what has just happened here?

1. The canvasser got your attention by ringing your doorbell. You weren't expecting her, and as far as you're concerned, the evening would've been just as pleasant, if not more so, if she'd never shown up.

2. The moment you set eyes on her, barely conscious questions started welling up in your head in quick order: you wondered who she was, and why she'd come, and what she wanted you to do — and you answered most of those questions for yourself as quickly as they popped into your mind, because the obvious answers were staring you in the face.

3. The young woman was representing a charity that's working on an issue you care a lot about. If she'd asked your help for some other organization, or to address some other issue, you might just as well have smiled as politely as you were able and wished her better luck with the neighbors.

4. Her manner or her appearance — combined with something about your own mood and circumstances — induced you to let her into your home. You weren't planning to do so; it just happened. And you invited her in even though you knew perfectly well she was going to ask you for money.

5. Once inside, the young woman delivered her pitch, watching your body language all the while and answering every question you raised, as responsively as she could, some more fully than others.

6. Something she said triggered a strong reaction in you — enough, at least, to provoke a comment of your own and a substantive question. Right away, the fundraiser gave you all the details you asked for, and more.

7. As soon as she sensed your patience waning, the fundraiser moved quickly to ask for a gift. She knew perfectly well you support the work of [fill-in-the-blank]: her challenge was to make you admit it.

8. You declined to contribute the full amount she requested, but you did agree to give something. Since you had taken up so much of her time, it seemed the least you could do. Anyway, [fill-in-the-blank] does such valuable work!

9. The canvasser didn't just take your money and run: she thanked you for your support, reassured you it will make a big difference and promised you'll hear again soon from [fill-in-the-blank].

In short, you started the evening with absolutely no intention of giving a cent to [fill-in-the-blank] — or anybody else, for that matter — let alone a check

for $25. You've done so, anyway — and you know what? You feel pretty good about it!

Now what if, instead, you'd been approached by [fill-in-the-blank] *by letter?* Let's look at that experience as it might be viewed through the practiced eye of Professor Siegfried Vögele.

How people decide whether to open fundraising letters

You've just gotten home from a rotten day at the office. You toss the mail into a heap on the coffee-table, grab something to drink from the refrigerator, and collapse into the easy chair, flicking on the TV with the remote control in one hand and pulling the wastebasket close to your chair with the other. Now, one or two deep breaths later, barely paying attention in the flickering glow of the television screen, you retrieve a handful of mail and begin the daily ritual.

Plunk! into the wastebasket goes the fourth duplicate copy of the Spiegel catalog. *Plunk!* again, in one smooth, unhesitating motion: another American Express card offer. And again and again: that health charity that reminds you of things you want to forget . . . a packet of discount coupons from a store you wouldn't visit if your life depended on it . . . a promise of untold wealth from Publishers Clearing House . . . a picture of pathetic little children. Amid all this . . . *stuff* . . . is not. One. Single. Personal. Letter!

But wait: here's the gas and electric bill. And here's something else that may be worth a glance. At least they spelled your name right (unlike the Spiegel people and a couple of the others). This one's from [fill-in-the-blank] — the people who do all that good stuff about whatchamacallit. You know it's from them, because their name and address are right there in the upper left-hand corner, and, besides, there's a photo on the envelope that looks a lot like whatchamacallit. Anyway, it sure looks familiar.

Chances are, this is another fundraising appeal from [fill-in-the-blank] — but you never know for sure until you look inside. Maybe they have something interesting to say, even if it is a solicitation.

Before you know it, you've turned over the envelope from [fill-in-the-blank], slit it open with your finger, and pulled the contents out onto your lap. *Now* there's no question what these people want from you: the self-addressed envelope with those telltale broad stripes and the reply card with a hefty checkmark and a big bold "YES!" above a string of dollar amounts leave no doubt whatsoever this is a fundraising solicitation. But [fill-in-the-blank] is a fascinating group, and a photo and caption on the reply card give the impression this letter is definitely about whatchamacallit, so it's probably worth looking a little further.

Now let's take stock before we stumble deeper into the jungle of real-world fundraising. What's happening here, and how does it compare to the experience you've just had with that aggressive young canvasser?

1. You weren't expecting a fundraising letter from [fill-in-the-blank] any more than you were anticipating the young woman's visit to your home.

2. When you first glanced at [fill-in-the-blank]'s appeal, you weren't paying much attention at all — even less attention, no doubt, than you paid that canvasser. (After all, she was standing right there, in your face.) Vögele estimates we devote no more than *10 percent* of our attention to reading unsolicited mail!

3. Despite your lack of attentiveness, you noticed one thing without fail: they spelled your name correctly. That young woman didn't know your name, but she looked you in the eye, accomplishing much the same end.

4. Something else about the letter caught your attention, however, triggering curiosity or concern — enough, at any rate, to motivate you to open the envelope and pull out the contents. What did the trick? The [fill-in-the-blank] name? That photo of whatchamacallit? It's hard to know (but ultimately doesn't matter) exactly what made the difference, just as your decision to open your front door to that canvasser was impulsive and difficult to analyze.

5. As you opened the envelope and dribbled the contents onto your lap, a stream of questions started flitting nearly unnoticed through the depths of your consciousness, much like those that came to mind as the fundraiser delivered her pitch in your livingroom. These questions included the obvious ones ("What's this about? What do they want from me? What's it going to cost me?"), and many of them were answered at a glance as you observed the contents of [fill-in-the-blank]'s appeal. These casual little traces of wonderment or confusion are what Siegfried Vögele calls "unspoken readers' questions." As many as twenty such questions pop into the average reader's mind upon picking up a direct mail solicitation.

But all this slips by with amazing speed. So far, the whole incident — from your first glimpse of the [fill-in-the-blank] solicitation to your dumping the contents onto your lap — has taken up a maximum of five to eight seconds.

To get a better sense of just how quickly five seconds flit by, follow the secondhand on your watch, or count backward slowly by thousands. Those five *long* seconds spell the difference between the success or failure of a fundraising appeal. Tonight, for [fill-in-the-blank], they've been enough for a very good start.

Now, let's pick up the trail of our story again.

How a fundraising letter is like a face-to-face dialogue

Taking a sip of your drink, then turning up the volume on the television set, you now fish out [fill-in-the-blank]'s letter from the jumble on your lap. Dangling it before you between thumb and forefinger, you glance at the front page. Briefly you take in a dramatic little photo in the upper right-hand corner and note that the letter contains short paragraphs, subheads, and underlining. Then you quickly flip the letter over to the back page to see who's writing you.

Your eyes temporarily fix on the signature and the typed name below it, then drop down onto the postscript; it's only three lines long, so you read it through. Sure enough, [fill-in-the-blank] is hoping you'll send money to do something new about whatchamacallit. A whole new round of questions rushes to the surface — questions such as "How are they going to pull that off again? Will my twenty-five bucks make a difference? Are they going to send me something if I mail them a gift?" So now you scan the subheads and underlined words in the letter at a rapid rate, *first on the last page,* then, very briefly, on the two interior pages, and finally on the first page again.

Now, at last, you begin reading the letter's opening sentence. It's the beginning of a story, and before you know it you're hooked. You read first one longish paragraph, then another — but that's enough. You're satisfied. [Fill-in-the-blank] is up to its old tricks, all right, and you're just as eager to be part of the act this year as you were before. Out of long-ingrained habit, you grab the reply card and scan it to be sure you didn't misunderstand what [fill-in-the-blank] expected of you. Satisfied there was no miscommunication, you add the reply card to [fill-in-the-blank]'s postage-paid return envelope and drop them on top of the gas and electric bill: both will go into the "bills to pay" file. You'll write them both checks next Saturday — or so, at any rate, that's what you say to yourself.

Let's pause here to take stock again, reviewing what's taken place from the perspective of Siegfried Vögele.

1. You were still largely inattentive — after all, you had a drink in one hand and a TV set blaring in front of your face — but something about the letter from [fill-in-the-blank] persuaded you to turn it over for a second look rather than toss it into the waste-

basket along with the day's direct mail losers. Was it that little photo on the first page? The way those short paragraphs, subheads, and underlining suggested the letter would be quick and easy to read? No doubt both factors helped (and I'll have more to say about that in a moment).

2. Take careful note: your eyes may have skipped through quite a number of words in scanning the first page of the letter, but you didn't actually *read* anything. The first words you read were the signature; the first element of text, the postscript. In other words, *the P.S. was the lead of this letter!* Siegfried Vögele says his eye-motion research reveals the postscript is the first text read by more than 90 percent of all direct mail recipients!

3. But what was it you saw on the final page of the letter that motivated you, first to read the P.S. and then to scan the subheads and underlining? Was it the easy-to-read format and accessible language — or was there something genuinely involving in what you read? Was [fill-in-the-blank] making it worth your while to read on — by answering *your* unspoken questions with carefully crafted subheads, addressing *your* concerns through judicious underlining, spelling out the advantages *you* would receive by supporting their work? Vögele says yes: that only by answering *your* silent questions through such devices as these will a solicitation be involving enough to induce you to read on. If the letter doesn't answer those questions in the most obvious and accessible way, it's unlikely to be read at all.

4. Notice that the first time you actually read a complete block of copy was when you took in the P.S. The *second* time was after you read the opening sentence of the letter and learned it was interesting enough to engage you; then you read one or two complete paragraphs — and *that* was the point where you were really, finally, hooked. In Siegfried Vögele's way of looking at these things, there are two stages in a reader's involvement in a direct mail letter. As soon as you read one full block of text from beginning to end, you passed from the first stage into the second and final stage. At that precise moment, you began to participate in the "comprehensive second dialogue." Here's how Vögele himself describes the process: "We answer unspoken readers' questions in a simple, easily understood way, first through a short 'dialogue' which makes the reader aware of the benefit to himself, then through a [second and] more detailed 'dialogue' built along the same lines as a real personal sales conversation."

5. But what was it that caused you to glide so smoothly from the "short dialogue" to the "comprehensive second dialogue"? Vögele would say many factors contributed — everything in the content, language, and format that made the letter easy to read, accessible, informative . . . and directly responsive to *your* concerns. All are examples of the response boosters he calls "amplifiers" — little signs and gestures of positive reinforcement that help the reader spot encouraging answers to his unspoken questions.

In Professor Vögele's lexicon, "filters" are the polar opposite of amplifiers. They're the *negative* forces that come into play in a direct mail package: the elements of formatting or contents that make the package hard to read, uninteresting, off-putting.

Amplifiers provide you with little "yeses" to answer those unspoken questions. Filters produce "no's."

The canvasser used her own arsenal of amplifiers by speaking intelligently (but not over your head), answering your questions (whether vocalized or not), watching and responding to your body language, and shutting up quickly when your patience flagged.

She skillfully moved you to answer yes to your own unvocalized questions — again and again and again. She avoided all the little traps (or filters) — the distractions, the boring lists of facts, the self-centered emphasis on [fill-in-the-blank]'s needs. Instinctively, she knew those missteps were a surefire way to lead you to answer your own unspoken questions with no — over and over again. Whoever wrote that

letter for [fill-in-the-blank] did much the same thing, guiding you to answer yes far more often than you answered no.

As Vögele sees it, getting to that big YES! — a check-mark on the reply form, along with a check — is merely a matter of helping the reader answer yes a lot more frequently than he answers no.

But something else was going on here, too, something much more basic:

Both fundraisers — the letterwriter no less than the canvasser — took pains to engage you in a dialogue. They answered *your* questions (spoken or not). They both went out of their way to involve you in a conversation — silent and one-sided in the case of the letter, but nonetheless involving.

Neither the young woman nor the writer of the letter was engaged in a monologue, preoccupied with [fill-in-the-blank]'s needs and problems. Both made the effort to *relate the organization's needs to you* — the listener or the reader — in a style, language, and presentation format that subtly moved you to adopt [fill-in-the-blank]'s needs as your own.

Answering your reader's questions before they're even asked

The trick to this craft, Siegfried Vögele tells us, is to anticipate the questions that will be on the reader's mind — and answer those questions clearly and forcefully. He admonishes us to pay extra special attention to those questions that highlight the advantages the reader will enjoy (what we call *benefits*). Your answers must find their way into photos or drawings (and accompanying captions) or into subheads or underlined phrases or words — because those are the items in your letter that the reader will notice *before* actually reading what you've written!

Much of the skill that a letterwriter brings to the task, then, is to catalog those questions readers are sure to ask — and artfully weave the answers into the letter. Vögele says there are two types: "basic questions" and "product questions." (I told you the translation was less than artful!) Although Vögele's terminology is obviously derived from the experience of commercial direct marketing, both categories of readers' unspoken questions have their equivalents in the realm of fundraising.

Here, for example, are some of the "basic questions" that donors or prospective donors might ask themselves when they pick up one of your fundraising letters. These are questions that involuntarily leap to mind when someone picks up any fundraising letter.

- Where did this letter come from?
- What's inside the envelope?
- Who wrote this letter?
- Who signed this letter?
- Where did they get my address?
- What do they know about me?
- Why are they writing to me specifically?
- How much money do they want from me?
- Should I even bother to read this letter?
- Can they prove what they say?
- What happens after I respond?
- Do I have to sign anything?
- Do I have to put a stamp on it?
- What would my spouse think about this?
- What would my friends think?
- Can this wait?
- What would happen if I don't do anything?
- Can I throw this thing away?
- Have I received this before?
- Will they put my name on another mailing list?
- What's the catch?

Now consider some of the many "product questions" that might leap into your reader's mind at the first sight of your fundraising letter. Questions of this type relate specifically to your appeal and might not come to mind if your reader were instead examining an appeal from some other charity.

- Have I heard of this organization before?
- Have I given to these people before?

- Do they get any government funds?
- Do they really need my help?
- What difference will it make if I respond?
- Are they going to send me a newsletter?
- Will I get lots of other solicitations from these people?
- Will they expect me to give them money every year?
- How much of this gift will actually be used the way they say?
- How is this different from what other groups do?
- Are they going to send me a thank-you?
- Have they been doing this kind of work for very long?
- Is there a local branch of this organization?
- How do I know they're honest?
- Who runs this organization?
- Is there anybody famous who supports them?
- Is there a deadline?
- What do I have to do to fill out the reply card?
- Is there a better solution for this problem?

These questions are actually pretty straightforward, aren't they? Questions of both types are a natural human response to any unsolicited appeal, whether it comes by mail or in person. In a face-to-face visit, the fundraiser intentionally confronts the most promising of these questions — and tries to provoke yet more questions, knowing that engaging a prospect in *dialogue* is the straightest path to a gift. In a written fundraising appeal, too, the skillful writer seeks to anticipate these readers' unspoken questions, knowing that the more directly readers' true private concerns are met the more involved they'll become in *silent dialogue.*

But what happens if the writer doesn't properly anticipate and answer the reader's unspoken questions? Instead of a preponderance of little "yeses" that add up to one big beautiful YES!, the "no's" have it, Vögele says — and *plunk!* goes that letter, too! Rejection can come at any moment, he warns us. There are four possible stages in which the reader might give up on you.

The four waves of rejection

1. You've got up to twenty seconds to engage the reader — just long enough for her to open the envelope, examine the contents, and decide whether to spend any more time with your letter. Siegfried Vögele refers to this as the "first run-through." In this stage, you face your first and biggest hurdle; if your letter survives this test, the greatest danger is past. If, instead, the reader concludes, "I've never heard of these people before," or "I already sent them money this year," or simply "I'm not interested" — or any one of a thousand other possible excuses not to proceed — your appeal may well end up in the wastebasket. Most do. Even letters to your most loyal and generous donors may suffer this ignoble fate: few people have the time or the inclination to read everything they receive in the mail.

2. If your appeal survives the first wave of possible rejection, your chances of securing a gift are greatly improved — but you're not home free. All that's happened, from Siegfried Vögele's perspective, is that your reader has found satisfactory answers to the *first* round of silent questions. Now, reading more thoroughly, the reader looks for answers to a whole new round of questions. Previously, the reader has looked only at the pictures, read the subheads, and cruised through the underlined text. Now comes the true test: what you've written (or failed to include) in the blocks of text. What the reader encounters here, too, must respond to questions and spell out the benefits the reader will receive as a result of giving a gift. If the blocks of text in your letter don't speak to the reader and if your text fails to provoke a preponderance of little "yeses," chances are your appeal will make its way into the trash in this "second throw-away wave."

3. But even if your letter survives the second wave of rejection, there's yet more potential trouble

in store for you: for starters, the "filing-away or archive wave." If your letter succumbs to the near-universal human fondness to put off until later what could just as easily be done right now, it won't find its way into the trash — at least not immediately. But, Vögele points out, time acts as a filter: the reader who was impressed enough with your appeal to put it away for later reference may after a week or a month has gone by no longer remember why she was so moved. The effect achieved is little better than a big fat NO! Rarely will archived appeals result in donations. (So how, you might ask, can this tendency be avoided? Here's one suggestion: don't include such items as hole-punched newsletters or pamphlets that radiate the message "File me!")

4. Vögele distinguishes between the phenomenon of "archiving" (or filing away) and what he terms "putting to one side." The difference lies in the reader's intentions: in putting aside your appeal, the reader has resolved to do . . . *something* . . . but can't quite make up her mind. This may happen because you've presented her with a decision to make, a question to answer, a form to fill out, a comment or greeting to write — or because she simply doesn't have enough money in her checking account at the moment. Vögele estimates that 50 percent of solicitations that are "put to one side" will ultimately get lost. He explains: "One day, they may well end up in the wastebasket too, even if the advantage offered in them was once recognized. In the meantime, a long period of time has elapsed. New pictures and information have taken precedence."

Here's the key: the faster you get your reader to respond, the more likely she will. That puts an enormous burden on the first twenty seconds of your letter's exposure to the reader's indifference. So let's conclude by going back to the beginning of this process: the first twenty seconds.

A closer look at the first twenty seconds in your letter's public life

Vögele divides the crucial first twenty seconds into three phases:

1. In the first phase — before the envelope is opened — eight seconds go by on average. During this time, recipients turn over the envelope, note how they're addressed, read the return address and any text (or teaser), look for a way to open the envelope, and finally tear it open.

2. In a second phase, lasting approximately four seconds, the reader picks up and examines the contents. Even before she's read a single word, the materials have immediate impact on her. She unfolds them, forming a general impression of what they contain.

3. A third phase occupying another eight seconds is what Vögele refers to as the "first run-through." The reader examines the pictures and headlines, finding short answers to her silent questions. If the writer has done a good job, the reader is now fully engaged in the "short dialogue."

Now remember: the writer's objective is to involve the reader by persuading her to *read* some of the blocks of text in the letter — to become involved in the "comprehensive second dialogue."

"This means you need to get your reader's interest long before the twenty seconds are up," Vögele warns. The recipient will continue reading only if the benefits *to her* are obvious within the first few seconds. And that's why he insists a letter needs to "express the advantages to the reader by using pictures and headlines" and underlined words and phrases.

Now let's take a break from the quantifiable certainties of German research and venture into the realm of *qualitative* research — by taking a close look at "What Donors Really Think About Fundraising Letters." ▶

WHAT DONORS REALLY THINK ABOUT FUNDRAISING LETTERS

I took time out from writing this book to observe a focus group in Los Angeles. For two hours I cringed behind a two-way mirror while ten people sat around a table, picking apart a direct mail fundraising letter for Camp Fire Boys and Girls. I was present because Camp Fire had retained my firm to help them launch a nationwide direct mail fundraising program.

The worst part was that the letter those people were savaging was one I'd edited less than a week before. I'd thought the letter was pretty good to begin with, but I was convinced my brilliant editing had lifted it into the ranks of the fundraising Hall of Fame. Indeed, one of my senior associates went out of his way to congratulate me on my fine work (nonetheless pointing out — too late — a few embarrassing little editorial oversights). And, for the first time ever, Camp Fire staff approved the text without changing a single word. They *loved* the letter.

Of course, Camp Fire had agreed that, before mailing the letter, we would test our draft copy in focus groups and not rely exclusively on our own instincts. The Los Angeles group was the second of two organized exclusively for that purpose.

The group included seven women and three men. They were diverse in age, ethnicity, religion, and income level as well as occupation: among them were a couple of retired people, a housewife, a teacher, a banker, two business owners. Half had completed at least four years of college; most had done volunteer work in the past three years.

Despite their differences, these ten people had one crucial element in common: in interviews over the phone they said they had previously contributed money by mail to human service organizations such as the Girl Scouts, Boys' Town, Special Olympics, City of Hope, or Red Cross. In other words, they seemed to us like good prospects to support Camp Fire.

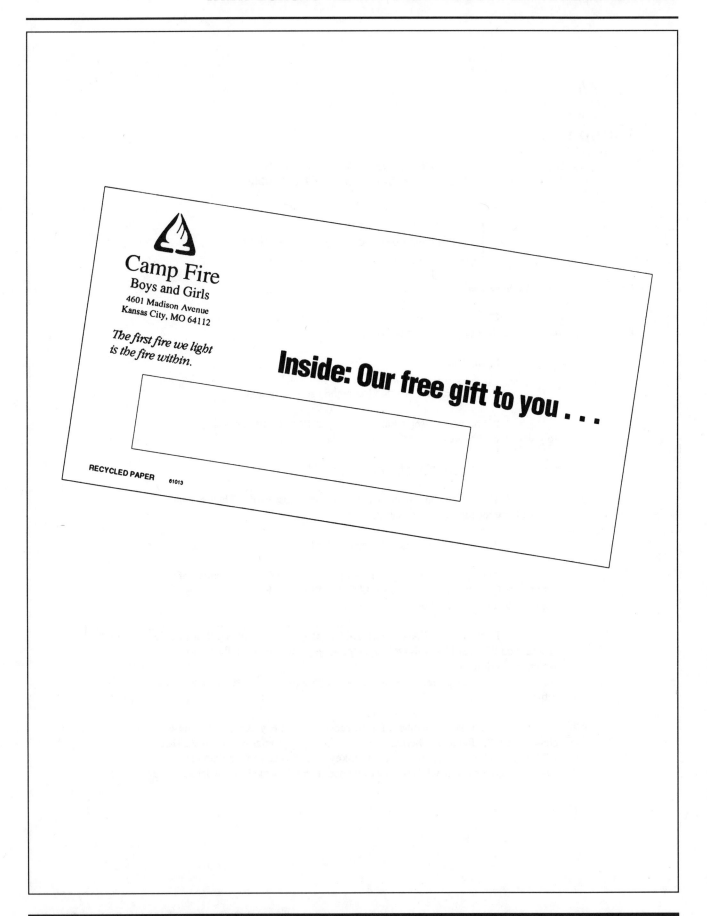

Camp Fire
Boys and Girls
4601 Madison Avenue
Kansas City, MO 64112

*The first fire we light
is the fire within.*

Inside: Our free gift to you . . .

RECYCLED PAPER   61013

Camp Fire
Boys and Girls
4601 Madison Avenue
Kansas City, MO 64112

**CAMP FIRE BOYS AND GIRLS
The First Fire We Light is the Fire Within...**

> **"I'm gonna be dead by the time I'm 18."**

Dear Caring American,

Chances are, you never had to cope with the things kids have to confront as they're growing up today.

I sure didn't!

Crack. Cocaine. AIDS. The nightly sounds of gunfire.

It's no wonder some kids as young as 10 or 12 attempt suicide. For too many kids the future's just too painful to face.

<u>But there is help and hope for these kids!</u>

That's why I'm sending you the enclosed post-cards. They're a message of hope for the children of this nation.

And that's a message of hope for <u>all</u> of us.

And I sincerely hope you'll join me today as a Charter Member of the CAMP FIRE BOYS AND GIRLS LEADERSHIP CIRCLE — to help bring new hope to children all over America.

By supporting CAMP FIRE BOYS AND GIRLS with a gift of as little as $12, you'll be reaching kids <u>while they're young</u>. Before they fall prey to violence and despair.
<u>You'll</u> help these kids find a way to <u>be somebody</u> — somebody with a future.

As a Charter Member of our Leadership Circle, you can guide these children into the future by offering them the life-saving programs of CAMP FIRE BOYS AND GIRLS. Programs for "latch-key" kids forced to spend hours home alone. Programs that teach kids how to defend themselves against the dangers you and I never had to face. Programs that show kids what life on drugs is <u>really</u> like.

I can tell you from personal experience that it's a wonderful feeling to be a grownup who's part of turning kids lives around.

And I want you to share that terrific feeling.

So, please, join the fast-growing circle of concerned Americans who are giving kids the strength — and the hope — to escape from gangs and drugs and guns.

Please send your gift of $12, $20, $25 or more to CAMP FIRE <u>today</u>.

Let these kids know you believe in them!

With high hopes for the future,

K. Russell Weathers,
National Executive Director

P.S. Remember how long a week lasted when you were eight
years old? I worry when kids in gang neighborhoods have to
wait for our programs. So I'm asking you to take a minute
<u>right now</u> to send your tax-deductible Charter Membership
gift to CAMP FIRE. Thank you for caring!

Camp Fire
Boys and Girls
4601 Madison Avenue
Kansas City, MO 64112

☐ **YES, I want to show today's kids that I believe in them.**
Here's my tax-deductible Charter Membership Gift to
CAMP FIRE BOYS AND GIRLS. Please put my
contribution to work right away. Help young boys and
girls learn to "be somebody" — and find hope again —
before they fall prey to gangs, drugs, AIDS and guns.

☐ $12   ☐ $25   ☐ $35   ☐ $50   ☐ $100   ☐ S_____

As a Charter Member of the CAMP FIRE BOYS AND GIRLS LEADERSHIP
CIRCLE with a gift of $12 or more, you'll receive a free subscription to our newsletter,
the CAMP FIRE **Digest**, plus special updates on our programs to restore hope to
America's kids.

The enclosed postcards are our gift to you. Please share that gift with someone you
care about.

— Russ Weathers

How ten people reacted to my pride and joy

Now here's what happened:

Under the skillful guidance of a professional moderator, the participants quickly warmed up to the subject at hand by discussing their views of direct mail fundraising and of youth programs. They revealed what they knew — mostly what they *didn't* know — about Camp Fire. Prodded by the discussion leader, they cited examples of "good letters" from charities (ones that were "interesting" and contained "local examples so you can see the money at work"). Their biggest concern about fundraising letters was "authenticity." They were worried about getting sucked into scams "like you hear about on TV."

The group analyzed Camp Fire's tagline — "The first fire we light is the fire within" — which most of them seemed to like. (A typical comment: "I'm not sure [what it means], but I like it.") Then they critiqued one of our two candidates for the outer envelope design. (You'll find it on page 55.) Here's what they had to say about that:

"Recycled paper." I like that.

Pretty good as an envelope.

Camp Fire caught my attention. The logo.

[For me, it was] the heart.

[I focused on] "Inside: Our free gift."

There might be too much on it.

*It's very feminine. Like Camp Fire **girls**.*

You get the feeling there's something they're going to tell you about the spark.

"Free gift"? I like that.

They want something.

I'd throw this away.

Why are they offering a free gift?

I'd open it.

So would I.

I'd toss it.

You think you have to send a gift and then they'll send something.

Mixed reviews, but not too bad for starters! Then the moderator passed out the fundraising letter reproduced on pages 47 to 49 and asked the group to read it.

The one-and-a-half-page letter the focus group participants received was the one I had edited; it was actually a version of a much longer letter my firm had drafted. My hunch was that a shorter letter would be better received in the market we expected to mail for Camp Fire, because appeals from many charities already competing in that market were typically short.

Now listen to what the group had to say about the letter:

I would throw it away.

There's nothing in there that says anything about the free gift.

There's not enough information in there.

How are they going to teach kids to "be somebody"?

I don't know Camp Fire.

I think it's very wordy.

How do I know it's an authentic program?

It didn't sell me.

There's a lot of programs out there that are trying to do the same thing.

I'd rather contribute to an L.A.-based organization.

[I'd contribute] if it said kids in L.A. would be helped.

[The letter] just doesn't flow very well.

I don't like this "Dear Caring American." Leave that out.

Are these kids from poorer areas, or is this like the Boy Scouts?

Is "kids" acceptable? Shouldn't you say "children"? "Teens"? "Youth"?

This doesn't sound like Camp Fire. There's nothing camp-y here.

They've been in business for over fifty years. Why don't they say that?

An 800-number? A hotline or somewhere you can call.

At various points along the way, the moderator turned the group's attention to specific elements in the letter copy:

- "I'm gonna be dead by the time I'm 18." – *It's not big enough. It wouldn't mean anything unless I read the rest.*

- "Leadership Circle" — *Too long a name." "Do I become a member?*

- "Charter Member" — *It sounds like the group [Camp Fire] is new. I'm not important enough [to be a Charter Member]. This letter's going to ten million people. Just ask me for the money. Does it mean they'll expect more money next year?*

To clinch matters, the moderator asked the group, "If you received this letter in the mail, would you consider making a contribution?" The unanimous response: "No."

Oh, ignominy! Oh, pain and suffering!

But, boy am I glad that answer came from a focus group, and not from an equally uncaring public — after Camp Fire spent a small fortune mailing 50,000 copies of the stupid thing all over the country!

Why did we set up that exasperating focus group, anyway?

Now listen to a few of the comments about the *four-page* version of our Camp Fire appeal our firm had drafted:

I personally like this. I would give.

It gives you an actual person.

It's lovely.

[The lead] grabs you – real hard.

A similar sentiment prevailed the evening before in a focus group assembled in Tulsa, Oklahoma. I'm told the Tulsa group had a somewhat different take on the first letter: They were much more familiar with Camp Fire, were much less critical of the copy,

and showed none of the L.A. group's cynicism about charity. But, emphasis and nuances aside, there's no question *both groups favored the longer letter* instead of the shorter, and by a huge margin.

However, Camp Fire didn't go to all the trouble and expense of organizing focus groups merely to choose between two versions of one appeal. Hearing unguarded comments from representative prospects helped us fine-tune our copy. We were able to answer major questions we hadn't anticipated and clear up ambiguities in the copy and artwork — any one of which might have profound impact on the results. In other words, we learned in advance what our readers' "unspoken questions" were likely to be — and made changes in the copy to answer those questions. For example, each of the following comments was helpful in making final copy revisions:

How come there's boys as well as girls?

What makes this organization different? What are they going to do?

Are there Camp Fire programs here [in L.A.]? (There are.)

What is AIDS counseling? As a parent, I would be very interested in knowing what approach they take.

If it were Girl Scouts, we wouldn't be as critical. We see them here.

Teaching kids how to survive. This is a key point.

It doesn't tell exactly where the money goes. Like, "thirty percent to this."

What's it going to do for my city?

There needs to be more interaction [in the photos on the postcards].

What those ten people taught me (all over again)

So, lest you, too, stumble into the wilderness of indifference — armed only with a pitiful little one-and-a-half-page fundraising letter — please keep the following lessons in mind:

1. Donors need lots of information to be persuaded to send gifts by mail. They may *say* they want to read only short letters, but what they really crave are answers to their questions. (Remember Siegfried Vögele's "unspoken readers' questions"!) And questions produce doubt or disinterest, the parents of inaction. If it takes an extra page or two to answer every question you can anticipate, increase the budget and stifle your natural tendency to keep your message short and sweet. The results will vindicate you.

2. Donors are skeptical. It's best to head them off at the pass by volunteering information about the unique character, the impact, and the cost-effectiveness of your work. And they want proof you're really doing the things you say you're doing: abundant details — facts — will get that point across.

3. An appeal is too long only if it doesn't convey the information that donors want. My one-and-a-half-page version was "wordy" because it lacked the particulars of the four-page letter. The longer version was *not* wordy.

4. Human interest sells — and probably doubly so in human service appeals! A story, especially about kids, is a great way to humanize a fundraising letter. (And that, by the way, is precisely what we did in the longer letter, which led with a gripping story about an inner city child whose life was turned around by Camp Fire.)

5. If there's a way to misunderstand your message, donors will find it. They'll miss important points if you don't emphasize them. They'll be thrown off by awkward transitions, unfamiliar words, poor word choice, and attempts to gloss over details. Words matter.

6. Format and design affect understanding, too. In a fundraising letter, the only tools you've got are: (a) words, (b) numbers, (c) typography, (d) pictures, (e) paper, and (f) ink. Use them all wisely: you have no other way to establish your credibility by mail.

Most of the time, I remember all those lessons when I sit down to work on a fundraising letter. Yet I still sometimes write letters that don't work well.

Raising money by mail is an endlessly tricky business, and no amount of knowledge will equip a fundraiser to avoid occasional nasty surprises. But experience, insight, and market research like the focus group reported in this chapter can all help narrow the uncertainties and enlarge the odds of success.

Focus groups may not be cost-effective for your organization, and they're certainly not needed for every fundraising letter. But your writing and the design of your package can be evaluated informally by friends, family, and coworkers. That way you, too, might find you're not achieving the effect you thought you were!

Now that we've examined what really happens to fundraising letters when donors receive them in the mail, let's take a close look at some of the many reasons they might send gifts in response. The next chapter is entitled, "Twenty-Three Reasons People Respond to Your Fundraising Letters." ▶

5

TWENTY-THREE REASONS PEOPLE RESPOND TO YOUR FUNDRAISING APPEALS

It's downright unnatural. Your fundraising letter must persuade the recipient to take an action that much of humanity thinks peculiar: to give money away.

To accomplish this seemingly unlikely objective, your appeal needs to be built on the psychology of giving. Forget your organization's needs. Instead, focus on the needs, the desires, and the concerns of the people you're writing. Your job is to motivate them.

The author of a popular book on writing fundraising letters says there are five "great motivators" that explain response: fear, exclusivity, guilt, greed, and anger. Advertising copywriters typically fall back on a similar short list. But I believe the truth is much more complex.

In my opinion, there are at least twenty-three reasons why people might respond to your fundraising letter. Any one of the twenty-three might suggest a theme or hook for your letter. It's likely that several of these reasons help motivate each gift.

1. PEOPLE SEND MONEY BECAUSE YOU *ASK* THEM TO.

Public opinion surveys and other research repeatedly confirm this most basic fact of donor motivation. "They asked" is the *most* frequently cited reason for giving. The research confirms, too, that donors *want* to be asked. Focus group research also reveals that donors typically underestimate the number of appeals they receive from the charities they support. These facts help explain why responsive donors are repeatedly asked for additional gifts in nearly every successful direct mail fundraising program. When you write an appeal, keep these realities in mind. Don't allow your reticence about asking for money make you sound apologetic in your letter.

2. PEOPLE SEND MONEY BECAUSE THEY HAVE MONEY *AVAILABLE* TO GIVE AWAY.

The overwhelming majority of individual gifts to nonprofit organizations and institutions are small contributions made from disposable (or discretionary) income. This is the *money left over* in the family checking account — after this month's mortgage, taxes, insurance, credit cards, and grocery bills have been paid. Unless you're appealing for a major gift, a bequest, or a multi-year pledge, your target is this modest pool of available money.

For most families, dependent on a year-round stream of wage or salary income, the pool of disposable income is replenished every month or every two weeks. That's why most charities appeal *frequently and for small gifts*. If your appeal is persuasive, your organization may join the ranks of that select group of charities that receive gifts from a donor's household in a given month. If you're less than persuasive, or if competing charities have stronger arguments — or if the family just doesn't have money to spare that month — you *won't* get a gift.

For example, if you write me a letter seeking a charitable gift, you may succeed in tapping into the $100 or $200 I'll probably have "left over" for charity during the month your letter arrives. If your appeal is persuasive, I might send you $25 or $50 — $100 tops — because I decide to add you to the short list of charities I'll support that month.

Now, you may have the mistaken impression that, as a businessman, a snappy dresser, and an all-around generous guy, I have a lot of money. You may even be aware I've occasionally made much larger gifts to local charities. But, I warn you: you're unlikely to tap into me for more than $50 . . . because that's all I have available *right now*. Those few larger gifts I gave *didn't* come from my disposable income stream. They came from other sources and required a lot of planning.

3. PEOPLE SEND MONEY BECAUSE THEY'RE IN THE *HABIT* OF SENDING MONEY BY MAIL.

Charity is habit forming; giving by mail is a special variety of this benign affliction.

The Direct Marketing Association (DMA), a leading industry trade association, periodically surveys the American public to determine what proportion of the adult population is "mail-responsive" and thus susceptible to offers or appeals by mail. When

I first became involved in direct mail fundraising, in the late 1970s, I was told the DMA estimated approximately 25 percent of Americans were mail-responsive. Now, in the mid-1990s, the DMA's estimate tops 50 percent. Clearly, the American population is becoming increasingly mail-responsive. Almost gone are the days when people would insist on waiting in line to pay bills in person because they distrusted the mail.

Surveys also reflect the growing importance of direct mail appeals in the fundraising process. Research shows that fundraising letters are the number-one source of new gifts to charity in America.

4. PEOPLE SEND MONEY BECAUSE THEY SUPPORT ORGANIZATIONS *LIKE* YOURS.

Your donors aren't yours alone — no matter what you think. Because they have special interests, hobbies, or distinctive beliefs, your donors may support several similar organizations. A dog owner, for example, may contribute to half a dozen different organizations that have some connection to dogs: a humane society, an "animal rights" group, an organization that trains Seeing-Eye dogs, a wildlife protection group. A person who sees himself as an environmentalist might be found on the membership rolls of five or six ecology-related groups: one dedicated to land conservation, another to protecting the wilderness, a third to saving endangered species or the rain forest, and so on. There are patterns in people's lives. Your appeal is most likely to bear fruit if it fits squarely into one of those patterns.

5. PEOPLE SEND MONEY BECAUSE THEIR GIFTS WILL MAKE A DIFFERENCE.

Donors want to be convinced their investment in your enterprise — their charitable gifts — will achieve some worthy aim. That's why so many donors express concern about high fundraising and administrative costs. It's also why in successful appeals for funds, the impact of a gift is often quantified: $35 to buy a school uniform, $40 for a stethoscope, $7 to feed a child for a day. Donors want to *feel* good about their gifts.

Like everyone else on the planet, your donors are striving to be effective human beings. You help them by demonstrating just how effective they really are.

6. PEOPLE SEND MONEY BECAUSE GIFTS WILL ACCOMPLISH SOMETHING *RIGHT NOW*.

Urgency is a necessary element in a fundraising letter. Implicitly or explicitly, there is a deadline in every successful appeal: the end of the year, the opening of the school, the deadline for the matching grant, the limited press run on the book available as a premium. But the strong attraction in circumstances such as these is best illustrated if no such urgent conditions apply. If the money I send you this week *won't* make a difference right away, shouldn't I send money to some other charity that has asked for my support and urgently needs it?

7. PEOPLE SEND MONEY BECAUSE YOU RECOGNIZE THEM FOR THEIR GIFTS.

You appeal to donors' egos — or to their desire to heighten their public image — when you offer to recognize their gifts in an open and tangible way. A listing in your newsletter. A plaque, certificate, lapel pin, house sign, or armband they can display. Screen credit in a video production. A press release. If your fundraising program can provide appropriate and tasteful recognition, you're likely to boost response to your appeals by highlighting the opportunities for recognition in your letter or newsletter. Even if donors choose not to be listed in print or mentioned in public, they may be gratified to learn you value their contributions enough to make the offer.

8. PEOPLE SEND MONEY BECAUSE YOU GIVE THEM SOMETHING TANGIBLE IN RETURN.

"Premiums" come in all sizes, shapes, and flavors: bumper strips, gold tie tacks, coffee-table books, membership cards, even (in one case I know) a pint of ice cream.

Sometimes premiums (such as name stickers or bookmarks) are enclosed with the appeal; these so-called "front-end" premiums boost response more often than not and are frequently cost-effective, at least in the short run. In other cases "back-end" premiums are promised in an appeal "as a token of our deep appreciation" when donors respond by sending gifts of at least a certain amount. Either way, premiums appeal to the innate acquisitiveness that persists in the human race.

9. PEOPLE SEND MONEY BECAUSE YOU ENABLE THEM TO "DO SOMETHING" ABOUT A CRITICAL PROBLEM — IF ONLY TO PROTEST OR TAKE A STAND.

Today, we are bombarded by information about the world's problems through a wide variety of channels. Though we may isolate ourselves inside triple-locked homes, build walls around our suburbs, and post guards at gateposts, we can't escape from knowing about misery, injustice, and wasted human potential. Often, we feel powerless in the face of this grim reality. Charity offers us a way to respond — by helping to heal the sick or balm troubled souls, to teach new ways to a new generation or feed the hungry. Your appeal will trigger a gift if it brings to life the feelings that move us to act, even knowing that action is never enough.

If you offer hope in a world drowning in troubles, your donors will seize it like the life jacket it really is.

10. PEOPLE SEND MONEY BECAUSE YOU GIVE THEM A CHANCE TO ASSOCIATE WITH A FAMOUS OR WORTHY PERSON.

There are numerous ways that the identity, personality, or achievements of an individual might be highlighted in a fundraising appeal. For example, that person may be the signer of the letter, the organization's founder or executive director, the honorary chair of a fundraising drive, a patron saint, a political candidate, an honoree at a special event — or simply one of the organization's members or clients. If the signer's character or accomplishments evoke admiration — or even simply a past, personal connection — your donors may be moved to send gifts in response. The opportunity to associate with someone who is well known or highly esteemed may offer donors a way to affirm their noblest inclinations — or compensate for what they believe to be their shortcomings.

11. PEOPLE SEND MONEY BECAUSE YOU ALLOW THEM TO GET BACK AT THE CORRUPT OR THE UNJUST.

There are too few outlets for the anger and frustration we feel on witnessing the injustice and corruption that pervades our society. Both our moral sense and the secular law hold most of us in check, preventing expressions of violence or vocal fury that might allow us to let off steam. For many, contributing to charity is a socially acceptable way to strike back. Whether a public interest organization committed to fighting corruption in government or a religious charity devoted to revealing divine justice, your organization may help donors channel their most sordid feelings into a demonstration of their best instincts.

12. PEOPLE SEND MONEY BECAUSE YOU GIVE THEM THE OPPORTUNITY TO "BELONG" — AS A MEMBER, FRIEND, OR SUPPORTER — AND THUS YOU HELP THEM FIGHT LONELINESS.

Your most fundamental task as a fundraiser is to build relationships with your donors. That's why so many organizations use membership programs, giving clubs, and monthly gift societies. The process of solicitation itself can help build healthy relationships. For some shut-ins, for example, or for elderly people left with distant family and few friends, the letters you send may be eagerly anticipated. Most of us are social animals, forever seeking companionship.

13. PEOPLE SEND MONEY BECAUSE YOU ENABLE THEM TO OFFER THEIR OPINIONS.

The act of sending a gift to some nonprofit organizations might itself constitute a way to speak out. Consider, for example, the ACLU, or the Campus Crusade for Christ, or Ross Perot's United We Stand; support for such a group makes an obvious statement about a donor's views. But almost any charity can offer donors an opportunity to state an opinion by including in an appeal an "involvement device" such as a membership survey, a petition, or a greeting card that might later be sent to a friend or family member. Even though most donors may ignore the chance to offer suggestions, they may regard the invitation to do so as a strong sign of your respect and concern for them.

14. PEOPLE SEND MONEY BECAUSE YOU PROVIDE THEM WITH ACCESS TO INSIDE INFORMATION.

Even if your organization or agency isn't an institution of higher education or a research foundation, you still hold knowledge many donors crave. Nonprofit organizations are often on the front lines of everyday, hands-on research, gathering important data day after day from real-world clients, visitors, or program participants. Their staff members are likely to be specialists, often *experts* in their fields.

However, *every* nonprofit possesses information that is not widely known to the public and that donors may perceive as valuable. A loyal supporter may be vitally interested in the health and well-being of your executive director (who was ill lately), the progress of that project you launched last year (after a spectacular start), or what your field staff learned last month (three months after the hurricane).

Disseminating inside information, which is intrinsically valuable and thus constitutes a gift from you, also helps build strong fundraising relationships by involving your donors in the intimate details of your organization.

15. PEOPLE SEND MONEY BECAUSE YOU HELP THEM LEARN ABOUT A COMPLEX AND INTERESTING PROBLEM OR ISSUE.

In most advanced industrial nations, education, health care, and the arts are regarded as largely government's responsibility to provide. By contrast, the traditional American response has been to meet important needs such as these principally through private, voluntary action. Nonprofit organizations in the United States are established to tackle issues or problems that society otherwise ignores or under-values. Don't just think of all the private schools and colleges, nonprofit hospitals, museums, and symphony orchestras. Think about Mothers Against Drunk Driving, Disabled American Veterans, Planned Parenthood, the Nature Conservancy — and the hundreds of thousands like them that are far less well known. Often, these organizations are on the front lines of research or public debate — on the most challenging, the most controversial, the most engaging issues. If that's true of your organization, the emphasis you place in your appeal on your special knowledge may help motivate donors to give.

Your donors may even perceive the appeal itself as a benefit. As research frequently reveals, donors regard the letters they receive from charities as a source of special knowledge. I believe that helps explain why long letters containing hard facts and intriguing ideas often outpull more emotional appeals.

16. PEOPLE SEND MONEY BECAUSE YOU HELP THEM PRESERVE THEIR WORLD VIEW, BY VALIDATING CHERISHED VALUES AND BELIEFS.

The very act of giving affirms a donor's dedication to a charity's worthy aims. Donors support your organization's work because you act on their behalf, pursuing your mission with time and effort they could never bring to bear themselves. In this passionate pursuit, you act out their values and beliefs — the deep-seated convictions that lead them to join in your mission. But you must constantly remind them of the connection.

If your organization's mission is congruent with widely shared values and beliefs — a commitment to piety, for example, or saving dolphins, or promoting efficiency in government — you face an obvious marketing opportunity. But if your nonprofit is dedicated to an unpopular cause, you possess a similar (if unenviable) advantage: for that small number of donors willing to take a stand on an issue others reject, the values and beliefs that make the act of giving a form of personal affirmation suggest to the fundraiser a language both may speak.

17. PEOPLE SEND MONEY BECAUSE YOU ALLOW THEM TO GAIN PERSONAL CONNECTIONS WITH OTHER INDIVIDUALS WHO ARE PASSIONATELY INVOLVED IN SOME MEANINGFUL DIMENSION OF LIFE.

A charity is an intentional community of sorts — a cooperative venture, an institutional expression of a shared creed or common hopes. Your job as a fundraiser is to strengthen the bonds that tie your community together. Your greatest asset may be some person within your "community" whom donors may regard as an inspiring example: a selfless, dedicated staff member; a passionately committed trustee; a model client or beloved beneficiary of your work. If you bring such a person to life through your fundraising appeals, you enable your donors to live vicariously through him or her — and that can be a meaningful and rewarding experience for them as well as profitable for your organization.

18. PEOPLE SEND MONEY BECAUSE YOU GIVE THEM THE CHANCE TO RELEASE EMOTIONAL TENSION CAUSED BY A LIFE-THREATENING SITUATION, A CRITICAL EMERGENCY, OR AN ETHICAL DILEMMA.

The charitable impulse is often precipitated by special circumstances that cause pain, fear, or even embarrassment. Consider the enduring popularity of memorial gifts to commemorate the passing of friends or loved ones. Or the spontaneous outpouring of gifts to aid crime victims or the families of kidnapped children. People want to help relieve pain and suffering, if only because they share these feelings. And they want to respond to grave emergencies, if only because they fear death. Your appeal for funds may afford them an opportunity to ease their affliction.

19. PEOPLE SEND MONEY BECAUSE THEY ARE AFRAID.

Fear motivates. The American public has been subjected to billions (yes, billions!) of fundraising letters expressly conceived to evoke fear. Fear of death. Fear of poor people or foreigners. Fear of Social Security benefit cuts. Fear of higher taxes. Fear of Democrats or Republicans, liberals, or reactionaries. No Pollyannish view of human motivation can erase the evidence that vast sums of money have been raised by such appeals. Fear sells. Yet I believe with all my heart that it's often unseemly, at times ethically questionable — and ultimately counterproductive to use this obvious stratagem.

Consider the would-be prophet who predicts Armageddon next year. Who will heed the prophet when next year's come and gone? A fundraiser who builds the case for giving on the worst-case scenario may be building on quicksand.

20. PEOPLE SEND MONEY BECAUSE YOU ALLOW THEM TO RELIEVE THEIR GUILT ABOUT AN ETHICAL, POLITICAL, OR PERSONAL TRANSGRESSION, WHETHER REAL OR IMAGINED.

Guilt undeniably plays a role in prompting some gifts. Think of the $1 or $2 cash contribution mailed in response to direct mail packages containing name stickers or greeting cards. Or the belated membership renewals that follow a long series of increasingly insistent demands. Or the millions of small gifts sent every year in response to pathetic photos of skeletal children. Our complex society allows few of us the luxury of acting out of purely ethical motives. Compromise is woven through the fabric of our daily lives. The simple fact is, none of us is likely to feel guilt-free at any time. Sometimes, giving to charity, like coins thrown into the poor box in an earlier era, will help release the pressure.

Yet I believe guilt is highly overrated as a motivator; rarely will donors moved primarily by guilt prove loyal over the years, and larger gifts are relatively rare. As a fundraising strategy, then, guilt may be just as counterproductive in the long run as fear.

21. PEOPLE SEND MONEY BECAUSE YOU GIVE THEM TAX BENEFITS.

No list of motivating factors for charitable giving is complete without at least passing reference to tax benefits. Without question, the charitable tax de-

duction has played a major role in stimulating many large gifts and planned gifts because the benefits to the donor are substantial. (This is particularly true of gifts of artwork or other forms of appreciated property to such institutions as museums, because the tax laws are specifically structured to encourage such gifts.) However, many small donors also mistakenly believe they gain a great advantage from the tax-deductibility of their gifts. That's why it's always advisable when requesting a gift to inform the donor that it may be deductible: it may not help, but it can't hurt!

Still, it's dangerous to construct an appeal exclusively on the basis of tax benefits — even an appeal to buy into a tax-reduction program such as a charitable remainder trust. Experts in planned giving advise that "donative intent" — the desire to help, to do good, to make a difference — is usually of far greater importance than any financial considerations. Anyway, there are lots of tax-reduction schemes available to well-to-do people from institutions with no charitable purpose whatsoever!

22. PEOPLE SEND MONEY BECAUSE THEY FEEL IT'S THEIR DUTY.

Many of our religious traditions teach us that it's wrong to live life without observing our duty to others: to relieve their pain, to enlarge their opportunities, or to brighten their lives. There is also a secular belief, widely shared in the United States, that, as citizens in a democracy, we have an obligation to help make things better for our fellow citizens. Those who benefit from military training may acquire a heightened sense of duty.

Not every nonprofit organization can appeal explicitly to donors' sense of duty (though many charities can do so). But duty may nonetheless play a role in inspiring the gifts they receive, for by its very nature duty is self-activating.

23. PEOPLE SEND MONEY BECAUSE THEY BELIEVE IT'S A BLESSING TO DO SO.

The Christian belief that "it is more blessed to give than to receive" is deeply ingrained in Western civilization and far from limited to practicing Christians. And in the Jewish concept of *mitzvah,* for example, many Americans find justification for believing that doing good is its own reward. Clearly — at least in our idealized vision of ourselves — we Americans celebrate the notion of charity. Our self-image as "nice people" derives in no small part from our generous response to charitable appeals.

Now that we've got a handle on nearly two dozen of the reasons donors might respond to that fundraising letter you're writing, let's take a look at what might make that letter more effective. ▶

THE CHARACTERISTICS OF AN EFFECTIVE FUNDRAISING LETTER

ost fundraisers apparently think fundraising letters are all pretty much the same. Here's how their definition of a fundraising letter seems to run:

A fundraising letter is an appeal from a nonprofit organization, describing needs and requesting charitable gifts to fill them.

Right?

Wrong! Wrong on every count.

Banish that ill-conceived and misleading definition from your consciousness. Better yet, copy it down onto a sheet of scratch paper, cross it out with bold strokes of your pen, slice it up with scissors, and deposit the whole revolting mess in the nearest wastebasket.

Now you're ready to get started on the right foot!

Okay now? Read this next part carefully:

An effective fundraising letter possesses three attributes:

1. *An effective fundraising letter is an appeal from* **one person** *to another.*

2. *An effective fundraising letter describes an* **opportunity** *for the recipient to meet personal needs by supporting a worthy charitable aim.*

3. *An effective fundraising letter invites the recipient to take specific and immediate* **action.**

I'm sure you noticed that one all-important word is missing here: *money.* Money — a request for a charitable gift — is an indispensable element in the overwhelming majority of fundraising letters. Omit that request for funds, and your letter will fail the most basic test of effectiveness. What's worse, you'll almost certainly fail to raise much money.

But the action requested in a fundraising letter doesn't *always* consist of sending money, at least not right away. The specific action requested might be to complete and return a survey . . . to use a set of stamps, name-stickers, or greeting cards . . . or to authorize regular bank transfers. There are hundreds of possibilities. The letter-writer's first responsibility is to determine what that action is. That's always the writer's responsibility when writing for results! And understanding that duty leads to what I call the First Commandment of Fundraising Letter Writing:

> *When you set out to write a fundraising letter, make sure you know precisely to whom you're writing, and why — and be certain your letter makes that point just as clear to them as it is to you.*

That "point" — the equation that expresses the who, what, why, when and how of your appeal — is what I've fallen into the bad habit of calling the "Marketing Concept." I'll discuss this murky but all-important notion in more detail in Chapter 9, where I sum up the central message of this book. For starters, though, let's take a stab at a working definition:

◆ The Marketing Concept embodies the *purpose* you're writing: to secure a gift of $500 or more, for example.

◆ The Marketing Concept identifies the *person* to whom you're writing: a donor who's previously given your organization at least one gift of $100 or more, to extend the example.

◆ The Marketing Concept incorporates the *benefits* the person you're writing will receive as a result of responding: in this example, great satisfaction from knowing how much your organization can accomplish with $500, plus special recognition for giving such a generous gift.

The First Commandment, then, is to work out the Marketing Concept *before you write a single word* — and then to be sure every word you write speaks to that concept.

Fundraising letters: one size WON'T fit all

In fact, fundraising letters are of many different types, serving a broad variety of ends and thus involving a great many different Marketing Concepts. To write an effective appeal, you must first determine the target audience and specific purpose you want to serve:

◆ Are you writing to people who've never before supported your organization, asking them to join? That's an *acquisition* (or prospect) letter. I cover that topic in Chapter 11.

◆ Is your letter to be mailed to new members or donors, welcoming them to your organization? I call that a *welcome package*; others may describe it as a welcome packet or kit. See Chapter 12.

◆ Are you writing to previous donors, appealing for additional gifts for some special purpose? That's a *special appeal.* You'll find examples in Chapter 13.

◆ Are you writing to proven donors at the end of the year? That's a *year-end appeal.* The topic is covered in Chapter 14.

◆ Are you writing to some of your most generous donors, seeking large gifts? I refer to an appeal of that sort as a *High-Dollar letter,* the subject of Chapter 15.

◆ Is the specific purpose of your letter to induce previous donors to increase their support? If so, you're writing an *upgrade appeal.* You'll learn about that topic in Chapter 16.

◆ Are you writing your new and regular supporters to ask they renew this year's annual gift or membership dues? Then you're writing a *renewal.* That's the theme of Chapter 17.

The case studies in Chapters 11 through 17 include examples of all seven of these types of fundraising appeals. Studying them will prepare you for many letter-writing challenges — but hardly all. There are important types of fundraising letters that don't appear in this book. Monthly sustainer requests, upgrades or renewals, for example. Lapsed donor reactivation letters. Planned giving letters. Cultivation letters. And dozens more. No author can anticipate every need you may face. No book can supply you with models to follow in every contingency.

In fact, there's such great variety in fundraising letters that it's difficult to speak except in general terms about what they have in common. The only things common to all appeals, I believe, are an *offer* (or proposition) that incorporates the Ask, if any, as well as the benefits to the donor, and the *case,* which is the argument that justifies the offer and spells out the benefits. If the appeal is framed as a letter, as are almost all successful fundraising efforts, it's likely to include a *salutation* and *signature* that clarify the relationship between the letter signer and the person to whom the letter is addressed, a *lead* that starts off the letter, a *close* that ends it, a *P.S.,* and a *response device* (or reply device) the donor may use to return a gift. That's about it.

Many fundraisers relate these elements to a formula, insisting there's a standard structure or sequence a writer may follow in constructing an appeal. I disagree. To understand how to write successful fundraising letters, I believe, you must study appeals that have worked well, attempt to determine what made them successful — then put them aside and focus on your own donors and your own organization. Your fundraising letters will be successful only if they reflect what's unique about your organization and uniquely attractive to your donors.

To bear down hard on this important point, let's take a leisurely stroll through the pages of *one* well-written fundraising letter. If you accompany me on this paragraph-by-paragraph tour, you'll gain an overview of the approach I'll spell out later in more detail, while seeing how the principles I've already laid out have been artfully put into practice in a real-world fundraising project. In the process, I hope, you'll gain insight about how to frame the unique attractions of your own organization in ways that will be compelling to your donors. ▶

7

A LEISURELY TOUR THROUGH ONE SUCCESSFUL APPEAL

My colleague and friend Bill Rehm wrote the fundraising appeal for the San Francisco Conservatory of Music that's reproduced beginning on page 75. The conservatory had retained our firm, Mal Warwick & Associates, Inc., to assist them in building their membership base — part of a broader development strategy to lay the foundation for a significant capital campaign at the turn of the century.

Ready? The ten-dollar tour starts . . . *now.*

The outer envelope

1. Your eyes may leap first to the signature in the upper left-hand corner (called the "corner card"). Colin Murdoch signed the appeal inside, and printing his signature on the envelope lends a personal touch that, as previous testing suggests, may improve results.

2. Or you may focus on the extraordinary woodblock print in the corner card: the conservatory's logo. [Note: The signature is printed in blue ink, contrasting with the red of the logo and return address.]

3. Notice the typefaces used in the Conservatory's name and address. You'll see those typefaces consistently repeated throughout the contents of the package. That's as it should be. A typeface can be an organization's signature as surely as the most distinctive logo design.

4. You'll also notice a postage meter has been used instead of a postal indicia (permit imprint). Testing sometimes shows metered postage will outpull an indicia (but both are usually far less successful, though not necessarily less cost-effective, than first-class stamps).

5. Now, *you* may have noticed all four of the features of this envelope I've enumerated above — but, as a recipient of this appeal, *I'm* much more likely to have found my eyes leaping first to the mailing label. The so-called Cheshire label, a strip of plain paper machine-affixed to a card inside, shows

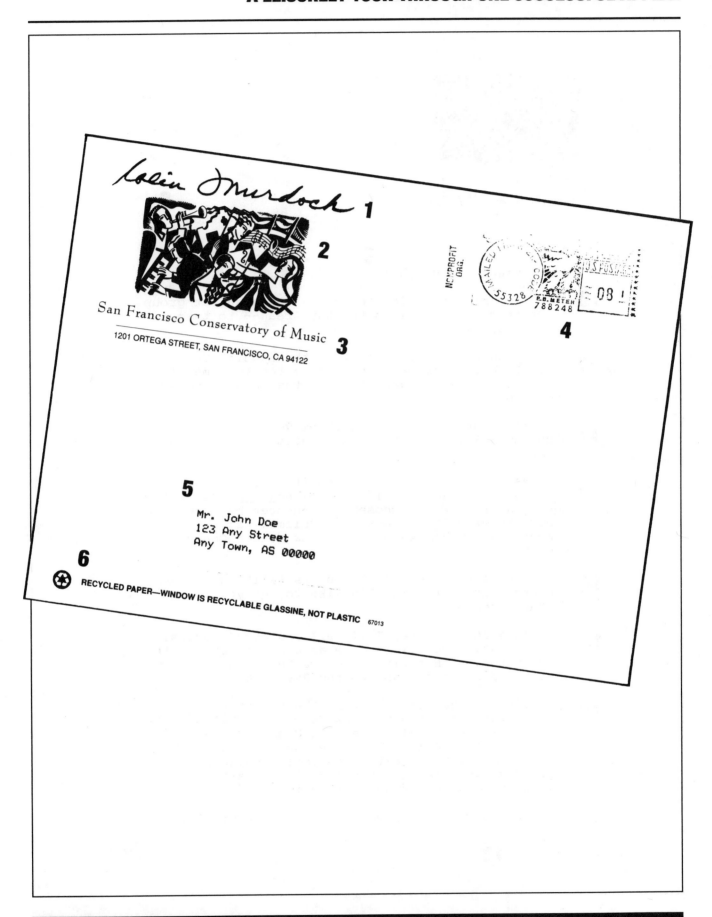

7

San Francisco Conservatory of Music

1201 ORTEGA ST., SAN FRANCISCO, CA 94122
415/759-3463

8

Thursday afternoon

9

Dear Friend and Neighbor,

10   I'm writing to invite you -- and a select group of other music lovers in the Bay Area -- to take your seat, please.

11   Sit down, as our guest, at the Faculty Trio Concert this November 15th, and listen to some of the most beautiful chamber music that San Francisco has to offer.

12   It's our way of saying thank you -- for becoming a Friend of the San Francisco Conservatory of Music.

13   As the Conservatory begins its 76th season, we've set a goal of enlisting <u>333</u> <u>new</u> <u>Friends</u> <u>of</u> <u>the</u> <u>Conservatory</u>. We've chosen that number because there are exactly 333 seats in Hellman Hall -- the concert hall where we hold our New Member Concert each year.

14   I'd like to see all 333 seats filled with new members this year. And I'd like to see you in one of those seats.

15   In just a minute, I'll tell you about several other benefits you'll receive as a new member of the Conservatory. But first, let me tell you what your membership support means to the Bay Area.

16   Like the Bay Area itself, the San Francisco Conservatory of Music represents many things to many people. But above all else, the Conservatory is a community of musicians who experience the joy, the promise, and the pursuit of musical excellence. Every day, we celebrate the teaching, learning, composing, and performance of music.

17   That's been our proud mission for over 75 years

RECYCLED PAPER   67011 **18**

19

Page two

20 -- ever since the Conservatory was first founded by pianists Ada Clement and Lillian Hodghead in 1917.

21 Today, the San Francisco Conservatory of Music is one of the most respected institutions of music education in the country, offering instruction to more than 1,500 students ranging from pre-school to post graduate levels.

22 Conservatory students, faculty and guest artists perform more than 300 concerts on campus each year.

23 And over the past seventy-five years, the Conservatory has trained some of our country's most brilliant musicians -- violinists Isaac Stern and Yehudi Menuhin, pianist Jeffrey Kahane, and guitarist David Tanenbaum, to name just a few.

24 The Conservatory's faculty of 78 professional musicians are drawn from some of the finest musical organizations in the country, including 32 musicians who are currently playing with either the San Francisco Symphony, the San Francisco Opera, or the San Francisco Ballet.

25 It goes without saying that all of us at the Conservatory share a love for music. But more than that, we possess the desire to help talented and motivated students realize their dreams.

26

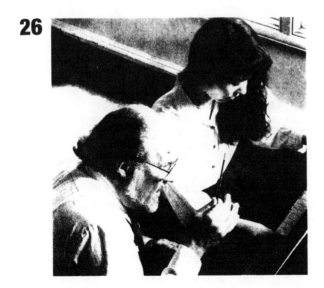

With a student-faculty ratio of just six to one, teachers give special attention to every student.

27

Page three

28   I see our role at the Conservatory as one of helping to nurture and develop the creativity, skill, and genius residing within each musician.

29   I also see it as the responsibility of the Conservatory to share the music we help create with the community.

30   Through the Conservatory's Community Service Program, our students give more than 400 performances each year. We bring music to hospitals, convalescent homes, day care centers, retirement homes -- reaching people who otherwise would never have the pleasure of hearing live classical music.

31

Conservatory students contribute to our community by performing more than 400 free concerts each year.

32   The San Francisco Conservatory of Music has a long, proud tradition of teaching and providing musical excellence to the Bay Area. And, I assure you, this will continue to be our overriding mission in the years ahead.

33   But the Conservatory is only as great as its supporters. Tuition and fees cover just 59% of our annual budget. The remainder must come from generous individuals in our community.

34   Currently, we have a very special group of Friends -- people like you -- who help support the Conservatory with a tax-deductible membership contribution each year.

35   That's why I hope you'll accept my invitation to become a Friend of the San Francisco Conservatory

Page four

36 of Music today -- and support one of San Francisco's oldest and most respected institutions.

37 When you become a Friend of the Conservatory, you'll receive <u>all</u> <u>these</u> <u>membership</u> <u>benefits</u>:

38 o A subscription to <u>At</u> <u>the</u> <u>Conservatory</u>, the monthly newsletter and calendar of events.

39 o Free tickets to the special Faculty Trio Concert for new members on November 15.

40 o Free attendance at the "Friends Only" Tour and Concert in January, 1994.

41 o Membership discounts for Conservatory concerts throughout the year and special discounts for Conservatory extension classes.

42 o Advance ticket purchase for the <u>Sing-It-Yourself</u> <u>Messiah</u> concerts at Davies Symphony Hall this December.

43 Perhaps the greatest benefit you'll receive, though, is knowing you're helping to ensure that students will continue to get the best musical instruction available.

44 So please, right now while everything is in front of you, take a minute to write your tax-deductible check and send it to the San Francisco Conservatory of Music.

45 With many thanks.

46 Sincerely,

Colin Murdoch
President

47 P.S. To reserve your free ticket to the Faculty Trio Concert at the Conservatory's Hellman Hall on November 15, we must receive your membership contribution by November 8. Please send your gift <u>today</u>. Thank you very much.

48

YO-YO MA

49 Dear Friend and Music Lover,

50 Some of the finest cello teaching in the country today takes place at the San Francisco Conservatory of Music, where high standards are combined with an openness to new trends.

51 The San Francisco Conservatory of Music has a sense of tradition in the best sense of the word. Generations of great cello teachers from Margaret Rowell to Bonnie Hampton and Irene Sharp have nurtured some of the finest young cellists today.

52 The Conservatory is a working community -- it not only functions as an institution, but it participates as a vital member of the Bay Area community.

53 The high standards, tradition and a sense of community are the reasons why the San Francisco Conservatory of Music continues to be such a strong, creative force in producing the next generation of musicians.

54 I urge you to support this fine institution.

55 Sincerely,

Yo-Yo Ma

56 # *BRAVO!*

57 I accept your invitation to become a Friend of the San Francisco Conservatory of Music. I want to help continue the long, proud tradition of musical excellence in San Francisco. Enclosed is my membership gift of:

58
- ☐ $40   Regular Membership
- ☐ $100   Special Friend of the Conservatory
- ☐ $_____

59 ☐ Send me my FREE ticket(s) to the Faculty Trio Concert on November 15. Request must be received by November 8.   ☐ one ticket   ☐ two tickets

60 Mr. John Doe
123 Any Street
Any Town, AS 00000

61

San Francisco Conservatory of Music

1201 ORTEGA ST., SAN FRANCISCO, CA 94122
415/759-3463

62 Your contribution to the San Francisco Conservatory of Music is fully tax-deductible. Thank you very much.

63 ▲ DETACH HERE

- -

64 ## Your Membership Entitles You to Receive:

65
1. A subscription to *At the Conservatory*, the Conservatory's monthly newsletter and calendar of events.
2. A special New Member Fall Concert.
3. Membership discounts for Conservatory concerts throughout the year—and for Conservatory extension classes.

4. Advance ticket purchase for Sing-It-Yourself Messiah Concerts at Davies Symphony Hall.
5. Free attendance at the "Friends Only" Tour and Concert (January 1994).

66 Please detach top portion, fold and return with your check in the enclosed postage-paid envelope. Keep bottom portion for your records.

RECYCLED PAPER   67012B

through a glassine (recyclable) window, revealing a computer-imprinted name and address plus a five-digit keycode (upper right in the window) and a postal barcode. The barcode enabled the Conservatory to mail this particular envelope at a savings of three cents off what was then the standard nonprofit bulk rate (8.1¢ versus 11.1¢).

6. The envelope advertises "recycled paper," though testing may show that doing so doesn't improve results, even among donors who describe themselves as environmentalists. So what? As my grandmother would have said, "What can it hurt? And it might help!" Besides, it's the right thing to do.

Page one

7. First, notice the size of the page: 7 x 10", a so-called Monarch letter; this has a more personal feel to it, because it's notably smaller than standard business size (8-1/2 x 11"), much more like personal stationery. And there's that lovely logo again! It appears above the address — a street address, mind you, not a post office box — and a telephone number. Using the conservatory's actual address and phone number may help inspire confidence in me as a prospective donor. (It may also lead me to pay an unexpected visit or place a phone call out of curiosity or suspiciousness — but that's very unlikely.)

8. The use of "Thursday afternoon" is a copywriter's conceit, and probably not taken seriously by anyone. Still, it may subliminally convey an illusion that the letter bears a specific date. There's no real date here because this appeal was mailed via bulk rate.

9. "Dear Friend and Neighbor" is a neat variation on the standard "Dear Friend." I like the added touch — a signal this appeal was mailed only locally. This is, in its way, a form of personalization, shortening the distance between the conservatory and me. However, since this letter is *not* addressed to me personally, it's obviously not personalized

within the generally accepted meaning of that term. This is a bulk appeal, mailed in quantity, and there's no way around that.

10. In its five opening words, "I'm writing to invite you," this appeal simply and directly establishes the basis of a relationship between the signer and me. (If I'm like most people who receive this letter, I'll probably take a peek now to see who that is — by turning to the bottom of page four to view the signature. But let's be orderly about this, and stick to our paragraph-by-paragraph story.) The opening sentence (the "lead") also identifies me in two important ways — as a music lover and a resident of the San Francisco Bay Area — and seizes my attention with an unfamiliar request: to take a seat.

11. The second paragraph quickly explains that unfamiliar request with specifics: *what* (a concert), *when* (on a particular day, and *where* (in San Francisco), in time-honored journalistic fashion. You'll note, too, that the conservatory is appealing to my love for chamber music. (How do they *know* that? They don't, of course. But they know how popular chamber music is among classical music buffs.)

12. Now Colin Murdoch makes clear exactly why he's writing me this letter. He wants me to become a "Friend" (and, since I receive lots of letters like these, I've got a pretty good idea what he means).

13. Now come more facts. Details that tell me this is a letter *about something specific*. Numbers and capitalized words that hold my interest because they supply information that answers questions I may have about a topic that (as we've already established) is of general interest to me. The unusual number "333" is itself engaging, because it's unexpected.

14. That intriguing number is repeated. And so are the words "you" and "I," each for the third time so far. This is *not* an impersonal institutional appeal. It's a letter from Colin Murdoch to me. You'll also note that "333 new Friends of the Conservatory" is underlined — the *only* underlining on this page, so it really stands out. You or I might have chosen different words to emphasize, but what's most important is that underlining is used sparingly here, to lessen the impression this is simply one more stereotypical direct mail appeal.

15. There's "you" again: three more times. And "me" counts as a form of "I." Just as important, the concept of membership — broached in each of the two preceding paragraphs — is introduced in terms of its benefits, both to me and to the area where I live. (Not San Francisco, you'll notice: the entire, much larger "Bay Area.")

16. In this seven-line paragraph — the longest on all four pages of the appeal, by the way — the conservatory is described in emotional and conceptual terms, not as brick and mortar. Murdoch is connecting with me where I really live — on the plane of *values*: "joy," "promise," "excellence," "teaching," "learning," "music."

17. Note that only one line of this paragraph appears on this page: that's a device to draw my eye onto the second page. The mind abhors an incomplete thought!

18. There's that "recycled paper" again!

Page two

19. This letter consists of two sheets of paper that form four pages. The notation "Page two" at the top helps orient me, minimizing the possibility I'll be confused (and thus less likely to send a gift).

20. Take note: specifics again. Facts and figures (used with reasonable restraint) heighten reader interest.

21. This reference to the conservatory's nationwide reputation helps establish credibility. The additional facts lend added authority to the reference, making it more than a boast.

22. Here's a significant and surprising fact. Most concertgoers are aware that 300 performances per year is a very *large* number for any arts group.

23. More facts here, and interesting ones at that. These names — familiar to classical-music lovers — help reinforce my interest while enhancing the credibility of the appeal.

24. Facts *again!* Numbers! By now, I'm really getting acquainted with the conservatory.

25. Now we're back to values and abstracts again: "love," "desire," "talented," "motivated," "dreams." This fellow Murdoch isn't sending me a term paper. He's connecting with me about things that matter!

26. This intense and charming photo and its handwritten caption convey important facts about the conservatory and its work. They also lend added human interest to the appeal.

Page three

27. The words "Page three" reassure me that I'm on the right page. But I haven't been hit over the head with a "Next page, please" or the equivalent on the bottom of page two. (No doubt some direct marketer somewhere, sometime, has tested that obnoxiously condescending device and found it improves response; as a matter of taste, however, I tend to avoid using it. I doubt it makes much difference other than to serve as one more subtle but unwanted reminder that an appeal is really, after all, just an impersonal letter sent to large numbers of people via direct mail.)

28. Again, Colin Murdoch reveals his personal feelings. He uses the lofty language that gets to the heart of the subject: the teaching of music.

29. Continuing in the first person, Murdoch now reveals the outward-looking dimension of the conservatory's mission: relating to the community — *my* community.

30. Now, I see that by supporting the conservatory I won't just be helping to bring out the genius in future world-class performers. I'll also help support my community's social safety net.

31. This photo depicts an obviously diverse group of schoolkids, and the caption repeats the number 400. The effect is to drive home the point that the conservatory serves far more than its own students and faculty or affluent concertgoers like me. Those 400 concerts are "free."

32. Now we're back to values again: "tradition" and "musical excellence." Even the word "mission" connotes passion and an orientation to values.

33. Citing the central financial fact about the conservatory brings me back into the picture once again. There's little doubt in my mind I'm (supposedly) one of those "generous individuals"!

34. Now any doubt I may have is quickly dispelled: Murdoch's talking about "people like" me. But the contribution he wants is more than simply that. It's "tax-deductible," it buys me a "membership" — and it's to be annual.

35. That, obviously, is what Murdoch means when he asks me to become a "Friend." But I'm going to have to go on to the next page to learn whether there's some qualification or exception to his request.

Page four

36. Nope: no exception here — just another argument for supporting the conservatory: its long and respected institutional history.

37. Here — in the first underlined words since that phrase on page one — Murdoch introduces the subject of "membership benefits". (Please note that the words are individually underlined. Some people prefer continuous lines, but I think the underlining of spaces distracts the eye from the message and focuses it on what's less important: the fact of the underlining itself. It also eliminates the spaces between words, which readers use to "swallow" words and phrases.)

38. As a "Friend," I'll receive a monthly newsletter *and calendar*. Murdoch cites the newsletter's name, further emphasizing the unstated promise of events I may want to attend at the conservatory.

39. In fact, I'll receive "free tickets" to a specific concert — one that's coming up very soon.

40. More free tickets, and another event that's not too far off.

41. I'll get discounts — not only on admission to other concerts but for extension classes too. Here's a potentially important benefit that piques my curiosity. (I gave up trying the clarinet in fifth grade, but maybe I could learn it after all!)

42. Now — underlined again and deliberately placed last in the series, where it's most likely to be remembered — is a membership benefit that could well be the most attractive of all: the conservatory's wildly popular sing-along Messiah concerts at San Francisco's elegant Symphony Hall.

43. However, despite all these tangible benefits of membership, Murdoch rushes to remind me I'll get something even more valuable: the satisfaction of knowing I've helped achieve something I value highly — to teach good music.

44. If I'm tempted to set this appeal aside and make my mind up later about whether to respond, Murdoch's suggestion I do it now may have no effect on me; but this, too, can't hurt. And I'm reminded once again my gift will be tax deductible, a fact that may be of special interest to me since the end of the year is fast approaching.

45. Ever hopeful, Murdoch thanks me.

46. He signs off "Sincerely," rather than a more formal "Yours truly" or a flamboyant "See you at the Conservatory!" He is, after all, the president of a respected institution. His flowery signature has an artful flair; it's printed in dark blue ink, to set it off from the typed text and reinforce the illusion of personal (or, rather, business) correspondence.

47. As you'll remember, most readers read the P.S. *first*. This P.S. makes good use of that opportunity. It restates the date of the fast-approaching faculty concert and, for the first time, lays out a *specific deadline* for membership contributions. To be sure I'll beat that deadline, I may really have to mail in my gift *today,* as I'm asked to do! (While I rarely recommend including specific dates in letters written to recruit new members — or, for that matter, in *any* letters mailed at bulk rate — this case is an exception. The appeal was mailed within a narrow region and likely to be delivered well in advance of the concert date. And conservatory faculty and students perform so frequently that similar offers can be made almost any time of the year.)

The lift letter

48. Yes, that intense-looking fellow in the upper right-hand corner photo is actually named Yo-Yo Ma. If you're a classical-music lover, you probably knew that. Unusual as his name is, however, it's likely to be the photo that first caught your attention. That's what the eye-motion studies reveal. *Then* your eyes swept leftward to take in his name, and finally down to the salutation and lead.

49. While Colin Murdoch addressed me as a "Neighbor," Yo-Yo Ma finds common cause with me as a "Music Lover." It's a flattering reference.

50. From this first paragraph until the fifth and last, this testimonial "lift letter" from Yo-Yo Ma is a credibility-building exercise. It means a lot for one of the world's most illustrious cellists to write about the conservatory's "high standards."

51. Similarly, it's useful — and impressive — for a celebrity in the world of music to name several of the conservatory's faculty members, who are far less likely to be known to the readers of this appeal. (I certainly knew none of the three names cited.)

52. In a longer letter, Mr. Ma might have revealed how frequently he visits the conservatory and how much time he spends at the conservatory, thus establishing his authority as a judge of the conservatory's participation in the Bay Area community. In

this context, I'm not impressed with the claim he makes in this paragraph.

53. However, he's back on more solid ground in the following paragraph, speaking about musical tradition and the "next generation of musicians."

54. Most celebrities try to get off easy in lift letters like this one, omitting explicit endorsements such as the last paragraph. But without such a direct statement, a lift letter's value is limited. Now I know Yo-Yo Ma really wants me to lend a hand. (His appeal would have been even stronger if he had written, "I urge you to join me as a Friend of the San Francisco Conservatory," thus leaving not a shadow of a doubt about his own deep commitment.)

55. He signs off "Sincerely," his name alone sufficing to identify himself. His signature (like Colin Murdoch's) is printed in dark blue ink to set it apart from the typewritten text.

The reply device

56. "BRAVO!" What an appropriate variation on the more commonly used "Yes!" (The applause line is printed in dark red, as are the check boxes and suggested gift amounts;,the logo, name, address, and phone number, and the headline below the line of dashes near the bottom. That bottom portion is tinted a gentle shade of red. All the text and every other element on this reply device is printed in black.)

57. In three terse sentences, the response device sums up the essence of "offer" spelled out in Colin Murdoch's letter.

58. I'm offered three choices here. (Unfortunately, I have to read closely the text at the bottom of this reply device to be certain "Regular Membership" really entitles me to all the benefits I'll get as a "Friend" of the conservatory. It might have been better to label the $40 option "Friend of the Conservatory" and devise a new name for the $100 option, while spelling out special benefits for the higher level of support. But no appeal's perfect.)

59. Here I'm reminded of the deadline (November 8). It's also clear to me that the offer of free tickets to the Faculty Trio Concert is a serious one: this is an excellent and appropriate use of a premium in membership acquisition.

60. Here's the Cheshire label (noted in paragraph number 5, describing the outer envelope).

61. That wonderful logo again!

62. I'm reminded — for the third time — that my gift will be tax deductible.

63. It's almost always wise to include instructions such as "Detach Here." Obviously, I could figure out that the reply device is perforated along the line of dashes, but it's courteous to relieve me of the (admittedly very slight) burden of determining that for myself. Instructions of this sort also reinforce the action-oriented nature of direct mail appeals.

64. Now any lingering doubt I might not actually receive the wonderful benefits described in Colin Murdoch's letter is totally dispelled.

65. Those benefits are listed. Note that they're described in the same words as in the letter.

66. The last thing I want to do when signing up for a membership in the conservatory is to fumble around with unfamiliar slips of paper of odd shapes and sizes, so I'm pleased to be told exactly what to do.

The reply envelope

67. Once again I'm reminded that my gift to the conservatory entitles me to membership (with its attendant benefits). This handwritten tagline is printed in dark blue like that of the signatures on both letters.

68. "Recycled paper" again!

69. This five-digit code helps our production staff and envelope printers keep this envelope apart from those used with hundreds of other jobs.

70. These vertical ruled lines are for the electronic scanning equipment used by the U.S. Postal Service to route the mail.

71. The indicia and the horizontal ruled lines are for the naked eye: unmistakable signs that this envelope is, as the words to the left explain, "Business Reply Mail." It will cost the Conservatory approximately 40¢ per envelope returned.

72. The envelope is addressed to the conservatory. In a more personal appeal — a membership renewal letter, for example — it might be appropriate to type the name Colin Murdoch above the institutional name. Its omission here is not a significant oversight: somehow, I would find it a little difficult to believe that the president of the San Francisco Conservatory of Music would be opening envelopes containing new memberships. Still, typing Murdoch's name on the reply envelope would reinforce the personality of this appeal; on balance, I would favor doing so.

73. This barcode enables the Postal Service to sort returning envelopes with minimal human intervention: the vertical lines are computer language for the letters and numbers contained in the address.

This fundraising letter for the San Francisco Conservatory of Music is a singular appeal; it was written for a particular purpose on behalf of a particular organization at a particular time. As a result, there are several ways this letter may not work well as a model for your own fundraising efforts. The package was written to *acquire members,* whereas most fundraising letters are written to proven donors. The letter is *benefit-driven* — even to the point of offering prospective members admission to a specific performance — and most nonprofits have to reach far to come up with tangible donor benefits. There's a *celebrity lift letter,* a device that's appropriate for most nonprofits only in unusual circumstances.

Why, then, is it worthwhile for you to study this package? *Because it does its job so well.* I chose this fundraising letter because its varied contents illustrate how to meet so many different letter-writing challenges — and, more to the point, because it dramatizes how different a fundraising letter can be from every other fundraising letter. There's no question what the Conservatory is offering. The Marketing Concept couldn't be clearer.

By contrast, let's take a look at an appeal that's much closer to the dysfunctional definition of a fundraising letter that I referred to at the beginning of the previous chapter.

A shorter journey through a letter that doesn't work well

A. Glance at the outer envelope pictured on page 72. You can't miss the return address rubber stamped in the upper left-hand corner or the incomplete (and, in many parts of the country, undeliverable) address on the mailing label. The only thing this envelope's got going for it is a first-class stamp. (But you probably guessed, just as I did, that the reason this was mailed first class was one of the following. (1) the quantity wasn't large enough to qualify the appeal for bulk mail. (2) the organization didn't have or couldn't get a nonprofit bulk mailing permit. Or (3) the list was in such bad shape they couldn't bundle the mail properly to suit postal personnel.

B. Now take a look through the text on the first page. It has its positive points: short paragraphs, white space, underlined subheadings, language that's clear and relatively readable. But there are precious few personal pronouns anywhere in sight — except for a few "we's" — and the rest is argumentative and rhetorical. It's not even really clear this is an appeal for funds because I'm asked if I can "assist in other ways." But there's no way I can tell how my "financial contribution" — or any other sort of help I might give — is connected to anything else in this letter.

C. The second page continues in the same vein, compounding the problems of the first page: more statistics, more rhetoric, a laundry list of organiza-

tions (some of them little known), a dual signature — and *no Ask*. It's hard to imagine a letter better calculated *not* to raise money!

D. Apparently, the Federal Jobs Program outlined in the top two-thirds of this reply device is the principal program of the organization that sent this appeal, although I'm forced to guess that's really the case. Only at the bottom of the page do I find a way to respond to the letter (assuming I'd be so inclined). You'll note it's called an "Endorsement Form." However, there's no way for me to indicate my endorsement (for the Federal Jobs Program? the Campaign to Abolish Poverty?). There's also no suggested gift amount — and no return address (in case the form becomes separated from the letter or the return envelope).

E. This rubber-stamped little reply envelope doesn't inspire confidence. Major gift fundraisers speak of an organization's "readiness" to receive big gifts. This organization doesn't appear ready to receive *little* gifts!

Throughout the journey you've just completed, you must have recognized the emphasis I placed on the *relationship* between the conservatory and the donor. Relationship-building is the central subject of the next chapter, "Why You Need to Write Thank-Yous Even Though Every Fundraising Letter Is a Thank-You." ▶

B

Campaign to Abolish Poverty

942 Market Street, #708, San Francisco, CA 94102 ● Ph: 415-397-4911 Fx: 415-434-3110

November 6, 1992

Dear Friend:

Electing Bill Clinton President certainly creates new opportunities in Washington, D.C. The pendulum is beginning to swing in the opposite direction.

But it remains to be seen how much difference Clinton will make, particularly for the poor and near-poor. If history is any guide, strong grassroots pressure will be necessary to push Clinton beyond his election-year program.

The Campaign to Abolish Poverty (CAP) aims to push the pendulum as hard as possible. Our current focus is to build support for the Federal Jobs Program -- a proposal to create two million new, permanent, public service jobs -- as a first step toward ending poverty in this country.

We urge you to help this effort by sending a financial contribution now, and letting us know if you can assist in other ways.

Clinton has committed himself to a number of good positions. But there is a downside to most of them.

Jobs

On the one hand, for example, it is encouraging that Clinton proposes federal funding for public works jobs. But he's only talking about one-shot infrastructure repair -- temporary jobs which largely would exclude women, minorities and low-income people who need them the most.

We need to persuade Clinton and Congress to support <u>sustained</u> federal funding for local human service jobs -- jobs for which the poor and near-poor would qualify, with relevant on-the-job training.

Tax Reform

It is also positive that Clinton advocates increasing taxes on the wealthy. But his proposal would roll back only one-fifth of the tax breaks received by the top 2% of all households during the last fifteen years. If these families with annual incomes over $200,000 paid 34% of their income in federal taxes, as they did in 1977, $80 billion in addition to the $20 billion targeted by Clinton could be generated.

We need to persuade Clinton and Congress to restore 1977 tax rates for the wealthy. All other income groups are now paying higher federal taxes (including payroll taxes). The wealthy could pay what they paid in 1977 without undue hardship.

C

FEDERAL JOBS PROGRAM

<u>Purpose</u>: **To appropriate $50 billion to create 2 million new public service jobs in both urban and rural areas, as the first step toward guaranteeing every adult the opportunity to work at a living wage. Each year, funding should increase by 20% until these jobs go begging due to lack of applicants.**

<u>Types of Work</u>: These funds shall be used to hire workers in repair/maintenance/ rehabilitation of publicly-owned facilities, conservation/rehabilitation/ improvement of public lands, child care, health care, in-home caregiving, education (including tutorial services), peer counseling, housing and neighborhood improvement, recreation, arts programs, community centers, and other vital public services.

<u>Wages</u>: Wages shall range from $7-$12 per hour, plus benefits, and shall be indexed to inflation. The compensation for these positions shall not be less than the prevailing compensation for individuals employed in similar occupations.

<u>Allocation of Funds</u>: Two and one-half percent of all funds shall be allocated for Native American tribes and Alaska Native villages. Remaining funds shall be allocated by the Secretary of Labor to the states based upon the number of people living in poverty in each state.

<u>Administration</u>:   The Secretary of Labor shall distribute the funds to the states for distribution to local governments. The cost of administration shall be no more than the standard for similar programs. Each recipient of funds shall be responsible for ensuring equal employment opportunities, equal pay for equal work, and the full participation of traditionally underrepresented groups, including women and racial and ethnic minorities.

<u>Displacement</u>: The following shall be prohibited: a) any displacing of current employees, including partial displacement such as a reduction in the hours of nonovertime work, wages, or employment benefits; b) impairing of existing contracts or collective bargaining; c) filling of openings created by related layoffs or terminations; or d) infringing on promotional opportunities of current employees.

<u>Oversight</u>: Prior to submitting its plan to the State, each eligible entity shall conduct an open public review and comment process, and during the year, shall conduct at least one public hearing to receive input into its evaluation process. Workers hired by these funds shall be encouraged to participate in this review process.

<u>Source of Funds</u>: The funds needed for this program shall come from increasing personal income taxes on the richest 2% of households and from reducing the military budget.

D

ENDORSEMENT FORM

___Please find enclosed a check for _____ (made payable to: Campaign to Abolish Poverty) to help with building support for the Federal Jobs Program. (Contributions are tax-deductible.)

___I would like to volunteer some time to help.

___Please send me more information about CAP and the Federal Jobs Program.

Name (print) _____

Organization (if any)_____

Address _____

City_____State_____Zip_____

Day Phone_____Eve Phone_____Fax_____

<u>Military Spending</u>

Clinton's proposals for reductions in the military budget are inadequate. **We need to persuade Clinton and Congress to move in the direction of a 50% cut in military spending,** which could free almost $150 billion per year to help put Americans to work.

<u>Federal Jobs Program</u>

In consultation with a wide range of recognized experts and community organizations, CAP has developed a specific program -- the **Federal Jobs Program** -- that would appropriate $50 billion to create two million permanent public service jobs, paid for by higher taxes on the wealthy and reductions in the military budget (see enclosed).

A broad range of community-based organizations, community leaders, and elected officials have already endorsed this program, including American Friends Service Committee, Catholic Charities of San Francisco, California Legislative Council for Older Americans, Coleman Advocates for Children and Youth, San Francisco Lawyer's Committee for Urban Affairs, and Maryland United for Peace and Justice. Considering that we have been gathering endorsements only since early October, this support is very encouraging.

But in order to influence the next session of Congress, the Campaign to Abolish Poverty and its membership must broaden its base and press its case effectively in Washington. We have recently begun encouraging discussions with a number of national organizations with lobbyists in Washington to build support for our jobs program.

The desperation and misery experienced by growing millions of Americans compel us to make this effort and to continue until economic security for all is established as a human right.

So please give what you can financially, and if possible contribute time and energy as well. Please complete the form enclosed and return it with your tax-deductible donation as soon as possible.

With your help, we have a chance.

Sincerely,

Wade Hudson
Chair

Barbara Arms
Director

WHY YOU NEED TO WRITE THANK-YOUS

You probably figured this out a long time ago: writing fundraising letters is no way for your organization to get rich quick. Raising money by mail, like fundraising conducted by any other means, is a long-term process. As you'll recall from earlier chapters, I think of that process as comprising three overlapping stages (acquisition, conversion, and upgrading). The fundraising letters you mail during these three stages may differ dramatically from one another, because your *relationships* with donors change over time. You know much more about your donors at the later stages than you do at the earlier, and your letters will reflect that knowledge in ways that are both obvious and profound. But there's one element *all* effective fundraising letters share:

They show appreciation.

Even when you're writing a prospective donor who's known to you only as a name on a list, it's sound practice to find a way to compliment her while you make your case for a gift — and then to thank her in advance for agreeing to help. It's the *polite* thing to do.

When you write a proven donor to solicit additional support, it's important to reinforce her goodwill (and her memory) by thanking her for her past generosity. It's not only polite to do that — it's sure to make your letter work better.

And when you're asking a donor to make an extra special effort to *upgrade* her support — by joining a High-Dollar club or a monthly sustainer program, for example — you'll get the best results when you include repeated, heartfelt thanks in your letter. After all, the donors you select as prospects for most upgrade campaigns are very special people who've *already* given you more money, or given more frequently, or for a longer period of time, than all the rest of your supporters. It's polite, effective — and *natural* — to thank them in an upgrade appeal.

In other words, every fundraising letter is a thank-you!

Even so, that's not enough.

Focus group research constantly turns up comments like the following, over and over again:

I sent them some money over a year ago, but I never got a thank-you. Well, never again!

I've been giving to them for years, twenty, twenty-five bucks at a time. They got a hundred bucks from me recently – and all they sent back was the same preprinted postcard they always send. How much do you think they're going to get the next time around?

The thing that burns me up is getting a thank-you about two months after I send a check – after they've already asked for more money! I won't give to a group that's that disorganized . . . or rude.

Why do comments like these so commonly turn up in focus group research? Because so many charities defy the Golden Rule of Donor Acknowledgments. In the following section, I'll tell you what I mean by that.

The Golden Rule of Donor Acknowledgments

Readers of my newsletter, *Successful Direct Mail & Telephone Fundraising,* are familiar with the Phantom Donor. This generous soul sends $15 or $20 gifts once or twice a year to some of the nation's top nonprofit organizations – and studies the mail that comes in return.

Not long ago, the Phantom paid special attention to the donor acknowledgment practices of his (or her) favorite charities. The experience was sobering. Eight weeks after a round of $15 checks to twenty organizations, all mailed on the same day with the most recent reply device and reply envelope received from each of the mailers, the Phantom Donor had been thanked by only fifteen of the twenty groups. One of them, the American Red Cross, got out a thank-you (admittedly only a postcard) within less than one week. But few others arrived within the first month. The average response time was five to seven weeks.

Okay. Let's not pussyfoot around here: that performance was *pathetic.* And we're not talking about the mom-and-pop charity down on the corner. These were some of the most successful nonprofit mailers in America — groups such as The Humane Society of the U.S., Common Cause, and the Christian Appalachian Project.

In fact, *most* direct mail fundraisers do a downright poor job of thanking their donors. The donor acknowledgment practices of those big charities simply mirror what goes on throughout the independent sector.

Charities that cut costs by refraining from mailing thank-yous — or by sending such cut-rate items as preprinted postcards — are *all* missing the boat. But it's not enough simply to send a thank-you. As far as I'm concerned, The Golden Rule of Donor Acknowledgments is this:

Thank your donors quickly!

The most heartwarming and informative thank-you copy will be wasted on a donor who already may have forgotten that he sent you a check. (If you doubt donors react this way, run a couple of focus groups, and ask donors what they think.)

In fact, I'm so concerned about the widespread failure to heed The Golden Rule of Donor Acknowledgments that I'll offer a corollary:

Send even a "bad" thank-you — if you can get it into the mail faster than a "good" one!

Here, now, are a few other pointers for effective donor acknowledgments:

◆ Reassure your donors it was a good idea to send gifts. Don't let them suffer from "buyer's remorse." Reinforce their original belief that your group is effective, caring, and worthy of their support.

◆ Be warm and friendly. If they're new donors, welcome them to the "family."

◆ Praise their generosity. Tell them how, by joining with other supporters, they're having a significant impact on your work.

- Reaffirm your gratitude at the end of the letter or in a P.S.

- Give examples of recent successes they can feel proud of.

- Finally, consider not just saying thank you but using the opportunity to suggest another gift, even if it's a "soft Ask" that no one could possibly interpret as arm-twisting. (Normally, I don't recommend this. But it's worth considering. In emergencies, and with important deadlines approaching, it might be unnatural *not* to ask for additional support!) Unless there's some good reason not to do so, enclose a reply envelope for a future contribution.

Now, to explore some of the numerous possibilities opened up by thank-you packages, let's take a look at the diverse styles and approaches followed by those fifteen mailers who (eventually) thanked the Phantom Donor.

How some of the country's top fundraising mailers thank their donors

A #10 window envelope was far and away the preferred choice of the fifteen mailers. Not a single one used a closed-face (non-window) envelope, although CARE opted for a self-contained "fast-tab" envelope. There were also two postcards, from the Red Cross and from the National Organization for Women.

Of the envelope packages received, fewer than half featured teasers. Nothing flashy, just a simple "Thank you" in five out of six cases. But the sixth got fancier: "A special note of thanks."

Many direct mail pros argue that a thank-you is the best time to solicit another contribution — a "get 'em while they're hot" mentality. All the thank-you packages sent to the Phantom (except for the two postcards) included return envelopes to be used for subsequent gifts. However, only seven of these thirteen mailers directly pitched for funds by also including reply devices. The most aggressive approach was the attempt to seek an immediate upgrade via

membership in a monthly giving club. Two environmental groups opted for this stratagem: Greenpeace and the National Audubon Society. Significantly, in both cases letter copy emphasized the long-term commitment needed in the day-to-day battle to save our environment.

Most of the packages consisted of copy that was short and to the point. Aside from the two postcards, the Phantom received six short-form receipts, one of which also incorporated a membership card. Of the seven actual letters, five were of the one-page variety. The exceptions were the two monthly sustainer packages: Greenpeace used a two-page letter, Audubon a three-pager.

One intriguing point about the two longer pieces: these were the only letters that were *not* personalized. Both instead used a variation on the "Dear Supporter" salutation — ironically a rather impersonal way to elicit a substantial upgrade.

Almost all the acknowledgments straightforwardly and profusely thanked the Phantom — from a simple "your gift makes a difference" to the gushy "you are special to us and we hold you in our hearts and minds." Religiously-oriented groups were apt to add a "God bless you."

Generally, the message was upbeat and gracious, reminding the Phantom Donor of the good work being accomplished by the group (to make her — or him — feel better about parting with 15 bucks!). Occasionally though, the tone was more downbeat, and the Phantom was treated to a lecture on the ills faced by our organization of choice. The Republican National Committee, for example, was up in arms about the "Clinton/Democrat tax and spend frenzy," while the World Wildlife Fund informed the Phantom that many species "are on the brink of extinction."

Four of the thirteen letter packages contained inserts. What was particularly striking was that *all four* were on the subject of planned giving. In each of these pieces, a return coupon was provided to receive additional information. In two other instances — where a planned giving brochure was *not* enclosed — a checkoff box was included on the reply device to request further material.

Most of the Phantom's charities avoided sending premiums. The Billy Graham Evangelistic Association was a notable exception. As in previous acknowledgment packages, the Graham organization included a 300-page paperback book and a reprint from its monthly magazine. Only two other groups mailed premiums, apart from The Nature Conservancy's membership card. St. Joseph's Indian School sent a prayer card and Father Flanagan's Boys' Home included an excerpt from a book by its executive director. The latter enclosed a "handy" wallet calendar that was "made in our own print shop."

Father Flanagan's also alerted the Phantom to be on the lookout for a future premium. The personalized copy declared, "In my next letter, because you are one of our family, I'm sending you an honorary certificate of citizenship." Two weeks later the certificate arrived — with another appeal for funds!

Now, despite bells and whistles and occasional high-pressure requests for additional donations, few donor acknowledgments generate even enough revenue to pay their costs. So why do such savvy (if far from speedy) fundraising mailers go to all this trouble and expense?

Two reasons are obvious and easily confirmed by testing:

1. *Thank-yous increase response to subsequent appeals.*

2. *Thank-yous increase donor loyalty.*

But there's a third, more fundamental reason to invest in timely and appropriate donor acknowledgments:

3. *Thank-yous help build long-term relationships with donors.*

To give you a better sense of what I mean, I'd like you to examine closely a thank-you package from another major fundraising mailer — not one on the Phantom's charity list.

A great example of a thank-you letter

Check out the letter from the Southern Poverty Law Center (Montgomery, AL) reproduced on pages 98 to 101. What you see there — an outer envelope and two notebook-sized pages, printed on one side only — were the entire contents of this masterful donor acknowledgment package. Many fundraisers insist you should include a self-addressed reply envelope in *every* communication with your donors, but there was none in this package (much less a personalized reply device that might generate a "bounce-back" gift). I'll bet, though, that this warm, informative acknowledgment generates gifts at least an order of magnitude greater than the few, paltry bounce-back contributions that might result if the package were to include a reply envelope.

[Note: this package was mailed first class. Had it been mailed bulk rate instead, the Southern Poverty Law Center couldn't have used Bobby Person's name and address as the return address on the outer envelope. Under postal regulations in force at this writing, a nonprofit organization must correctly identify itself on the outer envelope to qualify for the nonprofit postal discount.]

Clearly, the Southern Poverty Law Center has chosen to invest in its future relationships with its donors by spending what is, after all, a modest sum on thank-yous like these. You'd be well-advised to consider whether this technique makes sense for your own organization, too. It probably does. Why? Because the revenue you generate from future appeals to new donors is apt to dwarf the investment you've made in acquiring and "converting" new donors through such techniques as this. And far more of your new donors are likely to respond to those future appeals (and more generously so) if they feel you've treated them like part of the family.

It's really that simple. Treat every one of your donors like Grandma or Uncle Paul, and your organization will reap the rewards for many years to come. ▶

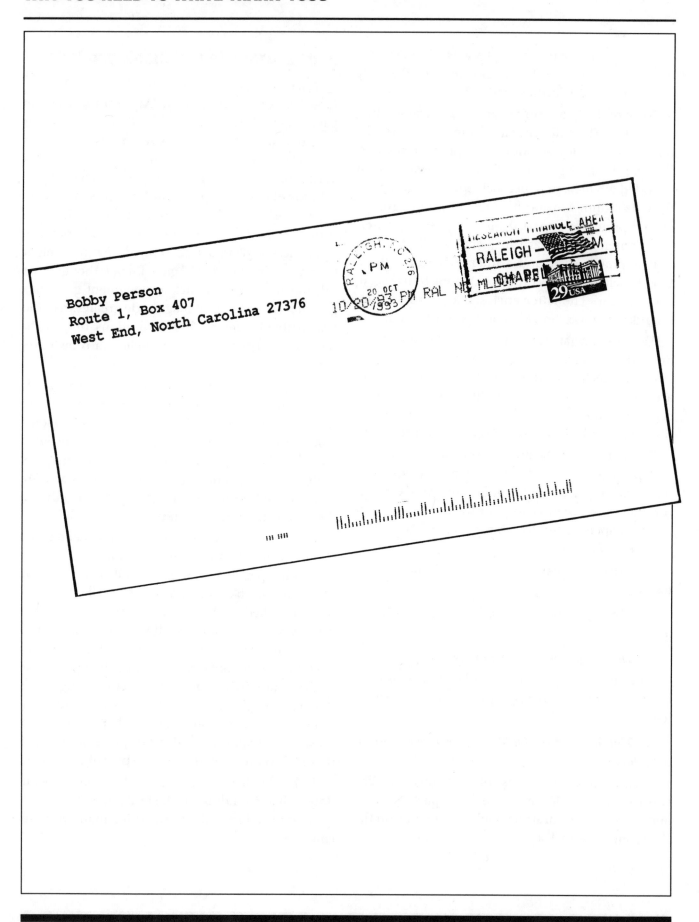

Bobby Person
Route 1, Box 190
West End, North Carolina 27376

October 15, 1993

Ms. ⌐⌐⌐⌐⌐⌐⌐⌐⌐
⌐⌐⌐ ⌐⌐⌐⌐⌐⌐ge Ave.
⌐⌐⌐⌐ny, CA 9470⌐

Dear Ms. ⌐⌐⌐⌐ ⌐,

I understand from my friends at the Southern Poverty Law Center and its Klanwatch Project in Montgomery that you recently sent a gift to help in their work.

I wanted to show some appreciation for the work the Center did for me and I wrote them a letter of thanks. They asked if I would share my feelings with you so that you might better understand that their work touches the lives of real people in a meaningful way. I was more than glad to help by writing you directly.

When I needed their help to protect me from harassment from members of the Ku Klux Klan, they spent hundreds of hours and several thousand dollars to protect my family and me.

Let me tell you about my case.

I am a black person living in a small rural North Carolina community and work as a guard at a state prison. I wanted to advance myself and asked my supervisor for permission to take the sergeant's examination. No black man had ever been sergeant of the prison guard.

I did not know at the time that one of the white guards was a Klansman. That night, a Klan cross was burned in the dirt road in front of my house. My wife and children were terrified. A few nights later, several Klansmen wearing sheets and paramilitary uniforms, and carrying guns, drove up in front of my home and threatened to kill me. My children were so frightened that they did not sleep well for months. Later, shots were fired at the guard tower at night from cars passing on the road.

The lawyers from the Southern Poverty Law Center filed suit against three Klansmen suspected of this harassment. They also filed suit to stop the Carolina Knights of the KKK from operating their paramilitary army. After a few months, they received a court order stopping the Klan paramilitary training. The three Klansmen who harassed me and my family also stood trial and were ordered to stop.

Since the Center came to my aid, I am proud to tell you that I won the promotion to sergeant.

You may have heard of some of the big cases the Center has handled. Many of these cases receive national publicity and many have made significant advances in human rights. My case is not very important in the long run and you may not ever have heard about it, but it was important to my family and me to be able to call on a group of lawyers who had the money to go after the Klan and who are experts in how to stop Klan terrorism. Funds were available to help me only with help from people like yourself.

Now the Center has expanded its work with a new educational project to encourage the teaching of tolerance in our schools.

For the first time in history, an organization exists that is not only fighting the Klan in the courtroom, but also in the classroom by helping teach children the value of tolerance.

Please continue your financial support of the Center. This is a long, hard fight that needs people like yourself committed to working for a future when all people live in peace and harmony.

My family and I want to thank you personally for the generous gift that you gave the Center.

Sincerely,

Bobby Person

9

WHAT TO DO *BEFORE* YOU WRITE A FUNDRAISING LETTER

Now what? You know the rules of style and English grammar (and how to break them). You understand how to write for results, and how to apply that understanding to the writing of fundraising letters. But how do you get *started* writing that fundraising letter that's due at the printer's next month?

Think.

Effective writing begins with clear, uncluttered thinking. Before you set down on paper a single word of your next fundraising appeal, you must understand precisely who and why and what you're writing.

That's what the following twenty questions are about. Asking yourself these questions won't guarantee you'll write a better letter (much less a more successful letter). But these questions may help you think clearly about the task at hand and focus your writing on the specific points you most need to make.

Answering these questions will enable you to construct a powerful *Marketing Concept*. Remember that awful-sounding phrase? It's advertising jargon for the idea that's at the core of any piece of writing conceived to produce results. The Marketing Concept is a tapestry woven of need, opportunity, and circumstance. It's the pure essence of the message you're conveying. Or think of it as an executive summary of your letter.

The Marketing Concept is at the heart of the dialogue that Siegfried Vögele describes (see Chapter 3). Incorporated into the Marketing Concept are the answers to many of your reader's unspoken questions.

Never forget this: the *words* you write will not yield results. You'll obtain the objectives you desire only to the extent that your words convey a Marketing Concept powerful enough to motivate your donors. You must appeal to them clearly and unambiguously — which requires that you begin with an absolutely clear understanding why you're writing a

How to Write Successful Fundraising Letters

letter in the first place. That's where my twenty questions start.

First, think about why you're writing this particular letter . . .

1. What is the purpose of your appeal? Are you writing to acquire new donors or members? To solicit larger gifts — or major gifts? To urge your donors to consider Planned Giving? To reactivate lapsed members or donors? Or to meet any of a multitude of other specific fundraising needs?

Now, think about the people you're writing to . . .

2. What do they have in common with each other? For example, do they share a powerful experience: an earthquake, religious conversion, new citizenship, a crushing personal loss? Are they patriotic . . . or dedicated to a particular cause? Are they all likely to be concerned about "family values"?

3. What fact, or facts, may be true about (almost) all of them — facts to distinguish them from the rest of the world's population? Are they all over the age of sixty? Do they all live in a single community? Were they all once patients in your hospital? Are they all women? Baby Boomers? Donors? Nondonors? Members?

4. What do you know about the people you're writing? Are they likely to be angry (or elated) about a recent turn of events in the world, or in your local community? Have recent economic setbacks made life more difficult for them, or changes in tax laws made them more comfortable? Are they likely to be skeptical about charity? Concerned about declining family values? Fearful of old age?

5. What's the relationship of the people you're writing to your organization? What do they know about you, your organization, or the issue or problem you're addressing? What don't they know? What do they *want* to know? Have they been contributing regular gifts for several years and demonstrated

interest, even commitment to your agency? Is the typical reader of the letter you're about to write a longtime subscriber to your newsletter . . . or a new donor who lacks basic information about your work? Is there likely to be a personal relationship between her and your executive director or a member of your board?

6. Consider the typical recipient of your letter. What experiences, feelings, and thoughts is that person likely to have that would help her understand the issue or problem you're addressing? Is it likely that the typical reader of your letter will feel very deeply — based on her own personal experience — about some issue or problem that underpins your agency's work? For example, if you serve the homeless, is she likely to come into contact with homeless people on a daily basis . . . or almost never? Put yourself in her position, and think how she might think and feel about the challenges your organization faces every day.

7. What leads you to believe that the typical person you're writing will respond favorably? Does she have a long history of supporting your agency — or, at least, organizations like yours? Has she expressed interest in knowing how she might help? Is there some personal connection, such as a child who was a patient, a parent who benefited from your services, or an old school tie? Is this a time of crisis, and have earlier appeals to the same or similar groups amply demonstrated that people like those you're writing are likely to respond?

Now, think about what you'll ask people to do . . .

8. What is it — exactly — that you want recipients to do? Renew their memberships? Send larger annual gifts than they did last year? Join an exclusive giving club? Sign up for Electronic Funds Transfer? Support a special new project? Respond to an emergency with an additional $10 or $15?

9. What is the minimum amount of money (if any) that you hope to receive from each recipient? Few questions are more important in appeals sent by mail, as the amount you *ask* — particularly the minimum amount — will often predetermine the amount you receive. A prospective donor may gag at a request for $1,000, while a long-loyal supporter thinks the same sum too small. (That's why the same appeal usually can't be sent to both prospective and proven donors.) To be successful, your appeal must ask for a specific amount — and that must be the *right* amount.

10. Is there anything else you want recipients to do right now? Will your appeal ask for a cash contribution and nothing more? Or will you request a three-year pledge, a monthly commitment, a signature on a credit card authorization form — or something entirely different? For example, will your appeal include an "involvement device" such as a postcard to the governor . . . a membership survey . . . or an offer to supply information about wills and bequests?

Now, think about the circumstances in which you're writing this appeal . . .

11. What problem, need, issue, or opportunity prompts your agency to send this appeal? Be specific: don't state the need as simply that "funds are tight" or "we need money." Think about the particular set of circumstances that makes it necessary for your agency to raise funds *right now*. Is there a profoundly exciting new opportunity that your organization wants to meet by launching a new program? Has there been an unanticipated demand for your services . . . or a shortfall in funding from corporate and foundation donors? Is a trustee or a friendly foundation offering a challenge grant (or willing to do so)?

Think about the person who'll sign the appeal . . .

12. What is the signer's name? It's dangerous to draft an appeal not knowing who will sign it. A fundraising appeal — a letter from one individual person to another — is most powerful when it reflects the personal views and feelings of both people. The appeal will be most effective if you can bring it to life with a relevant anecdote or two, or a typical statement that will ring true — something that might cause a knowledgeable reader to nod and say, "Yep, that's ol' Fred in a nutshell, all right!"

13. What is the connection between the signer and the problem, need, issue, or opportunity that prompts the appeal? If the signer is your president or executive director, the connection may be obvious — and rife with possibilities to bring that opportunity to life. If the signer is, instead, someone who has no day-to-day connection with the events or circumstances that prompt your appeal, think about what might move the signer to write an emotional appeal at this particular time. Is there something in his past: his education, perhaps, his childhood, his experience as a soldier at war, his business achievements?

14. What is the connection between the signer and those who will receive the appeal? Do they share the experiences of a generation? For example, are most of them over the age of fifty-five — or under forty? As loyal members of a single organization, have they shared a particular event or intense experience: the death of a president, a Superbowl victory, the landing on the moon? Or are they all well-to-do . . . or members of a very special community? Have they received similar honors, attended the same school, watched the same shows on TV?

15. What are the signer's feelings and thoughts about the problem, need, issue, or opportunity that underlies the appeal? If you don't know the answer to this question, ask it! Sometimes, the signer — even an in-house, staff, or board signer — can suggest a powerful line of argument, or an evocative story that will bring your appeal to life. Emotional copy is usually more effective than intellectual copy, but a powerful fundraising letter is built on ideas and facts as well as feelings. Look for both to flesh out your appeal.

Consider what benefits people will get if they respond to your appeal . . .

16. List all the *tangible* benefits, if any. Are you offering a newsletter, for example, or discounts on products or services — or the promise of invitations to events with celebrity supporters? Or have you enclosed a premium such as a bookmark, namestickers, photos, or a calendar?

17. List the *intangible* benefits of sending a gift in response to your appeal. Will donors help you change the course of human history . . . or save the life of a tiny child? Will they be ensuring that their values and beliefs will be passed along to generations of descendants . . . or raising the quality of life in their community? Will donors gain salvation, learn about a headline-grabbing issue, prevent the abuse of pets?

Now, why do the readers of your appeal need to respond *right now*? . . .

18. Is there an especially urgent need or opportunity that justifies this appeal? Is Thanksgiving approaching, and with it increased demand for the hot meals your agency serves to the poor? Is a regional war about to break out, shutting down communications with your field office? Is the Congressional debate drawing to a close? Will the board of directors be forced to shut the program down soon if funding goals aren't met?

19. Is there a deadline by which you must receive responses? For instance, have you arranged — or can you arrange — a challenge grant with an imminent deadline? Is the end of the calendar year approaching, and with it the opportunity to save on

this year's taxes? Is Easter special to your organization, representing a traditional time for your supporters to demonstrate their compassion for the less fortunate?

20. What will happen if you don't receive responses before that deadline? Will you lose the challenge grant? Will poor people go hungry? Will children be turned away from the door to your agency? Will small animals die, or the supply of autographed books run out, or people with AIDS suffer needless pain?

How to write a Marketing Concept

Once you've answered the twenty questions listed above, sum up all this information in *one paragraph*. Be as specific and precise as possible. Write the paragraph in the first-person singular (just as you'll have to do when you write the letter itself). And address it to that one typical *individual* who will be receiving your letter.

The paragraph you write will be the Marketing Concept for your appeal. Once you've written it, the *rest* of your job will be a piece of cake!

Keep in mind that the Marketing Concept is not the letter itself, or even its opening paragraph: it's simply a way to get started. Others might call it the "copy platform." It's the foundation on which you'll construct your appeal. It's what you'll write *about:* Facts. Information. Feelings. Circumstances. *Specifics.* The Marketing Concept is the skeleton on which you hang them all together. In writing your letter, you'll put flesh on those bones.

Now, to help you get the hang of it, here are examples of two typical Marketing Concepts.

Marketing Concept #1

Because you've been so generous to The Center in the past, you've heard from me from time to time about exciting new developments here. I've told you before how far we stretch your contributions to serve the underserved in The Community. Now, a renewal gift from you of as little as $25 will go twice *as far as before! Your $25 will help house the homeless children of The Community by enabling The Center to buy $50 or more worth of lumber and tools – because your gift will be matched, dollar for dollar, by an anonymous donor through The Center's new Matching Gift Program. That way, you'll get double the satisfaction from your act of generosity – and bring new hope to twice as many of your neighbors in The Community.*

Marketing Concept #2

You may not know me, but I'm sure you're familiar with The Museum, which has been the centerpiece of my life during the past twenty years of my tenure as its Director. I'm writing you, a fellow resident of The City, because I want you to be among the first to know about The Museum's unique new Charter Membership program. As a person who appreciates the finer things in life, you'll cherish for many years to come each magnificent issue of our new bi-monthly magazine on the visual arts. You'll receive the magazine absolutely free of charge as a Charter Member of The Museum. And you'll have the satisfaction of knowing that your Charter Membership contribution of $45, $75, $150, or more will help us to showcase the exciting new work of emerging new artists in our region.

Often but not always the reply device restates the Marketing Concept in a successful direct mail fundraising package. That's why many experienced direct mail copywriters (myself included) *start* with the reply device when they set out to write a package.

To get a stronger grip on this point, study the reply devices pages 107 to 111. You'll soon get the gist of the Marketing Concept behind each of the fundraising appeals from which these response forms were selected. They stare you right in the face. That's what your Marketing Concept needs to do, too — *every time you write an appeal!*

Why am I so adamant about this? Simple: your reader has only twenty seconds to get the message. (Remember Siegfried Vögele's eye-camera research!) If your message — the central reason why your readers should respond — isn't clear at a glance, then there's little chance your letter will be read at all, much less generate contributions.

Join me now on a step-by-step journey through the route I usually take when setting out to write a fundraising letter. ▶

Captain Cousteau,

I care, too. And I want to do my share to help you carry on your much-needed work to protect this planet, its waters, its environment, and its people. Please enroll me as the newest member of The Cousteau Society. Enclosed is my check for:

☐ **My $25 family membership fee.**
☐ **My $15 annual membership fee.**

(Facsimile. Full-size free decal enclosed.)

```
Z7A02
MAL WARWICK
BERKELEY,          CA
IlılııılılıllıılıılılıIlılılıllllıllıılıllılI
```

THE COUSTEAU SOCIETY

 Recycled Paper

Your membership benefits include ...

- The *Calypso Log*, an informative, colorful bimonthly membership magazine that keeps you in touch with the Society's expeditions and projects.
- Your personalized Cousteau Society membership card and decal.
- The Gift Gallery, which offers Cousteau Society videotapes, art prints, books, posters and T-shirts.

And with a Family Membership ...

- In addition to all of the above, you receive our award-winning *Dolphin Log*, a spectacularly illustrated bimonthly publication which introduces young readers to life in and around the sea. But its fascinating stories, facts, games and experiments are enjoyed by people of all ages.

Please allow 6 to 8 weeks for delivery of your membership card and Society publications.

Join The Cousteau Society Today! 870 Greenbrier Circle, Suite 402
Chesapeake, Virginia 23320

Please make your check payable to The Cousteau Society. The Cousteau Society attempts to eliminate all duplicate mailings. However, if you happen to receive two mailings, please pass one on to a friend.

Dear Vivian,

Yes, I want to help provide the gift of a better world for our children.

Enclosed is my special gift to help launch MADRE's important life-affirming programs for 1993. Please use it to provide a gift of hope for the future to the women and children who suffer from war, poverty and repression. I know they depend on our friendship.

Mr. John Doe
123 Any Street
Any Town, AS 00000

[ ] $200   [ ] $100   [ ] $_____

Please see other side ▶

FOR THE CHILDREN

42DOE
121 WEST 27th ST., ROOM 301
NEW YORK, NEW YORK 10001

Please fold and return this reply memo with your check payable to MADRE in the enclosed postpaid envelope. Thank you.

RECYCLED PAPER   53422

Your special year-end gift to MADRE will help fund these crucial projects for 1993:

-- Shoes, school supplies and post-traumatic stress therapy for the children of El Salvador who are returning home after the war.

-- A women's and children's clinic in Guatemala City for those who've fled the violence in the countryside

-- Ongoing support for street vendor children in San Marcos, Nicaragua

-- A kindergarten for children who suffer from war and repression on the West Bank

TOTAL PROJECTED COST FOR 1ST QUARTER OF 1993: $122,000

Yes...

I value commercial-free, mind-enriching public television!

And I realize it's time I did my share to help support Northern California's leading public television station — KQED. Therefore, please enroll me as the newest KQED Member and begin all my membership benefits immediately. Enter my Membership for:

☐ $35   ☐ $50
☐ $100   ☐ $200

As part of your KQED Membership, you receive *San Francisco Focus* magazine, including the "Fine Tuning" member and program guide, every month... AND the KQED Membership Card, entitling you to an array of discounts around town — at Bay Area museums, theater presentations, the aquarium, planetarium, and zoo, and at KQED's own popular Special Events.

KQED

MEMBERSHIP ACCEPTANCE FORM

FDG D04D28
MR. MAL WARWICK
BERKELEY, CA
94102

☐ My check is enclosed

☐ Please charge my
☐ VISA   ☐ MasterCard   ☐ Discover

FDG

Account Number_____

Expiration Date_____ Signature_____

Your contribution is tax-deductible except for $12 which applies to a year's subscription to *San Francisco Focus* magazine.

Plus...FOR A LIMITED TIME ONLY
the Bay Area restaurant guide, *Dining Out*, will be sent to you as a special introductory offer.

KQED

P.O. Box 340
San Francisco, CA 94101

01FAJP

090309

1990 NATIONAL
REPUBLICAN SENATORIAL COMMITTEE
STRATEGIC OVERVIEW

RECEIPT VERIFICATION REPLY

May 4, 1990

Report ID # 01117228 – 9D19

Issued to: Mr. Mal Warwick
Berkeley, CA 94___

I hereby verify that I received my copy of the National Republican Senatorial Committee Strategic Overview,

_____ _____
Signature   Date

INSTRUCTIONS: Due to the highly confidential nature of this report, we must have verification that you, and only you, received this copy. Please complete and sign this receipt verification and return it immediately.

☐ Please let me know as soon as possible whether or not we've solved this budget crisis.

Dear Senator Nickles,

   I realize the immediate necessity of meeting our critical budget shortfalls in the fourteen states noted in the Overview. To make certain that we get out of this dangerous situation and bring our campaign budgets up to schedule, I'm sending my special contribution today of:

Please make your check payable to the National Republican Senatorial Committee.
425 Second Street, N.E. • Washington, D.C. 20002

☐ $20   ☐ $30   ☐ $_____ Other

CHARTER MEMBER ACCEPTANCE FORM

Yes, I want to send American doctors to the world's most troubled areas—regardless of the obstacles. Enclosed is my tax-deductible contribution to enable Doctors of the World to answer desperate calls for help from around the world. I understand that every dollar I send will provide 50 times its value in medical care.

☐ **$20 = $1,000 value in medical care**

☐ **$35**   ☐ **$50**   ☐ **$100**   ☐ **$250**   ☐ **$ _____**

*Your gift to
Doctors of the
World is tax-
deductible.*

*Thank you for
your caring and
compassion.*

Mr. John Doe
123 Any Street
Any Town, AS 00000

75022B

PHOTO © COLART-ODINETZ SIGMA

Please detach here and return top portion with your
tax-deductible Charter Membership gift to Doctors
of the World in the pre-paid envelope provided. ▲

*Human suffering knows no national
boundaries or political allegiances.*

*We will not let politics or borders
stop human compassion.*

DOCTORS OF THE WORLD
625 BROADWAY, 2nd FLOOR
NEW YORK, NEW YORK 10012

EIGHT STEPS TOWARD SUCCESSFUL FUNDRAISING LETTERS

Not long ago, a man who's been raising money by mail for more than thirty years bragged to me that he rarely spends more than an hour or two writing a fundraising letter — and he's been responsible for some big winners. Some of the most successful appeals he's ever written, he claimed, took no more than forty-five or sixty minutes of work.

You may choose to believe his claim or not. (I, for one, am skeptical.) But you won't hear me making similar assertions. I've been known to spend hours — even, occasionally, days — wrestling with a Marketing Concept before I set a single word down on paper.

In other words, I sometimes spend just as long *thinking* about what I'm going to write as another writer might require to do the job from start to finish. It's usually time well spent, as far I'm concerned. Once I know what I'm going to write, the rest goes much more smoothly. (Well, most of the time, at least!)

And developing the Marketing Concept is just the *first of eight steps* I take when writing a fundraising letter, but it may occupy half or three-quarters of all the time I spend on a project.

The eight-step sequence I follow may not work for you. In fact, you may believe you're better off working like my colleague Stephen Hitchcock, who swears he writes *in order to* think (rather than the other way around). I suspect the truth is that Steve simply thinks a lot faster than most of the rest of us. You may, too. Nevertheless, I hope you'll try it my way at least once. There's a method in this madness!

So let's run through the eight steps, one by one. Assume, for the sake of argument, that you've been assigned the task of writing a simple, straightforward special appeal to the active donors of a charity called "Hope Is Alive!" Here, now, is the way I recommend you go about the job.

Step #1: Marketing Concept

Write a complete Marketing Concept, so you'll know the offer you'll be making in the letter. Writing this down will force you to decide how much money to ask for, who will sign your letter, and whether you'll include a donor involvement device (such as a survey), a premium or a deadline — in short, all the things you're writing the letter *about*. In this case, let's say you've determined that the Marketing Concept runs as follows:

> *As Executive Director of Hope Is Alive!, I've written you many times in the past about the terrible challenges faced by the homeless in our city. Now I'm writing you, as one of our most loyal and generous supporters, to tell you about a challenge that's a wonderful **opportunity**: two members of the Board of Trustees have volunteered to match your gift on a dollar-for-dollar basis if we receive it before January 15 – up to a total of $10,000. The money raised in this Challenge of Hope will be used to outfit our new shelter, so that thirty more homeless families can find a warm and secure place to sleep in the difficult weeks still to go before winter ends.*

Now you're *almost* ready to start writing the appeal itself.

Step #2: Contents of package

But what — exactly — are you going to write? A long letter . . . or a short one? A window envelope with text (a "teaser") on the outside . . . or a businesslike, "closed face" (no window) envelope with no printing except the name Hope Is Alive! and the return address? In other words, it's time to determine how your Marketing Concept will be implemented as a fundraising *package*. What will the appeal consist of? For example, in preparing this particular appeal, you might decide the following components are adequate to the task:

◆ #10 closed-face outer envelope printed in black on the front only, with the addressee's name and address laser-printed on the front and mailed first class with a live postage stamp

◆ Two- or three-page letter, 8-1/2 x 11", printed in two colors, one side only on two (or, if necessary, three) sheets, with page one laser-personalized and subsequent pages printed to match but not personalized

◆ Reply device, approximately 3-1/4 x 8-1/2" (to fit unfolded in a #10 envelope), printed on one side only in two colors on card stock, with name, address, and Ask amounts laser-personalized

◆ #9 Business Reply Envelope printed in one color on one side only

I suggest you write all this information down on a sheet of paper. Label it something like "Contents of Package." And take the time necessary to describe in some detail the paper stock and other specifications for each of the items you've decided to include in the package.

These aren't casual choices. You've settled on a closed-face outer envelope with no teaser because you reason that committed donors will be inclined to open an appeal from Hope Is Alive! without an extravagant promise on the envelope. You've picked a two- or three-page letter with no brochure or other graphic enclosures because (a) the story of the matching gift challenge is easily told and (b) the January 15 deadline fosters a sense of urgency that might be undermined by a photo-brochure that takes time and trouble to design and print.

Note how much closer you're getting now to knowing exactly what you're going to write. If you were writing a package to acquire new members rather than solicit support from proven donors, you might feel the need for a longer letter, a bigger reply device (to accommodate a full listing of membership benefits, perhaps), plus a brochure or other insert, and maybe a premium such as name-stickers as well. You might also find laser-personalization is impractical in such a member-acquisition package (because it's unlikely to be cost-effective). Before you actually write a letter, you need to know such things. Why? For two reasons: (a) whoever's in charge of getting the letter printed and mailed will need to secure printing and lettershop bids and (b) you need to know the space limitations you'll be facing when you write.

Even what might seem like inconsequential details can make a big difference in the way you go about writing a letter. For example, the choice of laser-personalization on the reply device and on the first page of the letter but not on subsequent pages means you can only include specific Ask amounts on page one, and not repeat them on the final page (as is customary and advisable). If the final page of the letter is to be reproduced on an offset printing press rather than a laser printer, the Ask amounts will all be identical.

But now your choices have been made. You know what you're writing, and you're ready to start.

Step #3: Reply device

Begin by drafting the response device. This task may take no more than a minute or two, since you've already written a complete Marketing Concept. But writing the response device may force you to flesh out the Marketing Concept. For instance, if there are to be several different Ask levels (or segments) in your appeal for Hope Is Alive!, now's the time to think through the implications. A gift of $500 might require a dramatically different justification than one of $25. Waiting until later to figure that out might oblige you to do a lot of rewriting — and if you're anything like me and have a distaste for writing, you probably *despise* rewriting!

But *this* appeal, we've said, is simple and straightforward. So let's assume different versions of the letter aren't needed for different segments. The language on the reply device, then, will read somewhat as follows:

Yes, I'll help meet the Challenge of Hope, so that thirty more homeless families can find a safe, warm place to sleep in the difficult weeks remaining before winter ends. To beat the January 15 deadline – so my gift is matched dollar-for-dollar by the Trus-

tees – I'm sending my special tax-deductible contribution in the amount of:

☐ *$(Last + 50%)* ☐ *$(Last + 25%)* ☐ *$_____*

Step #4: Outer envelope

Here's the point where I'm likely to get hung up all over again — even after developing a gem of a Marketing Concept! If a letter I'm writing requires an outer envelope teaser, I might find myself dithering for hours before I can get past this crucial fourth step in the process. (I'll devote a chapter in Part Three to the topic of teasers.)

But you're lucky. You've decided the appeal you're crafting for Hope Is Alive! will be mailed in a closed-face, personalized outer envelope with no teaser. You're off the hook and ready to move along to the fifth step.

Step #5: The lead

Here's another one of those points where I'm likely to stop dead in my tracks. Because research shows the lead of the letter has higher readership than any other element but two (the outer envelope copy and the P.S.), I've been known to clutch in writing an opening paragraph.

You won't clutch, however. You know *exactly* how you're going to lead off your letter for Hope Is Alive! You'll begin with a brief, inspiring story about a six-year-old client of the agency who personifies everything that's best about its work. Something like this:

Jennifer just <u>knew</u> things were going to get better. Molly told her so.

Jennifer was only six years old, and she'd spent most of those years on the streets. Drifting from town to town with a dad who could never find work that lasted. No school. No friends, really. No pretty clothes like the other girls she saw sometimes.

But one day Jennifer and her dad showed up at our Front Street shelter. Molly D'Alessandro was on duty and greeted the new arrivals. You might say it was love at first sight.

While you're engaged in writing this lead, you might find it convenient to write the close of the letter as well. Just as the lead must almost always be directly connected to the outer envelope teaser, the close should relate to the lead. If you began by asking a question, answer it now. If you started by challenging the reader, refer to the challenge again — and note how the offer you've made will enable the reader to respond in a meaningful way. Complete the circle; round out your letter with a satisfying close. In this case, you'll want to be sure that Jennifer and her dad and Molly D'Alessandro all figure in the way you wind up the letter.

Step #6: The P.S.

We've learned from Siegfried Vögele that the postscript is the real lead more than 90 percent of the time. So we know this step deserves our full attention.

After a lot of thought, you've decided to use the P.S. to emphasize the deadline for receipt of matching gifts in the Trustees' challenge grant campaign. The postscript, then, would go something like this:

P.S. Your gift will be matched dollar-for-dollar — but only if we receive your check by January 15. In this difficult winter, please help us outfit the new shelter and take thirty more homeless families off the streets!

In this way, you've conveyed three of the strongest elements of the appeal — the deadline, the dollar-for-dollar match and the thirty families who will benefit — at just the place in the letter that's bound to have the highest readership of all.

Now you're ready to move along to the body of the letter itself.

Step #7: Subheads and underlining

Do you remember Vögele's observations about the behavior of real-world direct mail recipients? If so, you'll want to decide at the outset what *points to highlight visually* within the body of the letter. Let's assume you've decided that subheads are inappropriate for the appeal you're writing for Hope Is Alive! (Perhaps they're out of character for the signer, the executive director, who tends to be a bit stuffy, or you think subheads detract from the upscale image the agency wants to convey.) There's still an easy way for you to accent the benefits offered in your appeal, answer readers' unspoken questions, and make your letter easier to read: by underlining. Do it sparingly. Choose only a few key words and phrases. But, if possible, choose them *before* you write the body of the letter!

In this case, you'd be likely to decide that among the points requiring underlining are the following:

If you respond by January 15, your gift will be matched dollar-for-dollar.

With your generous support, Hope Is Alive! will be able to open the new shelter on time – and thirty homeless families will be off the streets for the rest of the winter.

One way to determine which points warrant underlining (or subheads) is to outline the letter before you write it. If you construct your outline paying particular attention to the *benefits* you're offering, the appropriate words and phrases may come jumping off the page.

Keep this in mind: the items to underline — or to feature in subheads — aren't necessarily the ones you think will break up the text at the most convenient intervals or help convey your tone of voice. Rather, subheads and underlining must *appeal directly to the reader.* For example, instead of emphasizing Hope Is Alive!'s $10,000 budget to outfit the new shelter, you've wisely chosen to stress the thirty homeless families who will have a warm and secure place to sleep. Obviously, your readers will care much more about Jennifer and her dad and the other families than about an agency's budget!

Step #8: At last! The text

This is the easy part.

You've already written the reply device; you've developed the lead, the close, and the P.S.; you've drafted the subheads and principal underlined points. What else is there to do? A game of fill-in-the-blank!

Take care, though: it's all too easy to stumble off-course in the stretch. Tell the story you started about Jennifer and Molly — but don't turn it into a novelette. Make sure the story shows the benefits the reader will receive if she accepts your offer. (Jennifer now has hope for a better life; so will dozens of other good people trapped in terrible circumstances.) Stick to the points you selected for the subheads and underlining. You picked those points because they *answer the unspoken questions* you know your reader will have — and because they emphasize the benefits that will motivate the reader to send a gift without delay. If you stay on this course, Hope Is Alive! will raise its $10,000 and more, those thirty families will be off the streets, and you, the author, will be a hero.

Now let's begin a longer journey through the pages of the case studies I've selected from the files of EditEXPRESS™. We'll start where every new direct mail fundraising program begins: by considering how to recruit new donors. ▶

PART TWO

Case Studies

RECRUITING NEW DONORS

Starting Intimate Conversations with Strangers

*he reply device reproduced on the opposite page is typical of those used to accompany "acquisition" letters mailed to prospective donors. How do you **know** the form comes from an acquisition (or prospect) package? Because the statement in large type – in the first complete sentence at the top – reads in part, "I'm joining Bread for the World." But this form is typical of acquisition packages in several other ways as well:*

◆ *For example, the language of the main headline and the sentence that follows is general. While it refers specifically to "the 1992 legislative campaign," the accompanying letter (not illustrated) makes clear that lobbying is the principal activity of Bread for the World. In effect, the appeal asks the recipient to buy into the organization's mission and goals. That's what "joining" means. This is not an appeal to support a specific project.*

◆ *Look at the suggested gift amounts. You'll note they're typeset – so the amounts are probably the same for "John Doe" as they are for other recipients of this letter. The amounts are comparatively small, too, affording an easy entry level for new members. But there are four gift choices, covering a wide range, because little is known about those to whom the letter was mailed: they're strangers.*

◆ *Another clue that this reply device is part of an acquisition package is the way it's addressed. As you can see, the name and address appears in a computer typeface that's different from the other type on the form. The name and address were first imprinted on a small, white paper mailing label (called a Cheshire label) and then affixed with glue to the form. This inexpensive addressing technology is commonly used in prospecting, less frequently so in other types of fundraising letters (where "personalization" is often routine).*

◆ *Note also that the "Citizen Endorsement" form in the center of the page provides an opportunity for the prospect to become directly and immediately involved in Bread for the World's then-current lobbying campaign. "Involvement devices" of this sort aren't unique to acquisition letters, but they're more commonly found in that context. Involvement typically boosts response. It's a way to get strangers to pay attention.*

I want to help end hunger for children in the U.S.

I've signed the Citizen Endorsement below, and I'm joining Bread for the World—
to support the 1992 legislative campaign on behalf of "Every Fifth Child."

☐ $35   ☐ $50   ☐ $100   ☐ $_____

Mr. John Doe
123 Any Street
Any Town, AS 00000

Bread for the World
802 Rhode Island Avenue, N.E.
Washington, DC 20018
(202) 269-0200

See other side for important information.

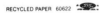
RECYCLED PAPER 60622

CITIZEN ENDORSEMENT

WHEREAS every fifth child in our country faces hunger, and every 53 minutes an American child dies of poverty-related causes;

WHEREAS the end of the Cold War provides a once-in-a-generation opportunity to redirect our nation's resources from military spending to helping hungry children in our country; and

WHEREAS programs such as the Women, Infants, and Children nutrition program have proven effective in reducing infant mortality and saving medical costs as children grow, yet 45% of those eligible are not receiving benefits because of inadequate funding;

THEREFORE, I endorse Bread for the World's legislative campaign on behalf of "Every Fifth Child."

I CALL upon the Administration and the Congress to fully fund the Special Supplemental Food Program for Women, Infants, and Children (WIC) so that all those eligible are able to benefit from this effective program.

AND I urge our nation's leaders to reduce military spending and redirect some of those funds to benefit the more than 35 million poor and hungry people in this country.

SIGNED _____

CITY, STATE _____

Please tear off here and return the entire form along with your membership contribution to Bread for the World.

In our country, every fifth child faces hunger

Your Citizen Endorsement can help end hunger among children in the U.S.

How donor acquisition letters differ from other fundraising appeals

Successful letters written to recruit new donors or new members come in all sizes, shapes, and flavors. They may be fat or thin, colorful or drab, up-to-the-minute or timeless. They're sometimes mailed using third-class bulk postage, sometimes (though less often) with first-class stamps. But there are five characteristics shared by the majority of donor acquisition letters:

1. Acquisition letters are often long. Occasionally they contain lots of additional material, too: brochures or folders, flyers, lift letters, buckslips — not to mention those little free gifts called premiums. Many charities fare better without using any of this stuff. Some well-known groups can get away with short letters, too. Chances are, though, that a letter you write to prospective donors will need to be at least a little longer than the letters you usually write to previous donors — because otherwise prospects may not have enough information about your organization to decide whether they'll make a gift.

2. Acquisition letters typically appeal to prospects to support a charity's larger agenda: its goals, the full range of its programs (though one project or aspect of the work may get the lion's share of the attention in the letter). If prospective donors send gifts in response to such a letter, they're more likely to respond favorably when later asked for additional support.

3. In an acquisition letter, the references to "you" (the reader) are normally vague and general. Though you may know a great deal about the people on *one* of your prospect lists, you'll probably know next to nothing about those on other lists. With them, there isn't much to hang a relationship on. Chances are, the demands of economy will require that you mail the same letter, unchanged, to all your prospects lists.

4. Typically, an acquisition letter is undated and makes few references to time or the calendar. That's because you'll probably want to use it over and over again. Not just because of the need to economize, but because it normally takes repeated trial and error to write a really successful acquisition letter.

5. The minimum suggested gift amount tends to be low. Most charities seek to maximize the number of new donors: asking for less at the outset may serve that purpose.

Case Study: Food for the Poor Donor Acquisition Package

Food for the Poor (Deerfield Beach, FL) asked me to edit this new-donor acquisition package. The most significant change I made was to clarify the offer. In the draft, there were a *lot* of numbers: several different examples of how much a modest-sized gift might accomplish, plus two different and unrelated sets of Ask amounts. ("$25, $40, $50, $100 or more" in the letter, "$10, $25, $5, $100, $500, other" on the reply device). I settled on one "string" of Ask amounts and related the numbers to the text of the letter.

These changes are significant for two reasons:

♦ Eliminating the inconsistencies in the numbers used makes it that much easier for readers to understand what Food for the Poor wants from them. This helps answer the unspoken questions rather than raising new ones.

♦ The benefits offered by Food for the Poor in this letter are all intangible. Dramatizing the direct connection between giving a gift and feeding children is the equivalent of placing a photo of a book or other tangible membership benefit on the reply device. For only $12, you could "put food in the mouths of six hungry children!" Now *that's* a benefit!

As you can see at a glance, I made several changes in the format of the letter. I switched to typewriter-like Courier typeface — on the letter, but not on the reply device. I also indented every paragraph and double-indented the message from Raymonde so that it has more the appearance of a classic "Johnson box." (That's the part that appears on the first page of the letter above the salutation; it's a device named for a direct mail copywriter — named Johnson, oddly enough — and in fact it usually appears inside a box, often with a tinted background to set it apart from the text of the letter.) In this case, the Johnson box seemed like a way to avoid printing a separate insert to reproduce the telefax message from Raymonde. It also made it easier to dive right into the substance of the story. Otherwise, the letter might have had to begin with something like, "Take a look at the enclosed fax from my friend Raymonde." ▶

FAX:

TO FOOD FOR THE POOR PRESIDENT FERDINAND MAHFOOD
FROM RAYMONDE PUN, FOOD FOR THE POOR MANAGER IN HAITI

Ferdy,

I can't call because I'll cry.

Our neighbor, Sister Kamal from St. Teresa School, came begging for bread this
morning . . . to feed 450 hungry children. It broke my heart to tell her no, that I
had already given away all 710 loaves to other malnourished children in Port-au-
Prince.

Sister pleaded with me to help her feed even the littlest ones, but I had nothing to
give. And I don't have the funds to double our orders for bread and milk. The
situation here is desperate. . .

When can we tell Sister Kamal yes?

Dear Friend,

What would _you_ tell Raymonde?

I told her that Food for the Poor would do everything possible to feed those
students -- and as many impoverished Haitian children as we can. Somehow, I
know you'd say the same.

But that was just one request.

Every morning, thousands of youngsters throughout the Caribbean wake up
with the same hunger pains that gnawed at them the night before. Their parents
are too poor to provide their daily bread -- or any nutritious foods to grow
strong.

For many children, our simple lunch is their only meal of the day. In fact, most
are the family breadwinners.

Like little Simon Lavalier, a third grader at Living Christ College in Port-au-Prince who slips his peanutbutter sandwich and pint of milk into his tattered school bag. He sits, head lowered, as other classmates eat.

Simon will remain hungry so that he can share his food with two younger brothers at home.

Perhaps the boy is too young to know that his sacrifice reflects that of his namesake, Simon the Cyrenian, who carried the cross for our beaten, suffering Christ. (Mt. 27:32)

This little Simon carries the cross of his poverty-stricken family. Without Food for the Poor, he has nothing to give his brothers.

Without you, we have nothing to offer him.

About $2 provides a child with a healthy lunch for five days. Will you feed six children, or a whole classroom of 37? Maybe a school of 450?

You probably wonder how Food for the Poor can feed a child for only 40 cents a day. It's our buying problem.

For example, we purchase flour at 8 cents a pound. We do this by skillfully buying in bulk on domestic and international markets and by monitoring purchases at our four warehouses in Deerfield Beach, FL; Port-au-Prince, Haiti; Georgetown, Guyana, and Kingston, Jamaica.

In essence, we can quadruple the value of your gift. Through Food for the Poor, your $25 will buy $100 worth of goods.

Such efficiency keeps our ratio of administrative costs to value of good purchased at a low 10.51%! And that spells NO WASTE.

But low cost and ratios mean little unless we reach the poor.

Our non-profit ministry guarantees you that your donation goes directly to help God's poorest of the poor.

How? Because we work directly through those who serve the poor daily -- dedicated clergy, missionaries, nuns and educators of all denominations.

People like Sister Kamal.

That's why we beg your support today -- so that we can tell this dedicated servant of God and the poor that we will buy more bread and feed her 450 students every day.

Your gift of $25, $40, $50, $100 or more will help us tell Sister Kamal . . . and children like little Simon . . . YES!

Please send help today. . . so that the poor children of the Caribbean can look forward to tomorrow.

A servant of the poor,

Ferdinand Mahfood,
Founder and President
Food for the Poor, Inc.

P.S. I told Raymonde to go ahead and buy more bread. That's how much faith I have in the Lord . . . and in you.

[REPLY DEVICE -- FRONT]

YES! I'll buy bread

Tell Sister Kamal, Simon and hungry poor people throughout the Caribbean that I will help you!

(please circle one)

$10 $25 $5 $100 $500
(other) _____

"As often as you did it for one of the least of my brothers and sisters, you did it for me."
Mt. 25:40

Please make check payable to FOOD FOR THE POOR and mail in the enclosed envelope. Your gift is tax-deductible under IRS code Section 501 (c)(3).

Food for the Poor was founded in 1982 by Ferdinand Mahfood, a Jamaican businessman who became a "beggar for the poor" after a profound religious conversion.

Food for the Poor is an interdenominational, non-profit Christian organization. We directly respond to the needs of the poor by working through the clergy and missionaries.

Since inception, Food for the Poor has helped 24 countries and 19 cities in the United States. We also sent relief to Hurricane Andrew victims.

Food for the Poor believes in helping the poor to help themselves. Thousands of hard-working poor people own small businesses through 16 Food for the Poor sponsored self-help programs such as farming, tailoring, carpentry, fishing, auto repair and vending.

[REPLY DEVICE -- BACK]

Dear Food for the Poor,

Please pray for the health of all hungry children and for my special need:

_____

_____

_____

_____

_____

_____

_____

"What is your greatest need?" is the question Ferdinand Mahfood asks the poor on his frequent trips to the Caribbean. Our program is simple and efficient — working through missionaries and churches of all denominations Food for the Poor supplies the items that the people truly need and will use.

Since 1982 Food for the Poor has been able to supply more than $130 million worth of food, clothing, medical and educational supplies, building materials, job training equipment and agricultural tools to the Third World poor, with an administrative cost of only 10.51%.

Food for the Poor begs the support of individuals, like yourself, in order to reach the forgotten, suffering members of the human family.

FOOD FOR THE POOR
550 SW 12th Avenue #4
Deerfield Beach, FL 33442
(305) 427-2222

To date, Food for the Poor has shipped more than $130 million worth of goods to impoverished people throughout eight Caribbean countries: Haiti, Jamaica, Grenada, Guyana, Trinidad, St. Lucia, Dominica and St. Vincent.

Last year, Food for the Poor shipped 7.5 million pounds of food.

The average weekly pay for unskilled workers in Jamaica equals $20 U.S. and the per capita income of Haitians is $376.

Food for the Poor's ratio of expenses to market value of goods is 10.51%.

Food for the Poor is audited by independent auditors and is registered with U.S. AID. It is also registered in the State of Florida and 37 other states. Copies of audited financial reports are available upon request.

Since 1986, Food for the Poor has built 4,300 modest one-room houses for the poor.

URGENT ... TELEFAX ... URGENT ... TELEFAX ... URGENT

TO: Ferdinand Mahfood, President, Food for the Poor

FROM: Raymonde Pun, Food for the Poor Manager, Haiti

Ferdy --

I can't call because I'll cry.

Our neighbor, Sister Kamal from St. Teresa School, came begging for bread this morning ... to feed 450 hungry children. It broke my heart to tell her no, that I had already given away all 710 loaves to other malnourished children in Port-au-Prince.

Sister pleaded with me to help her feed even the littlest ones, but I had nothing to give. And I don't have the funds to double our orders for bread and milk. The situation here is desperate ...

When can we tell Sister Kamal yes?

Raymonde

Dear Caring and Compassionate Friend,

What would you tell Raymonde?

When her fax arrived this morning, I told her that Food for the Poor will do everything possible to feed those impoverished Haitian children. Somehow, I just know you would have said the same.

But that fax was just one request.

Every morning, thousands of youngsters throughout the Caribbean wake up with the same hunger pains that gnawed at them the night before. Their parents are too poor to provide their daily bread -- or any nutritious foods so they can grow up strong.

For many children, the simple lunch they receive from Food for the Poor is their only meal of the day. In fact, most are

- Page 1 -

the family breadwinners.

Like little Simon Lavalier, a third grader at Living Christ College in Port-au-Prince. Simon slips his peanut butter sandwich and pint of milk into his tattered school bag. He sits, head lowered, as other classmates eat.

Simon will remain hungry so he can share his food with two younger brothers at home.

Perhaps the boy is too young to know that his sacrifice reflects that of his namesake, Simon the Cyrenian, who carried the cross for our beaten, suffering Christ. (Matthew 27:32)

This little Simon carries the cross of his poverty-stricken family. Without Food for the Poor, he has nothing to give his brothers.

Without you, we have nothing to offer Simon -- just as we have nothing for our sister, Raymonde. Yet only $2 provides a child with a healthy lunch for <u>five days</u>, the length of a week in school.

<u>Will you feed a classroom of 37 children for a week?</u> The cost to you is just $74.

Or, can you possibly be so generous and caring as to feed an <u>entire school</u> of 450 children? A week's worth of lunches is only $900.

If such sums are out of your reach, will you put food in the mouths of just <u>six</u> hungry children? The cost is so very modest -- only $12!

You probably wonder how Food for the Poor can feed a child for only 40¢ a day. It's our buying power.

For example, we purchase flour at 8¢ a pound. We do this by skillfully buying in bulk on domestic and international markets and by monitoring purchases at our four warehouses in Florida, Haiti, Guyana and Jamaica.

In essence, we can quadruple the value of your gift. Through Food for the Poor, <u>your $25 will buy $100 worth</u> of goods.

Such efficiency keeps our ratio of administrative costs to the market value of the goods we deliver at an extremely low 10.51%! And that ratio spells <u>no waste</u>.

- Page 2 -

But low costs and ratios mean little unless we reach the poor.

Our non-profit ministry guarantees you that your donation goes directly to help God's poorest of the poor.

How? Because we work directly through those who serve the poor every single day -- dedicated clergy, missionaries, nuns and educators of all denominations.

People like Sister Kamal.

That's why we beg your support today -- so we can tell this dedicated servant of God and the poor that we'll buy more bread and feed her 450 students every day.

Your gift of $12, $25, $40, $74, $100 or more will help us tell Sister Kamal ... and children like little Simon ... that the answer to their prayerful question is YES!

Please send help <u>today</u> ... so that the poor children of the Caribbean can look forward to <u>tomorrow</u>.

A servant of the poor,

Ferdinand Mahfood
Founder and President
Food for the Poor, Inc.

PS   I told Raymonde to go ahead and buy more bread. That's how
     much faith I have in the Lord ... and in <u>you</u>.

- Page 3 -

Yes! Tell Sister Kamal I'll buy bread!

I want to help little Simon -- and hundreds of other poor and hungry children throughout the Caribbean. That's why I'm enclosing my tax-deductible gift in the amount of:

☐ $12 ☐ $25 ☐ $40 ☐ $74* ☐ $100 ☐ $_____

* Enough to provide nutritious lunches to a classroom of 37 children for a week.

☐ I want to feed an entire school of 450 hungry children for a week. I'm sending $900.

Please make your check payable to FOOD FOR THE POOR and mail with this form in the enclosed envelope.

IMPORTANT FACTS ABOUT FOOD FOR THE POOR

■ Food for the Poor is an interdenominational, nonprofit, Christian organization. We directly respond to the needs of the poor by working through the clergy and missionaries.

■ Food for the Poor was founded in 1982 by Ferdinand Mahfood, a Jamaican businessman who became a "beggar for the poor" after a profound religious conversion.

■ Food for the Poor has helped people in 24 countries plus 19 cities in the United States, including victims of Hurricane Andrew.

■ Food for the Poor is audited by independent auditors and is registered with the U.S. Agency for International Development. We are also registered as a charity in the State of Florida and 37 other states. Copies of our audited financial reports are available upon request.

■ To date, Food for the Poor has shipped more than $130 million worth of goods to impoverished people throughout eight Caribbean countries: Haiti, Jamaica, Grenada, Guyana, Trinidad, St. Lucia, Dominica and St. Vincent.

■ Last year, Food for the Poor shipped 7.5 million pounds of food. Food for the Poor's ratio of expenses to the market value of the goods we deliver is just 10.51%.

■ Food for the Poor believes in helping the poor to help themselves. Thousands of hard-working poor people own small businesses through 16 Food for the Poor-sponsored self-help programs. These businesses include farming, tailoring, carpentry, fishing, auto repair and vending.

- Since 1986, Food for the Poor has built 4,300 modest one-room houses for the poor.

FOOD FOR THE POOR
550 S.W. 12th Avenue, Building 4
Deerfield Beach, FL 33442
(305) 427-2222

[BACK OF REPLY DEVICE]

Dear Food for the Poor,

Please pray for the health of all hungry children and for my special need:

_____

_____

_____

Sincerely,

_____
Signature

"As often as you did it for one of the least of my brothers and sisters, you did it for me." (Matthew 25:40)

A copy of the official registration, etc.

12

WELCOMING NEW DONORS

Treating People Like Part of the Family

here's no doubt about it: the response device reprinted on the following two pages comes from a "new-member welcome package." Its distinguishing characteristics – typical in many ways of welcome packages – include the following:

◆ *The "Welcome!" message is impossible to miss.*

◆ *A membership card is included in the package.*

◆ *A "bounce-back" form offers the new member the opportunity to obtain information about important Bread for the World programs.*

◆ *There's space on the bounce-back form to supply information that will be useful to Bread for the World in targeting future requests for help – including telephone numbers that may be used in the organization's telephone fundraising program.*

◆ *On the reverse of the bounce-back form is information the new member may use when participating in future Bread for the World grassroots lobbying campaigns.*

◆ *There are three "donor options" on the reverse of the bounce-back form: opportunities to opt out of mailing list rentals and exchanges, special appeals, and telephone fundraising campaigns.*

How new-donor welcome packages are different from other fundraising appeals

In nonprofits' continuing search for heightened donor loyalty and higher renewal rates, new-donor welcome packages are becoming increasingly common. These packets of information mailed to newly recruited members or donors may be fat or thin, elaborate or simple. Typically, however, they share five attributes:

1. Welcome letters strive to be warm, emphasizing the charity's appreciation rather than its needs and offering additional information. Short copy is common. The welcome letter's purpose is usually to inform the new donor about the organization's programs and its donor benefits and services.

2. Any copy that refers to the new member personally is likely to be vague and general; usually, the

Welcome!

I'm pleased you've become Bread for the World's newest member. Your financial support and active involvement will help build a stronger movement to end hunger in the U.S. and overseas.

— *David Beckmann, President*

A CHRISTIAN CITIZENS' MOVEMENT ON BEHALF OF POOR AND HUNGRY PEOPLE

VALID THROUGH

DAVID BECKMANN, PRESIDENT

Detach here ▲

Tear off and keep this top portion. Please return the bottom portion to Bread for the World in the postage-paid envelope provided. Thank you.

You may wish to carry your membership card with you — or put it on your bulletin board. See the reverse side for information about contacting Congress and about Bread for the World's Legislative Update.

Want to be more involved?

☐ I'd like to be part of "Quickline"— Bread for the World's rapid response telephone network when urgent Congressional action is needed.

☐ Please let me know if there's a local Bread for the World group meeting in my area.

☐ I'd like more information about the **Covenant Church program** for churches and religious groups.

☐ Please send me a list of publications and other resources available from Bread for the World and from Bread for the World Institute.

☐ Please send me a **free** information packet about *Lazarus*, Bread for the World's musical on hunger and poverty.

PLEASE SEE REVERSE SIDE FOR IMPORTANT INFORMATION

The following information will help us provide improved membership services to you and others:

Please make sure your name is complete and spelled correctly — and your address is accurate. Thank you.

DENOMINATION/CHURCH BODY

OCCUPATION OR EMPLOYMENT

HOME PHONE

WORK PHONE

Bread for the World's 24-hour
Legislative Update: **202-269-0494**

How to contact your member of Congress:

U.S. House of Representatives
Washington, D.C. 20515

U.S. Senate Office Building
Washington, D.C. 20510

Phone for both House and Senate:
202-224-3121

Bread for the World **202-269-0200**
802 Rhode Island Avenue, N.E.
Washington, D.C. 20018

Your contributions are used wisely.

New York residents may receive a copy of the last financial report filed with the New York Department of State by writing to: New York Department of State, Office of Charities Registration, Albany, NY 12231

A copy of the official registration and financial information may be obtained from the Pennsylvania Department of State by calling toll free, within Pennsylvania, 1-800-732-0999. Registration does not imply endorsement.

Virginia residents may obtain financial information from the Virginia State Division of Consumer Affairs, Department of Agricultural and Consumer Affairs, P.O. Box 1163, Richmond, VA 23209.

Others may write to Bread for the World, 802 Rhode Island Avenue, N.E., Washington, DC 20018.

Please let us know . . .

☐ Bread for the World occasionally exchanges its mailing list with select organizations whose activities might be of interest to our members. Please check this box if you wish *not* to receive such mailings.

☐ From time to time, Bread for the World sends mailings to highlight special needs. Please check this box if you prefer *not* to receive such mailings.

☐ Some members may receive a phone call inviting additional financial support in response to an extraordinary opportunity or a special need. Please check here if you'd rather *not* receive such a phone call.

Bread for the World
802 Rhode Island Avenue, N.E.
Washington, DC 20018
(202) 269-0200

RECYCLED PAPER 60982B

charity knows too little to personalize the letter in any meaningful way. (One important exception: the amount of the initial gift, which may be inserted in the cover letter if it's personalized or noted on a gift receipt.)

3. Some charities use the opportunity to request a second gift or even to suggest that a new donor join a giving club, such as a monthly sustainer program. But it's more common — and, I think, more advisable — *not* to seek a gift with this package. For example, if you've decided that the best time to invite members to join a monthly pledge program is immediately after they join, I suggest you *first* mail them a welcome package and *then,* perhaps a week or ten days later, send the pledge invitation.

4. To introduce new donors to the charity's work, a recent issue of its magazine or newsletter is often enclosed. Sometimes, brochures about the organization's programs and services are included. Often welcome packages are heavy — and expensive. They're an investment in future fundraising efforts!

5. Welcome packages frequently offer new donors multiple opportunities to respond — through surveys, requests for additional information, "member-get-a-member" programs, donor options, or other involvement devices.

Six reasons you should mail welcome packages

Let's take a look first at the many roles that a welcome package is created to play. Then we can review several possible elements you might consider including in your own welcome package — or adding to your existing new-donor acknowledgment.

It seems to me there are six reasons to go to the expense and trouble of sending new members a special, initial package that's more than a simple gift receipt or thank-you note.

1. All donors expect to be thanked for their support. A simple receipt is probably not enough to make them think you're being nice. And treating members well increases the chances they'll renew their annual support. This is especially important if (like most charities these days) your first-year renewal rate is very low.

2. Donors are most receptive to your message immediately after making their first gifts. This is the best time to approach them about such fundraising options as monthly sustainer programs or "friend-get-a-friend" efforts. (However, it's not *necessarily* the best time to ask for a second gift.) If you can move a new member to take action right after joining — almost any action, in fact — you'll be well on your way to building a strong, mutually beneficial, long-term relationship. But timing is important here; receptivity fades fast, and donors can all too easily *forget* having contributed to a charity that's new to them.

3. Donors' *first* impression of your organization is likely to affect their views of all subsequent communications. A cheap thank-you may impress a few donors with its frugality — but far more donors are likely to be flattered by a carefully prepared, well-thought-out introductory package that underscores how very important their financial support really is. I'm convinced most donors secretly think you're wasting money on fancy packages to *other* people — not when you spend money on them.

4. Donors are too often skeptical about how their contributions are put to use. They sometimes need to be persuaded that their gifts accomplish more than raise additional money. By describing your work in detail — and by offering opportunities for members to contribute more than money — a welcome package can drive home the message that your organization is lean, hardworking, and cost-effective. This is true even if any given individual member has no interest at all in contributing volunteer time: the offer and the opportunities communicate an important message.

5. Donors probably won't understand your organization and its programs unless yours is a local group that provides a single, direct, easily grasped service. Any charity that's engaged in multiple projects — especially if it's a large, decentralized, complex nonprofit — will need a well-organized welcome package just so donors will understand your work and the role they can play in it. And, if they do understand you well, they're much more likely to respond favorably when you ask for additional support.

6. Not all donors are created equal. Some may be delighted to send a small monthly contribution. Others may want to contribute only once per year. Still others might be interested in joining a High–Dollar giving club. The welcome package is an excellent opportunity to test their preferences on these and other fundraising questions by giving them a questionnaire, or at least by clearly offering several different fundraising options and an easy way to sign up for them.

If your organization currently mails new donors more than a simple tax receipt or thank-you note, you may already be addressing some of the six opportunities I've just listed. But there may be a number of ways you can accomplish a whole lot more. Here are enclosures you might consider adding to your thank-you letter — or including in a full-fledged new-donor welcome package:

- Small brochure or folder that catalogs "Membership Services and Benefits"
- Involvement device that includes a *brief* "New Member Survey"
- Explanation of "How Our Organization Works," either in a brochure or flyer and/or in copy in the cover letter
- Membership card, with an abbreviated listing of membership benefits on the reverse
- Brochure about your monthly sustainer program
- Brochure about your Bequest and Planned Giving programs, if any
- Flyer that includes an order form for merchandise you sell, featuring a discount offer for new members

Case Study: Co-op America "Welcome Aboard" Package

Co-op America asked my help to overhaul the "Welcome Aboard Kit" they send new members. On the telephone and in two face-to-face discussions, we reviewed in detail my recommendations for upgrading the welcome process. Our shared hope, of course, was that new members exposed to a more intensive welcome process would be more generous and more loyal in the future. My recommendations are summed up in the chart on page 138.

Most of Co-op America's previous "Welcome Aboard Kit" is shown on pages 139 to 143. The revised version, incorporating the changes I specified, starts on page 144. As you can see, it's a two-part mailing that consists of a thank-you letter (mailed first class) and a follow-up welcome package (mailed nonprofit bulk rate).

In fact, this two-part treatment was just part of a year-long new-donor welcome *process*. The chart on page 138 shows how the process was intended to work. Here's how to read the chart:

- The left-hand column shows the approximate number of days elapsed since receipt of a new member's first gift. For example, about ninety days, or three months, after joining, a new member would be invited to join Co-op America's monthly sustainer program. From beginning to end, the whole process fills at least 210 days, or seven months.

- The second column from the left specifies the "segment" or group of new donors to be included at that stage of the process. For example, I recommended that Co-op America test a thank-you phone call to new members whose initial gift was $25 or larger.

- The third column from the left describes the nature of the contact — whether a letter, phone call, magazine, or whatever.

Obviously, Co-op America was starting at a point that few nonprofits have yet reached. The organization was already mailing a new-member welcome package! The most meaningful changes I introduced were to fit the welcome package into a year-long *process* — and to emphasize two-way communications between Co-op America and its new members.

Each of the two parts of the revised package includes an involvement device. There's a New Member Survey in part one, and a Feedback Form in part two. This is all part of the process of sustaining a *dialogue* between Co-op America and its members — a continuation of the dialogue opened up by the acquisition package.

Note: The Co-op America membership services offered in this new-member welcome package were in force when the package was first mailed. One of the services illustrated here was no longer in effect at the time we went to press, and other changes may have been made by the time you read this book. If you're interested in learning more, please call Co-op America directly. ▶

Proposed Co-op America New-Member Welcome Process			
Days Elapsed	Segment	Nature of Contact	Notes
None	All new members	Thank-you letter (welcome package, part one)	Ideally, a lasered one-page letter with closed-face outer and first-class stamp – revealing a special phone number and staff contact for member inquiries. Also included: New Member Priorities Survey and Business Reply Envelope.
Up to 15 days	All new members	Benefits package, mailed bulk (welcome package, part two)	Generic thank-you letter; folder or brochures on member services; copies of publications promised in acquisition package; information on donor programs
As available (15-30 days)	All new members	Quarterly magazine	
As available (15-90 days)	All new members	Merchandise catalog	
45 days	Test new members with initial gift of $25 or more	Thank-you call	An opportunity to test different approaches: pure thank-you vs. soliciting interest in member services vs. offering information about donor programs
90 days	Initial gift less than $50	Monthly sustainer program invitation	Fully personalized package; phone follow-up after 3-4 weeks
135-150 days	Current special appeal (i.e., whatever appeal is being sent to other, older members)		
180 days	All	Early renewal letter (i.e., beginning of the membership dues renewal series)	
210+ days	All	Return to membership mailstream (i.e., no more special new-member treatment!)	

Dear Member,

Welcome to Co-op America!

Thank you for joining. We're pleased to be working with you to build a sustainable economy based on peace, justice, cooperation and environmental responsibility.

Through your new membership you are supporting your commitment to positive social change. As a member of Co-op America, you are an economic activist -- helping to transform the economic system to one that values the earth and all its people.

Our commitment to you is to provide you with the **information, socially responsible products and services, and action programs** you need to make a difference.

As a member, you will receive practical **information** on economic strategies for creating social change through these publications, which are yours as member benefits:

* The <u>Co-op America Quarterly</u>, our magazine, covers the emerging ideas, institutions and strategies required by the sustainable economy. It offers you ideas, references and resources you can use to create positive social change. Your regular subscription will start with the next published issue (Spring, Summer, Fall or Winter). During the year of your membership, you will receive four issues.

* <u>Boycott Action News</u>, published within the <u>Quarterly</u>, gives you the background, news, status and "where to write and what to do" for social change boycotts.

* <u>Co-op America's Socially Responsible Financial Planning Handbook</u>, provides you with information about social investment strategies and the ABCs of social investing. Watch for it in the mail next quarter.

* Our <u>National Directory of Green Businesses</u> gives you instant access to all the businesses on the cutting edge of social and environmental responsibility.

Part of our mission is to provide you with <u>socially responsible products and services</u> that you can use to channel your money to building economic alternatives when you buy the things you need and when you invest. We're proud to offer you access to these socially responsible products and services as a benefit of membership:

* <u>The Co-op America Catalog -- your marketplace for peace, cooperation and a healthy planet</u> -- showcases socially and environmentally responsible organizations from around the world. You will get at least two catalogs a year. Your first catalog will be in the mail to you in either March or September, whichever is closer to the date you joined Co-op America.

(over, please)

2100 M Street, N.W. • Suite 403 • Washington, D.C. 20037 • (202) 872-5307   ♻ Printed on recycled paper

*   Travel-Links, our full service travel agency, will help you meet all your travel needs and assist you with a comprehensive range of culturally and environmentally sensitive travel options.

*   The Co-op America VISA Card gives you a way to support the sustainable economy by channelling a percentage of your monthly charges into Co-op America's programs. A postage paid application is enclosed.

*   Alternative Long Distance through Working Assets gives you monthly free calls to key decisionmakers on critical social and environmental issues, while offering top quality service and competitive rates.

We've enclosed a folder for you with brochures about each of these socially responsible products and services. Please send in the coupons for more information on those you're interested in now -- and save the folder for others you may need later on.

Here at Co-op America, we also launch **action programs** to create economic change on specific aspects of our economy. Your dues will help support -- and we hope you'll become actively involved in -- programs like these:

*   Rainforest Recovery -- We work with citizens in rainforest areas to find products that will sustain the rainforests, and help local farmers plant trees to reforest parts of Costa Rica -- we planted over 20,000 trees last year!

*   The Valdez Principles of Corporate Environmental Responsibility -- We encourage U.S. corporations to make a commitment to ecological stewardship by signing the principles.

Please write or call any time you have any ideas, suggestions -- or a problem with any of our products or services. Part of social responsibility is responsiveness to you.

Once again, thank you for your support. We look forward to working with you to help bring about a just, cooperative, sustainable economy.

In cooperation,

Alisa Gravitz
Executive Director

P.S. Enclosed you will find a dual-purpose postcard. Use it to tell us about friends to whom you'd like us to send information about Co-op America and/or to tell us to take your name off the mailing list we share with like-minded organizations.

Thank you for joining Co-op America. This handy member card has the numbers for Co-op America services listed on the back. Carry it with you for quick reference to socially and environmentally responsible products and services.

CO-OP AMERICA
2100 M Street, N.W., #403
Washington, D.C. 20037

Welcome!

"BUILDING AN ALTERNATIVE MARKETPLACE"

CO-OP AMERICA
Membership Card

2100 M Street, N.W., #403
Washington, D.C. 20037
1-800-424-2667   202-872-5307

Member Number

Member

Signature

Welcome Aboard! We value you as a member. Together, we are building a more co-operative, humane and sustainable economy. Along with being part of this crucial work, we hope you enjoy the benefits of Co-op America membership:

1) Your subscription to *The Co-op America Quarterly*. Your subscription will start next quarter — and you'll get four issues of this information-packed publication in your membership year.

2) Your annual Co-op America Catalogs.

3) Your copy of Co-op America's *Personal Guide to Socially Responsible Financial Planning* — on its way to you next quarter.

4) Access to Co-op America's socially responsible services — financial, insurance, VISA®, Working Assets Long Distance Phone Service, and travel. Refer to the back of your member card for the phone numbers, and review the enclosed brochures describing these services in detail, and look in *The Co-op America Quarterly* for new information on these and other Co-op America programs. Thanks for joining!

PLEASE NOTE: Send us your address change along with your member number when you move.

Keep These Numbers Handy
- Co-op America — 1-800-424-2667 or 202-872-5307
- Co-op America Catalog — 202-223-1881
-
-

- Travel-Links — 1-800-648-2667
- Co-op America's VISA® with Vermont National Bank — 1-800-367-8862
- Working Assets Long Distance Phone Service — 1-800-788-8588 ext. 840

This is not an insurance card

Co-op America's Socially and Environmentally Responsible Services

In this folder, you will find a wide range of services that can help meet your needs. When you use these services, you will help reallocate money to businesses that share your vision of a just, cooperative, sustainable economy. These companies are working hard to change the way America does business.

We offer these services to you in the spirit of expanding your choices. Our program of providing socially and environmentally responsible services is only a small part of our work. The center of our mission is providing education and action programs to help create a just and sustainable society. As a member supporting our work, you will receive our magazine, the *Co-op America Quarterly* which includes *Boycott Action News*, our directory of Green Businesses, our biannual catalog and our *Socially Responsible Financial Planning Handbook*.

Thank you for joining.
We look forward to working with you!

Co-o... ...ny • Suite 403

Co-op America is a member-controlled and worker-managed non-profit organization promoting a sustainable economy and educating consumers and businesses about how to align their buying and investing habits with values of peace, cooperation and environmental protection. By using our collective economic power, we can begin to change the American economic system to one that is just and sustainable.

We at Co-op America have an ongoing commitment to serve as a model for social responsibility. Should you experience a problem with any of the goods, services or programs we provide, or if you are not receiving all of your Co-op America publications, we urge you to call our Member Services Department at (800) 424-2667 or (202) 872-5307. Please call or write us — any time — if you have a suggestion or idea.

Please keep this folder as a handy reference.

Your Name _____   Your Member # _____

SHARE THE MESSAGE

❏ **Yes,** I would like to share the Co-op America message with my friends. Please send the following people more information about Co-op America.

Friend's Name _____
Address _____
_____

Friend's Name _____
Address _____
_____

OFF THE MAILING LIST

❏ Co-op America occasionally lets other like-minded organizations mail their literature to Co-op America members. If you do <u>not</u> want to receive additional mailings from organizations working on issues related to Co-op America's mission, check this box, and be sure to write down your name and member # above.

Welcome!

· ·

NEW
MEMBER
SURVEY
ENCLOSED

BUSINESS REPLY MAIL
FIRST CLASS   PERMIT NO. 18660   WASHINGTON, D.C.

POSTAGE WILL BE PAID BY ADDRESSEE

CO-OP AMERICA
1850 M Street NW, Suite 700
Washington, DC 20077-5983

NO POSTAGE
NECESSARY
IF MAILED
IN THE
UNITED STATES

Printed on recycled paper

COOP AMERICA

Dear New Member:

Welcome to Co-op America!

Thank you for joining us in the movement for a just and sustainable economy!

As a member of Co-op America, you are already helping change the way America does business. Your membership support makes it possible for us to encourage corporate responsibility ... help socially responsible businesses emerge and thrive ... build sustainable communities ... and provide people with the information they need to use their economic power to maximum effect.

Your complimentary copy of the National Green Pages and your Socially Responsible Financial Planning Handbook will be mailed to you within two or three weeks. You'll also enjoy many other valuable publications, including:

» Our quarterly magazine, the Co-op America Quarterly, packed with practical, down-to-earth economic ideas and information. Your regular subscription will start with the next published issue.

» Boycott Action News, published within the Quarterly, gives you background, news, "where to write and what to do" for social change boycotts.

» The Co-op America Catalog -- a showcase of socially and environmentally responsible businesses. Members receive the catalog every Spring and Fall.

Please write or call any time you have an idea or suggestion -- or if you have a problem with any of our products or services. For Co-op America, being socially responsible means being responsive to you.

Once again, thank you for your support! I look forward to working with you to create a just and sustainable economy.

In cooperation,

Alisa Gravitz

Alisa Gravitz
Executive Director

P.S. You and your views are important to all of us here at Co-op America. To get to know you and your needs, I'm enclosing your New Member Survey. Please take a few minutes right now to complete and return it to me. Thank you!

1850 M Street NW, Suite 700 ■ Washington, DC 20036 ■ 800-424-2667

printed on non-chlorine bleached, 100% recycled paper

CO-OP AMERICA MEMBER SURVEY

Please answer the following survey questions to acquaint us with yourself and your needs. The survey is divided into seven short sections and should only take you a few minutes to complete.

Your answers are strictly confidential.

ID# *(see your new membership card)* _____

Name _____

Address _____

City/State/Zip _____

Telephone _____

1 Please indicate your reasons for joining Co-op America *(check all that apply).*

☐ To support socially and environmentally responsible businesses

☐ To receive the *National Green Pages*

☐ To receive the *Co-op America Catalog*

☐ To learn more about using my buying power to create a better world

☐ To receive the *Co-op America Quarterly*

☐ To encourage corporate responsibility

☐ To learn more about boycotts from *Boycott Action News*

☐ To learn about socially responsible investment

☐ To receive Co-op America's *Socially Responsible Financial Planning Handbook*

☐ To learn more about sustainable lifestyles, work, and communities

☐ To get Working Assets Long Distance Telephone Service

☐ To apply for the Co-op America Visa Card

2 Please let us know how important each one of our main programs is to you.

Green Business Campaign — to help launch and support socially and environmentally responsible businesses; to publicize the success of Green Businesses and give people access to the growing Green Business sector, as consumers, investors and co-developers.

☐ *Very important* ☐ *Somewhat important* ☐ *Not important*

Consumer Education and Empowerment Program — to educate people about the power of their dollars to change the world; to help them use their savings and investments to prepare for their future while *supporting* a more just and sustainable future for all through socially responsible investing.

☐ *Very important* ☐ *Somewhat important* ☐ *Not important*

Corporate Responsibility Program — to provide information about boycotts and shareholder resolutions against irresponsible companies; to encourage corporations to become environmentally responsible citizens.

☐ *Very important* ☐ *Somewhat important* ☐ *Not important*

Sustainable Living Program — to educate people about practical measures they can take to make their personal, community and work lives more meaningful and sustainable.

☐ *Very important* ☐ *Somewhat important* ☐ *Not important*

5 More About You *(This section is optional. Your answers will help us decide which services to offer you.)*

- **Birthdate** _____ – _____ – _____

- **Gender** ☐ Male ☐ Female

- **Occupation** *(please check one only)*
  - ☐ Professional/Technical/Managerial
  - ☐ Sales/Clerical
  - ☐ Teacher/Professor
  - ☐ Craftsperson/Foreman/Other Worker
  - ☐ Farmer
  - ☐ Home Manager
  - ☐ Retired
  - ☐ Unemployed
  - ☐ Other_____

- **Education** *(please check one only)*
  - ☐ Elementary and/or some high school
  - ☐ High school graduate
  - ☐ Some college
  - ☐ College graduate
  - ☐ Graduate or professional degree
  - ☐ Post-college without degree

- **Number of adults in household**
  ☐ 0 ☐ 1 ☐ 2 ☐ 3 ☐ 4 or more

- **Number of children in household**
  ☐ 0 ☐ 1 ☐ 2 ☐ 3 ☐ 4 or more

- **Have you bought anything from a mail-order catalog in the last 6 months?** ☐ Yes ☐ No

- **Do you have a computer in your home?**
  ☐ Yes ☐ No

- **Is your computer equiped with a modem?**
  ☐ Yes ☐ No

- **Do you have a fax machine in your home?**
  ☐ Yes ☐ No

- **Do you have a VCR in your home?** ☐ Yes ☐ No

- **Household Income**
  - ☐ under $10,000
  - ☐ $10,000 – 19,999
  - ☐ $20,000 – 29,999
  - ☐ $30,000 – 49,999
  - ☐ $50,000 – 74,999
  - ☐ $75,000 – 99,999
  - ☐ $100,000 or more

6 Mailing List

Sometimes we share our mailing list with other like-minded organizations. If you would like us to take your name off the list we share with other groups check the box below.

☐ Please take my name off the mailing list you share with other organizations (**Important:** *be sure to include your ID# at the beginning of this survey*)

7 Suggestions and Ideas

Please let us know if you have any comments about our work in the space below.

_____

_____

_____

_____

_____

☐ check this box if you would like us to get back to you.

Thank you for completing this survey!

Co-op America • 1850 M Street NW, Suite 700 • Washington, DC 20036

non-chlorine bleached, 100% recycled paper (10% post-consumer)

CO-OP AMERICA • 1850 M Street NW, Suite 700 • Washington, DC 20036

Welcome! . . . .

"creating a just and sustainable society"

printed with
soy-based inks

Thank you for joining Co-op America. This handy membership card has the numbers for Co-op America's services listed on the back. Carry it with you for quick reference to socially and environmentally responsible products and services.

CO-OP AMERICA
MEMBERSHIP CARD

Member No.

Member

Signature _____

1850 M Street NW, #700 • Washington, DC 20036
800-424-2667 • 202-872-5307

Welcome aboard!

KEEP THESE NUMBERS HANDY

Co-op America 800-424-2667 or 202-872-5307 in DC

Co-op America Catalog 202-223-1881

Travel-Links 800-648-2667 or 617-497-8163 in MA

Co-op America VISA with Vermont National Bank
800-367-8862

Working Assets Long Distance Phone Service
800-788-8588 ext. 840

We value you as a member. Together, we are building a more socially just and environmentally sustainable society. Along with participating in our crucial work, we hope you enjoy your benefits as a Co-op America Member:

1 Your subscriptions to the **Co-op America Quarterly** and **Boycott Action News**

2 The **Co-op America Catalog**

3 Socially Responsible Services:

The Co-op America VISA® Card — get your credit card services from Vermont National Bank; **Working Assets Long Distance** — telephone service that lets you make free calls to government and corporate leaders; **Travel-Links** — a socially responsible travel service.

You will receive more information about these services in a separate package in 2-3 weeks.

Thanks for joining.

Please note: *Send us your address change along with your membership number when you move.*

Welcome aboard!

· ·

Your new member kit enclosed! Open immediately.

· ·

To:

COOP AMERICA

Dear Co-op America Member,

Thank you again for joining Co-op America! Enclosed you'll find your complimentary copies of <u>Co-op America's National Green Pages</u> and our <u>Financial Planning Handbook</u>. These are both essential tools for creating a just and sustainable economy. They're yours to keep. Use them well!

You'll also find a folder that contains introductory brochures on our membership services. Please look these over carefully to see which you would like to participate in. Each brochure has an easy-to-use reply device that you can send back to us or to the companies we work with.

Also included in this package is a Feedback Form you can send back to us if you have any comments, questions or concerns about your Co-op America Membership. You may also use the form to list the name of friends to whom you'd like us to send more information about Co-op America. Or, if it's more convenient for you to call, please don't hesitate to use our toll-free membership number, 1-800-424-2667.

We hope you enjoy all of these publications, products and services. These and all of our programs are designed to be used to transform the way business is done in America.

Thanks again for joining. It's good to be working with you to create a just and sustainable society.

In cooperation,

Alisa Gravitz

Alisa Gravitz
Executive Director

1850 M Street NW, Suite 700 ■ Washington, DC 20036 ■ 800-424-2667

printed on 100% recycled paper (10% post-consumer) with soy-based ink

FEEDBACK FORM

If you have any questions, comments or suggestions please use the space below or call our toll-free membership number, 800-424-2667.

_____

_____

_____

_____

_____

_____

_____

_____

_____

_____

If you think any of your friends would be interested in learning more about Co-op America, please list up to three names and addresses below.

If you'd like to give *gift memberships* to any of those you list below, please check the appropriate boxes. The first gift membership is $20. Each subsequent gift membership is $15. If you'd like you may also include any additional contributions in the enclosed reply envelope.

Your Name _____

Address _____

City/State/Zip _____

Your Membership No. _____
(on your membership card)

1 Please send more information to:

Name _____

Address _____

City/State/Zip _____

☐ Please send a gift membership in my name — $20

2 Please send more information to:

Name _____

Address _____

City/State/Zip _____

☐ Please send a gift membership in my name — $15

☐ *I'm enclosing an additional contribution of $_____.*

Total amount enclosed $_____.

3 Please send more information to:

Name _____

Address _____

City/State/Zip _____

☐ Please send a gift membership in my name — $15

Thanks again for joining Co-op America!

Co-op America • 1850 M Street NW, Suite 700 • Washington, DC 20036

non-chlorine bleached, 100% recycled paper (10% post-consumer) • soy-based inks

Co-op America

When you use Co-op America's Membership Services, you help reallocate money to businesses that share your vision of a just and sustainable economy.

These companies are working hard to change the way America does business.

Co-op America
1850 M Street NW, Suite 700
Washington, DC 20036
202-872-5307
800-424-2667

S E R V I C E S

Travel

Make Your Travel Dollars Count

Travel-Links
800-648-2667

CO-OP AMERICA

Long Distance

Use Your Phone Bill as a Tool for Justice

Working Assets
Long Distance
800-788-8588 x840

CO-OP AMERICA MEMBERSHIP·BENEFITS

13

APPEALING FOR SPECIAL GIFTS

Bringing Your Case Down to Earth

On the opposite page is a response device representative of thousands of "special appeals" mailed every year by nonprofit organizations to their previous donors. It could hardly be more obvious, with its italicized request for a "special gift."

You can tell this is a special appeal from some less obvious but equally telling clues:

◆ Bread for the World was seeking support for a specific purpose (a campaign to persuade President George Bush to sign and implement a specific piece of legislation). In other words, unlike an acquisition letter, this appeal could not be repeatedly remailed.

◆ The campaign that's the subject of this letter would soon come to an end. So this appeal was dated. the legislation, already passed by Congress, would reach the president's desk and be disposed of, one way or another, within a reasonably short time.

◆ The Ask amounts ($500, $100) are appropriate for donors who have established relationships with Bread for the World. Few nondonors would consider making such large gifts.

◆ The only general description of Bread for the World's mission is to be found in the lower right corner ("lobbies on behalf of poor and hungry people"). It's assumed that most readers of this appeal will be familiar with the organization's purpose.

How special appeals are different from other fundraising letters

Most special appeals share six characteristics:

1. There are specific time references — because special appeals are usually mailed only once, through a narrow window on the calendar. To emphasize urgency and underline how different they are from other solicitations from the same charity, most special appeals refer to passing conditions or one-time opportunities or circumstances.

2. The Ask amount is variable. Usually, a special appeal is "segmented," that is, different versions of the appeal are sent to distinct groups of donors. For example, those who've never contributed more than

YES, I want to make sure that President Bush signs and implements the Horn of Africa Recovery and Food Security Act. Here's my *special gift* so Bread for the World can continue to play a leadership role in bringing peace to the famine-ravaged Horn of Africa.

☐ **$500**   ☐ **$100**   ☐ $ _____

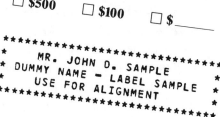

```
*********************************
*                               *
*    MR. JOHN D. SAMPLE         *
*  DUMMY NAME - LABEL SAMPLE    *
*      USE FOR ALIGNMENT        *
*                               *
*********************************
```

☐ I prefer that my gift be tax-deductible and that it support the research and education efforts of the Bread for the World Institute on Hunger & Development. I've made out my check accordingly.

Bread for the World
802 Rhode Island Avenue, N.E.
Washington, DC 20018

60472A

Since Bread for the World lobbies on behalf of poor and hungry people, contributions are not tax-deductible.

100% UNBLEACHED RECYCLED PAPER

$50 at any one time might be asked for $75, while previous donors of between $200 and $499 would be urged to send a minimum of $500.

3. There are specific program references. These are, after all, *special* appeals. More often than not, the funds requested are to support one particular project or program.

4. Special appeals are frequently short — just one or two pages. Many low-budget organizations — as well as some that are well heeled — include few inserts. The working assumption is that proven donors are well acquainted with the charity's work and need few reminders about its value. This assumption is questionable, but it's common, nonetheless. Also, inserts such as brochures or flyers may make a mailing seem less personal, blunting its effect. (There are many exceptional circumstances that justify such inserts. The "Dreamcatcher" package from St. Joseph's Indian School in Chapter 2 is a good example. But even that letter is a short one.)

5. A special appeal is far more likely to be "personalized" than a donor acquisition mailing. It's also more likely to include "live postage" (real stamps) and use high-quality paper. The extra expense is often considerable, and it's magnified by the lower volume that's also typical of mailings to proven donors. But the resulting higher cost per unit tends to be justified by the response, which is about five to seven times as great than from a donor acquisition mailing.

6. The copy in a special appeal is likely to be warm and personal. It's built on individual donor histories. A charity knows a few things about its donors. In a well-run fundraising program, those things are reflected in the frequent special appeals mailed in search of additional support.

Case Study: Family Service Agency Special Appeal

The Family Service Agency of Burlingame, California, is typical of many local human service provid-ers all across America in its dependence on government contracts (60 percent of its $3.6 million budget) and the relatively modest size of its efforts to raise funds from individuals (accounting for just 12-15 percent of the budget). Here's what development director Margaret Ann Niven wrote me when she sent along the draft appeal reproduced on pages 162 to 163:

We use a custom designed computer program based on Foxbase and a laser printer. The relatively simple database program doesn't let us make reference to past giving in our letters. Also, separate letters for renewals vs. prospects are complicated and time consuming. On the other hand, the database is easy to maintain and keep current. Thank yous go out within 48 hours. Production remains in-house, allowing us to print directly on the envelope rather than use labels.

The database hovers around 3,000, with about 700 donors annually. We consider the Spring mailing a clean-up for the annual campaign which begins in November. Last year the Spring mailing resulted in $37,770 from 92 donors. The Fall 1991 mailing brought $115,500 from 336 donors, both new and renewal gifts. About 1/3 of the donors are via designated United Way gifts.

Currently, we use one letter for the entire database and all letters are personalized (Dear Mr. and Mrs. Jones). Board members send the letter over their signature to their personal friends and business contacts with a hand written postscript. About 900 of the database is "linked" to a Board member. Of the remaining "unlinked" solicitation pieces, all but 500 have received at least one mailing in the past. Unlinked letters go out over the Board Chairman's signature without a postscript. All signatures are hand-written.

Linked letters go out First Class with oversized postage stamps. Unlinked letters go non-profit bulk rate in envelopes with a pre-printed indicia square.

This mailing will be preceded by a 6-page agency newsletter. The package includes: an outside enve-

lope, one-page letter, donor remit envelope and copies of two editorials on a two-sided sheet.

If you're reading closely, you've guessed that this mailing was intended to serve double duty — as both a special appeal (to proven donors) and an acquisition letter (to prospective donors). This presents special challenges to the writer. How can one fundraising effort meet the criteria for both types of letters, presenting the *general* case for making a first gift and the *special* case for additional support? In fact, one letter usually *can't* meet both needs adequately. Nonetheless, many nonprofits feel forced by limitations in their budgets or the size of their mailings to send a single version of a fundraising letter to both donors and prospects. Please keep in mind that this was one of those cases.

General comments

The Family Service Agency did an outstanding job of wordsmithing. I rarely make so few changes in wording — and, as you know by now, I'm a real nitpicker. The agency's staff told an engaging story and made a strong case for supporting their work. The lead was involving, and the closing tied the case and the story together. All good.

The only significant problem in the body of the letter was that they didn't directly ask for *money.* It's very important that a fundraising letter come clean on the subject of money. The earlier and the more straightforwardly the better.

Ideally, of course, they'd insert a specific, appropriate Ask amount in each individual letter. (That amount might be 15 percent or 20 percent higher than the donor's gift last year, for example.) Unfortunately, that wasn't feasible in this project: it was prohibitively costly to insert a specific amount of money tied to the donor's previous support. But a second-best alternative comes to mind: to ask for gifts within a certain range (say, $150, $400, $1000 or more). There's a pitfall in that approach, though: you've got to be sure not to send the same letter to everyone! You don't want to ask donors for *less* money than they've given you before.

A third-best alternative is to ask for "a generous gift" or something else nonspecific. But make sure there's no question you're asking for MONEY.

A lesser problem — occasioned by the shortness of the letter, perhaps — was that there was no P.S. With only the rarest of exceptions, I include one in every fundraising letter. As Siegfried Vögele teaches us, the postscript *is* the lead more than nine out of ten times! So I added one, and transferred one of the strongest elements of the agency's case to that location. In the case of what they call "linked" letters, board members could easily add either a P.P.S. or an unlabeled personal note.

The writer seems to have struggled to squeeze this letter onto a single page. To me, it's far more important to tell the story — and use the space necessary to do so — than to hold to some arbitrary length limit. In this case, that resulted in a two-page letter, with slightly broader margins. (Incidentally, since I know letter length is often a "political" question, I sliced up my own edited version and reduced the letter to a single page again when I did the original work.)

Format

I'm going to repeat here what I said to the Family Service Agency at the time. It's what I say to almost every other local and regional nonprofit organization that gives me the opportunity. Listing the members of your board of directors on the side of a fundraising letter is a distraction. And, unless your agency is very different from others, they're not nearly so well known as you — or they themselves — might think they are. (I'm supremely confident about this statement because I reviewed mounds of public opinion polling data firsthand quite a number of times during years of full-time involvement in local politics.)

So, if you don't have a closetful of letterhead and a high wall of political resistance to moving the listings off the letterhead (for fundraising letters only), you could list them on the back of a reply device, or — in some other appeal — on a brochure.

A fallback position is to place the listings more unobtrusively at the *bottom* of the letter, in the smallest type you can get away with.

As for the format of the text, you'll note in my edited version that I eliminated italics, using a limited amount of underlining instead . . . indented every paragraph . . . and broke up the text into smaller paragraphs. I made all these changes to enhance the readability of the copy and make the letter seem a little more personal and less institutional.

Outer envelope

I liked very much the use of laser addressing on a closed-face envelope, as the agency had planned to do. But I thought they'd detract from the personalized character of the envelope by using a postal indicia. I strongly recommend either first-class stamps (at least for prospects who aren't "linked" to board members but are past donors nonetheless) or a postage meter. Another alternative, which I don't favor highly but think superior to an indicia, is to use precanceled nonprofit bulk mail stamps.

Remittance envelope

I'm not a big fan of "bang-tail" remittance envelopes like the one the Family Service Agency was planning to use. (Those are envelopes with long, square flaps on the back, usually printed both inside and out.) Results are usually better with a detached, personalized reply device (so the donor doesn't have to write out all the information) and a Business Reply Envelope that's big enough to hold the reply device without folding.

The best reply devices are *involving*. They affirm the donor's eagerness to help (usually by using the word YES!) and repeat and underline the principal reason or reasons given in the letter for supporting the agency *at this time*. You can't achieve that with preprinted remittance envelopes.

The agency talked about "partnership level" on the remittance envelope but mentioned the concept nowhere else. Perhaps they had explained it in an earlier letter but left the copy on the envelope. (There's *another* reason not to pre-print remittance envelopes!) ▶

Family Service Agency
of San Mateo County

1870 El Camino Real   •   Burlingame, California 94010   •   (415) 692-0555

April 10, 1992

name
address
city/zip

Dear Mrs. ⸱ ⸱ ᴐᴑ,

Michael is going to see his Dad today and he is terrified.

*Michael is seven and hasn't seen his dad in four years. His
parents were divorced five years ago after a bitter fight.
First Michael lived with his mom, and his dad visited him
every week. Then his dad stopped coming because "seeing his
ex-wife was too difficult." Now Michael has a new stepfather
and a new last name. And his dad wants to see him again.*

If Michael is lucky, the court will order supervised visits at Family
Service Agency's Visitation Center. It's a cheerful, home-like place
where Michael can feel safe as he and his dad get to know each other
again.

Many families turn to Family Service Agency--for supervised visits in
custody cases or treatment for sexually abused children. For hot
meals for frail seniors or safe child care when parents work. And for
counseling when lives are devastated by conflict and abuse.

That's why I'm asking you to help Family Service Agency now.
During these difficult economic times, the demand for services has
exploded. In the last six months, for example, the number of people
in counseling has increased 40% over the previous six months. And
89 cents of every dollar contributed directly benefits the families who
need a helping hand.

I know that if you could help one just child like Michael, you would.
You and I agree that families are the backbone of our society and
that successful families build a healthy and strong community. Won't
you join me in making sure that no family is turned away for lack of
funds? Michael and his dad are counting on us to give them a second
chance.

Sincerely,

Arthur H. Bredenbeck
Board Chairman

NON-PROFIT
ORGANIZATION
U.S. POSTAGE
PAID
PERMIT #147
BURLINGAME, CA

Le Croix
Avenue, 3
San Mateo, CA 9

Family Service Agency
of SAN MATEO COUNTY

1870 El Camino Real, Burlingame, California 94010

Member of United Way of Bay Area

Burlingame   Redwood City

• Counseling   •   Child Care   •   Senior Services   •   Child Abuse Treatment

Serving families throughout the community since 1950

Family Service Agency
of San Mateo County

NO POSTAGE
NECESSARY
IF MAILED
IN THE
UNITED STATES

BUSINESS REPLY MAIL
BURLINGAME, CA

ADDRESSEE

NCY
NTY

9915

STRENGTH TO FAMILIES

I have checked the partnership level
I prefer and enclose my gift for:

❏ Director's Circle *($5,000 or more)*
❏ Benefactor *($1,000 or more)*
❏ Patron *($750)*
❏ Contributor *($400)*
❏ Family *($150)*
❏ Friend *(up to $149)*
❏ Endowment Trust Fund
❏ I wish this gift to be anonymous.

Thank You

Donor's Name _____

Address _____

City _____

State   Zip

Contributions to Family Service Agency are tax deductible.
❏ I'd like information on how to include Family Service Agency in my will.

April 10, 1992

name
address
city/zip

Dear Mrs. Cron,

Michael is going to see his Dad today -- and he's <u>terrified</u>.

Michael is seven and hasn't seen his Dad in four years. His parents were divorced five years ago after a bitter fight.

First Michael lived with his Mom, and his Dad visited him every week. Then his Dad stopped coming because "seeing his ex-wife was too difficult."

Now Michael has a new stepfather and a new last name. And his Dad wants to see him again.

If Michael is lucky, the court will order supervised visits at Family Service Agency's Visitation Center. It's a cheerful, home-like place where Michael can feel safe while he and his Dad get to know each other again.

Many families turn to Family Service Agency -- for supervised visits in custody cases or treatment for sexually abused children. For hot meals for frail seniors, safe child care, or counseling when lives are devastated by conflict and abuse.

During these difficult economic times, the demand for our services has exploded. In the last six months, for example, the number of people in counseling here <u>has</u> <u>increased</u> 40% over the previous six months.

That's why I'm asking you to help Family Service Agency today with a tax-deductible gift of $XXX or more.

I know that if you could help one just child like Michael, you would. You and I agree that families are the backbone of our society and that successful families build a healthy and strong community.

Will you join me in making sure that no family is turned away for lack of funds? Michael and his Dad are counting on us to give them a second chance!

With high hopes,

Arthur H. Bredenbeck
Board Chairman

P.S.   Your support for the Family Service Agency will make a big difference here in San Mateo County. <u>89</u> <u>cents</u> <u>of</u> <u>every</u> <u>dollar</u> you give will directly benefit the families who need a helping hand.

ASKING FOR YEAR-END CONTRIBUTIONS

Making the Most of the Holiday Spirit

Most year-end appeals resemble the fundraising letter from Bread for the World reproduced in part on the opposite page. You'll note there are at least five reasons this is obviously a year-end appeal to donors:

◆ *It says so: you can't mistake the words "Special Year-End Gift." No subtlety here (and none called for)!*

◆ *The reference to the "new year" implies that gifts will continue efforts the donor has (presumably) supported in the past.*

◆ *The Ask amounts are high enough to suggest that the people to whom this letter was mailed have a history of support for Bread for the World. Few outsiders would seriously consider gifts so generous.*

◆ *The offer of a tax-deductible option is likely to be of special interest because the end of the tax year is approaching. (Most nonprofits mention tax-deductibility year-round, but Bread for the World doesn't. As a lobbying organization, Bread for the World can offer tax-deductibility only for gifts earmarked for educational purposes.)*

◆ *The appeal is personalized. This package cost Bread for the World a significant amount of money for data processing. It's unlikely the group would spend as much on fundraising letters to nondonors.*

How Year-End Appeals Are Different From Other Fundraising Letters

The end of the year is a special time for most U.S. nonprofit organizations. A spirit of generosity holds sway and donors turn to thoughts of tax deductions for their charitable giving. Most charities therefore mail appeals to their donors at this time, even if they ask for renewed support at no other time of the year.

Year-end appeals are a major source of support for the nation's nonprofit organizations, because an estimated 40 percent of all charitable giving takes place during the final three months of the year. They can be either annual (or membership) renewal mailings or special appeals (seeking gifts for earmarked purposes). But the fundraising letters mailed by

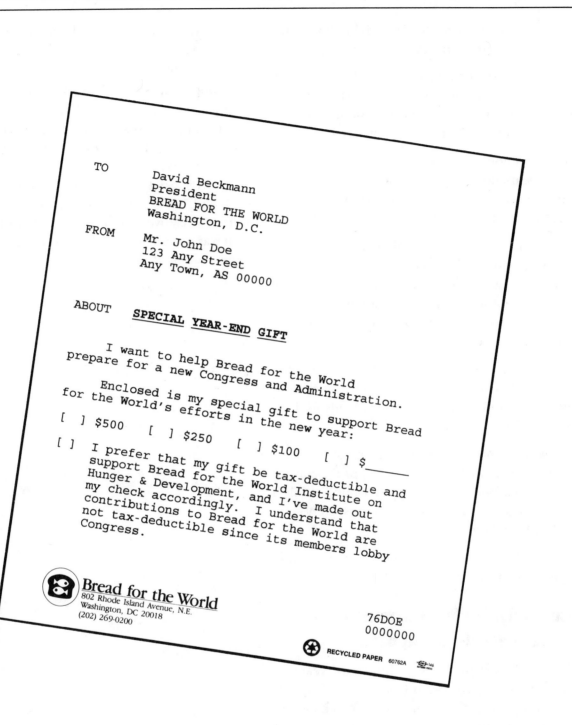

TO   David Beckmann
         President
         BREAD FOR THE WORLD
         Washington, D.C.

FROM   Mr. John Doe
         123 Any Street
         Any Town, AS 00000

ABOUT   **SPECIAL YEAR-END GIFT**

     I want to help Bread for the World
prepare for a new Congress and Administration.
     Enclosed is my special gift to support Bread
for the World's efforts in the new year:

[ ] $500   [ ] $250   [ ] $100   [ ] $_____

[ ]   I prefer that my gift be tax-deductible and
support Bread for the World Institute on
Hunger & Development, and I've made out
my check accordingly. I understand that
contributions to Bread for the World are
not tax-deductible since its members lobby
Congress.

Bread for the World
802 Rhode Island Avenue, N.E.
Washington, DC 20018
(202) 269-0200

76DOE
0000000

RECYCLED PAPER 60762A

charities during this time tend to exhibit most of the following six characteristics:

1. There are usually references to the season (particularly by religious organizations). The benefits of year-end tax deductions are commonly mentioned, too. Often the two are connected.

2. Ask amounts are usually variable. The generosity of year-end giving makes it possible for most groups to invest a little more in personalizing their appeals.

3. For the same reasons, many charities spend more on producing their year-end appeals than they do on fundraising letters mailed at other times of the year — not just on personalization but also on paper stock, ink colors, and premiums such as holiday greeting cards.

4. A favored theme is "looking back, looking forward." The widespread tendency in America to think about New Year's resolutions lends itself to this Janus-like approach.

5. More often than at other times of the year, charities may launch "multi-part" appeals, consisting not of a single fundraising letter but possibly a series of two or three letters, perhaps even combined with a telephone call.

6. Year-end appeals are often mailed to large proportions of the donor file.

Case Study: "Hebrew Women's League" End-of-Year Appeal

The draft text of this straightforward year-end appeal begins on page 169 to 171. My edited version follows on pages 172 to 174. Take a quick look at both versions, and you'll grasp the essence of what I did to strengthen this appeal:

◆ Changed the emphasis from "we" to "you."

◆ Altered the *look* of the letter, adding subheads, underlining sparingly, and switching typefaces from Times roman to Courier.

◆ Added a postscript, which had apparently been intended but wasn't part of the draft copy supplied to me.

◆ Dropped the credit card payment option.

If you actually read both versions, you'll also see that I reinforced the seasonal connections. To see what I mean by this, read the first paragraph of the reply device (above the string of Ask amounts). Note the words used there: "1993," "tax-deductible," "year-end." With these few, straightforward words and a few relatively subtle changes in the letter itself, what was originally a generic special appeal became a *year-end appeal.* ▶

"It's like a house of cards. Right now it is standing, but I feel like the slightest breath of wind, the merest breeze could knock down a wall, a room or the whole structure."

> A mother of two young boys talking about balancing her work and family responsibilities.

December 1992

Dear HWL Member:

Every day more and more American families juggle the demands of work and family commitments. And, in family after family, it is women who bear the major burden of this task. In one out of ____ families, women are the only adult parent in the home. In one out of ____ families they care for children and aging relatives. In one out of ____ families they have children and hold down a job. In one out of ____ families, they work and care for a frail elderly relative.

When I think of these American families, I think about all the talk we hear these days about strengthening the family, about how much of it is just talk. And, I know the difference, because our organization -- the Hebrew Women's League -- knows the difference between talk and action for American families. After all, come 1993, we will have been acting on behalf of families for 100 years.

We help. We help parents of young children give those children the gift of the joy of learning. HWL's Learning Is for Kiddies (LIKE) Program has become a national force in the arena of preparing children to succeed in school. We are now serving 9,000 families in 17 states and new requests for LIKE are dramatically increasing. Children and their families, educators, legislators and HWL members are forming an educational partnership that has become a force for the future.

We care. We know how parents feel when they leave their little children in child care and go off to work. Our American Family Project and the projects it nurtured are trying to make sure that affordable, quality daycare is there for families.

We lead by stimulating community action. It mobilizes communities to help employers assist their employees with their child and elder care needs.

We stand up for what American families need. On January 15, 1993, in every HWL community across the country, you will take part in a coordinated advocacy event for American families. On HWL's Women at Work Day, mayors and governors across America will be presented with "Food for Thought" lunchboxes filled with action information to help families care for their young and oldest members.

As 1992 draws to a close and you consider charitable contributions you want to make, please make a tax-deductible contribution... To support HWL's work for families. (Use the enclosed card to tell us where you want your money to go).

This letter also brings you my best wishes for 1993... our Centennial year.

With my warmest regards,

Marsha

P.S.

Hebrew Women's League, 255 East Lexington Avenue, New York, NY 10001

Dear Marsha,

☐ Yes, you may have my vote to support HWL's Family Agenda

$100 $75   *$50*   Other $

I want you to use my donation to increase HWL's work with:

☐ LIKE (Learning Is for Kids) Program
☐ Work/Family Project - Putting family values on America's Corporate Agenda.
☐ Women at Work Day ... January 15, 1993, when we draw national attention to the dependent care needs of working parents.
☐ HWL's Advocacy on behalf of legislation such as the Family and Medical Leave Act, the Violence Against Women Act, Women's Apprenticeship Bill and the Comprehensive Children's Initiative.
☐ You decide where its most needed for HWL's Family Agenda.

Card # _____
Visa ☐   MasterCard ☐   Expiration Date_____

Signature_____

Please make checks payable to Hebrew Women's League. Contributions may be charged to credit cards. Fill in your card number, expiration date and signature above. All contributions are tax-deductible to the extent allowed by law. Your canceled check is your receipt.

"It's like a house of cards. Right now it is standing, but I feel like the slightest breath of wind, the merest breeze could knock down a wall, a room or the whole structure."

      -- A mother of two young boys, talking about balancing her work and family responsibilities

December 1992

Dear Friend of American Families:

As a member of the Hebrew Women's League, you know the difference between talk and action when it comes to family values. Because you're already taking <u>action</u>.

** <u>You</u> <u>help</u>. **

Your membership support for HWL helps parents give their young children the joy of learning through the Learning Is for Kiddies Program (LIKE).

This model program has become a national force in the arena of preparing children to succeed in school. With your generous help, we're now serving over 9,000 families in 17 states -- and new requests for LIKE are increasing dramatically.

Children and their families, educators, legislators and HWL members are forming an educational partnership that has become a force for a more hopeful future.

** <u>You</u> <u>care</u>. **

You know how parents feel when they leave their little children in inadequate child care arrangements and go off to work. Your American Family Project and the projects it nurtured are trying to make sure that affordable, quality care is there for families.

** <u>You</u> <u>lead</u>. **

As an HWL member, you're taking the lead by stimulating community action. Your Women at Work Project helps employers assist their employees with their child and elder care needs.

** <u>You're</u> <u>standing</u> <u>up</u> <u>for</u> <u>American</u> <u>families</u>. **

On January 15, 1993, HWL members across the country will take part in a coordinated advocacy event for American families.

On HWL's Women at Work Day, mayors and governors across America will be presented with "Food for Thought" lunchboxes filled with action information to help families care for their young and oldest members.

As 1992 draws to a close and you consider how you'll direct your year-end charitable giving, please consider <u>how much more you can do</u> to help American families by sending a special, tax-deductible year-end gift to the Hebrew Women's League.

As you consider the size of your year-end gift, please think about the magnitude and the importance of the challenge you and I are facing:

Every day, more and more American families must juggle the demands of work and family commitments. And, in family after family, it is women who bear the major burden of this task.

In one out of xx families, a woman is the only adult parent in the home.

Women in one out of every xx families care for children and aging relatives, in one out of xx they have children and hold down jobs.

Please take a moment right now to write as generous a check as you can -- and return it to me today in the enclosed self-addressed envelope.

As I look ahead to our Family Agenda for 1993, I have to calculate how much funding will be available for each of our urgent and critical action programs. It will help so very much if I can have your year-end gift in hand <u>by the 31st of December!</u>

You may use the enclosed card to tell us which of the League's most urgent programs you want your gift to support.

With my warmest regards, and my best wishes for your health and happiness in 1993,

[sign "Marsha"]

Marsha [Lastname]

P.S. Come 1993, the Hebrew Women's League will have been acting on behalf of American families for 100 years! To commemorate the beginning of our Centennial year, and give an extra boost to our Family Agenda for 1993, will you consider a special, tax-deductible year-end gift of $100 or more?

To Marsha [Lastname], Hebrew Women's League

Dear Marsha,

Yes, you have my support for the Hebrew Women's League's Family Agenda for 1993! To help meet the most urgent needs, I'm rushing you my special, tax-deductible year-end gift in the amount of:

☐ $100   ☐ $75   ☐ $50   ☐ $_____

Please use my gift to give an extra boost to your work on behalf of American families in the following area:

☐ Learning Is for Kiddies Program (LIKE)

☐ American Family Project (putting family values on America's corporate agenda)

☐ Women at Work Day, January 15, 1993

☐ Advocacy (for legislation such as the Family and Medical Leave Act and the Violence Against Women Act)

☐ Please put my gift to work where it's most urgently needed.

Please complete and return this form with your check by December 31st

Please make your check payable to HWL and mail in the enclosed self-addressed envelope to: Hebrew Women's League, 255 East Lexington Avenue, New York, NY 10001. All contributions are tax-deductible to the extent allowed by law. Your cancelled check is your receipt. Thank you very much!

[NOTE: I do not recommend offering a credit card payment option. Many donors perceive this as commercializing charity.]

15

SOLICITING HIGH-DOLLAR GIFTS

Framing the Case for Major Contributions

he "Memorandum of Endorsement" on the opposite page was the response device used by Bread for the World in a High-Dollar appeal that's typical of the genre in many ways:

◆ John Doe (the addressee) is identified as a "leading private citizen." Clearly, this is a leadership appeal – a request that's far out of the ordinary. It is, in other words, an upscale, major donor appeal. Bread for the World is seeking John Doe's endorsement as well as his "leadership gift."

◆ The appeal requests a gift of $1,000 or more – obviously untypical of direct mail fundraising letters!

◆ The importance of the $1,000 Ask amount is underlined by a checkbox that describes the premium.

◆ There are two donor options, which are infrequent in appeals to small donors because they may cause confusion (and, thus, delay). This is a special case, however. The Internal Revenue Services requires the disclosure that most gifts to Bread for the World are not tax deductible. See page 166 for more information.

How High-Dollar appeals are different from other fundraising letters

A High-Dollar package (as I understand the term) may be used in the service of a great many fundraising purposes – even recruiting new donors. More typically, however, these high-cost efforts are directed at a nonprofit's most generous and responsive supporters – as special appeals or upgrade efforts, for example. But whether used in "housefile" mailings or in acquisition, High-Dollar fundraising letters usually share at least five characteristics:

1. The Ask amount is high. And that amount isn't just the highest in a string of suggested amounts that would let a donor off easy. If there's a choice of gift levels, *every* choice is a big number.

2. The packaging is often very expensive. These are upscale appeals, designed to communicate a feeling of exclusivity. High-Dollar packages accomplish this aim by looking and feeling different from most other direct mail fundraising letters. Some-

Bread for the World
802 Rhode Island Avenue, N.E.
Washington, DC 20018
(202) 269-0200

MEMORANDUM OF ENDORSEMENT

I am pleased to join other leading private citizens in endorsing Bread for the World's historic campaign to help end childhood hunger in the U.S. and abroad.

Our nation must shift resources from military spending to time-tested programs that benefit the 13 million children who face hunger in our own country. Foreign aid must be reformed -- to reduce hunger and poverty among the world's poorest people.

Please use my endorsement to enlist the support of other business, church, and civic leaders -- and to persuade Congress and the Clinton Administration to give priority to reducing childhood hunger.

I've enclosed my leadership gift to help underwrite this legislative campaign:

[ ] $1000   [ ] $_____

[ ]   I've made a gift of $1000 or more. Please include my name in Bread for the World's ANNUAL REPORT distributed to Members of Congress. I prefer that my name(s) appear as follows:

_____
Please print

[ ]   I prefer that my gift remain anonymous.

Mr. John Doe
123 Any Street
Any Town, AS 00000

☐ I prefer to make a tax-deductible contribution to support the research and education efforts of *Bread for the World Institute* and I've made out my check accordingly. I understand that contributions to *Bread for the World* are not tax-deductible since its members lobby Congress on behalf of poor and hungry people.

A21DOE

RECYCLED PAPER 60072

times they're different in size, shape, texture, and color as well as elegant design. High-Dollar appeals embody what Hollywood calls "high production values."

3. Almost always, High-Dollar appeals are personalized, often extensively so. Your chances of obtaining a $1,000 gift are slim with a letter beginning "Dear Friend."

4. The copy, too, is often "upscale" in tone and approach. Not to put too fine an edge on the matter, many High-Dollar fundraising letters are built around snob appeal (for example, through invitations to "exclusive" or "intimate" events or societies).

5. Most important, however, a strong High-Dollar appeal features a uniquely appropriate Marketing Concept — an offer to match the high-level Ask. In other words, a genuine High-Dollar letter doesn't just ask for a larger sum of money than other fundraising letters; it supplies the donor with a special and credible reason to send the amount of money asked for. In other words, a High-Dollar letter has a Marketing Concept all its own. (See Chapter 9 for a detailed discussion of this term.) And to reinforce the Marketing Concept, there may be only a *single* specified gift level. Often, the offer involves a "gift club" or "giving society" that entails unique benefits or privileges.

Case Study: Doctors of the World High-Dollar Acquisition Letter

I'm going to depart from the rules I've established for this section, which is otherwise devoted to Before and After case studies from the files of EditEXPRESS™. I want to share with you the full text of one High-Dollar fundraising letter — a new-donor *acquisition* letter — that worked really well.

The package was created by my colleague Deborah Agre and copywriter Judy MacLean for our client, Doctors of the World (New York, NY). The package is reproduced in full on pages 180 to 188. Here are the contents you'll observe on those pages:

◆ A 7-1/2 x 10-1/2", closed-faced outer envelope bearing first-class stamps (including a commemorative) and a 2 x 4" word-processed, pressure-sensitive ("peel-off") mailing label that was hand affixed.

◆ A four-page, personalized, dated letter on textured, high-quality paper, hand signed in dark blue ink. Pages two through four were pre-printed to match the first page, which was word processed.

◆ Three photographs with handwritten (printed) captions on the reverse side.

◆ A 7 x 14" response device in two parts, one of them a certificate of appreciation.

◆ A #7-3/4 preaddressed reply envelope bearing a live first-class postage stamp.

This letter certainly had an upscale look and feel — but it also offered prospective donors a chance to play a leadership role. That's an *upscale offer*, entirely consistent with the $200 Ask and the high production values. The same copy probably wouldn't work well with a $25 Ask in a more cheaply produced package. In fact, an equally successful small-donor version of this package used a significantly different offer.

But the writing style in this letter is *not* fundamentally different from that in other strong fundraising appeals. It's involving, liberally using the word "you." It's personal, even chatty. It uses short sentences, short paragraphs, underlining, and broad margins. There's no effort to impress the reader with obscure information or fancy language. In other words, this is a well-crafted High-Dollar appeal because it frames an appropriate offer in a setting that enhances its credibility.

If, like most educated people, you're accustomed to receiving lots of solicitations in the mail, you may have begun tuning out years ago. Chances are, you go through a routine a lot like the one I described in Chapter 3, when I reviewed Siegfried Vögele's research findings. Certainly, most of your donors go through routines like that!

Ask yourself this: if you come across a letter like the Doctors of the World appeal starting on page 180, would you toss it into the wastebasket along with all that unwanted "junk mail" . . . or would you open it, just to find out what all the excitement's about? And what would your donors do?

Packages like this are *not* suitable in most circumstances. They're rarely cost-effective using run-of-the-mill mailing lists. But with carefully selected lists of donors or prospects, High-Dollar letters like this outstanding example may help your organization raise far more money than would otherwise be possible. ▶

DOCTORS OF THE WORLD
625 BROADWAY, 2nd FLOOR
NEW YORK, NEW YORK 10012

```
From:   Jonathan Mann, M.D.
        President, Doctors of the World


To:     Mr. John Doe
        123 Any Street
        Any Town, AS 00000
```

RECYCLED PAPER

How to Write Successful Fundraising Letters

DOCTORS OF THE WORLD
625 BROADWAY, 2nd FLOOR
NEW YORK, NEW YORK 10012

February 16, 1993

Mr. John Doe
123 Any Street
Any Town, AS 00000

Dear Mr. Doe,

Every day we read in the newspaper about the terrible suffering in so many parts of the world.

I'm sure you often feel that it's difficult to see what to do to help.

I'm writing you today as the founding President of Doctors of the World to assure you that there is a great deal you can do to help.

I hope you'll play a leadership role in our efforts to bring desperately needed medical care to people around the world.

For several years I served as the director of the World Health Organization's AIDS program. I've seen firsthand how millions of people are suffering needlessly.

I've also seen how American doctors -- with their high levels of skill and expertise -- can do so much to ease the suffering and save lives.

I'm asking you now to join a special group of compassionate Americans, as a Founding Sponsor of Doctors of the World.

Doctors of the World is the new American affiliate of Médecins du Monde, the highly acclaimed medical relief and human rights organization, headquartered in Paris.

For over thirteen years Médecins du Monde (MDM) has sent medical professionals from around the world where

RECYCLED PAPER

Page 2

they're most needed -- because they go where other groups are unable or unwilling to go.

When other relief agencies pulled out of <u>Cambodia</u>, MDM set up a M.A.S.H. unit to treat people injured by <u>exploding</u> <u>land</u> <u>mines</u>.

When <u>Kurdish</u> <u>families</u> fled Saddam Hussein's bombing, doctors rushed to the Iran-Iraq border to staff an <u>emergency</u> <u>hospital</u> despite harassment from the Iranian authorities.

Now, over 1,000 American medical professionals have signed up with the U.S.-based Doctors of the World -- to serve, <u>without</u> <u>pay</u>, on life-saving missions like these.

One of our first efforts was in war-torn Yugoslavia last summer when a <u>polio</u> epidemic broke out. Doctors of the World medical volunteers went from village to village, house to house, vaccinating over 175,000 children -- to halt the spread of this crippling disease.

And last fall while the world was helplessly watching the unfolding tragedy in Somalia, a Doctors of the World trauma surgeon treated hundreds of war refugees in the northern part of the country.

As a Founding Sponsor of Doctors of the World you'll enable American doctors to treat victims of war, natural disaster, famine and political repression.

Through the support of caring people like you, Doctors of the World recruits American doctors who <u>donate</u> their time.

We purchase and deliver the medicine and equipment the volunteers need to save lives. And we work with local physicians and human rights groups to overcome political and bureaucratic obstacles.

Like Médecins du Monde, Doctors of the World is guided by the principle that <u>doctors</u> <u>have</u> <u>a</u> <u>duty</u> <u>to</u> <u>intervene</u> where people are suffering.

And we believe we have the responsibility to speak out when we witness <u>human</u> <u>rights</u> <u>abuses</u> <u>and</u> <u>political</u>

Page 3

<u>conditions</u> that lead to disease and misery.

Médecins du Monde provided the first eyewitness accounts of the massacre in Afghanistan. And told the world about the abandoned AIDS babies in Romania.

I'm writing you because I believe you share our commitment to human rights -- and our concern for those who are suffering.

I'm sure you agree, when a child is dying of malnutrition in Central America ... or of AIDS in Africa ... or of gunshot wounds in Eastern Europe ... <u>national borders</u> <u>and</u> <u>political</u> <u>concerns</u> <u>must</u> <u>not</u> <u>keep</u> <u>a</u> <u>doctor</u> <u>from</u> <u>that</u> <u>child's</u> <u>side</u>.

Your leadership now will enable American doctors to go where they're needed most -- regardless of the obstacles.

o Doctors of the World sent a reconstructive surgeon to Ethiopia to operate on civilians shot in the face during the civil war. Our volunteer was the <u>only</u> <u>doctor</u> <u>with</u> <u>these</u> <u>skills</u> in this tortured nation of over 60 million people.

o Doctors of the World physicians were on the scene within hours of the 1991 toxic gas explosion in Guadalajara, Mexico.

o Our doctors and nurses are working in clinics in the black shantytowns of South Africa to <u>address</u> <u>long-</u> <u>neglected</u> <u>medical</u> <u>needs</u> and expose the substandard care for black citizens.

When we read of the many tragedies in so many parts of the world it often seems overwhelming.

But, believe me, <u>you</u> <u>can</u> <u>do</u> <u>so</u> <u>much</u> by becoming a Founding Sponsor of Doctors of the World, with a tax-deductible gift of $200 or more.

Your Founding Sponsorship gift will enable <u>one</u> <u>volunteer</u> <u>doctor</u> <u>for</u> <u>one</u> <u>month</u> to serve in one of the world's most troubled areas.

All of our medical professionals donate their time

Page 4

so your contribution provides <u>over 50 times its value in medical care</u>. That's <u>$10,000</u> in desperately needed medical care.

As a Founding Sponsor, your name will be inscribed on our International Roll of Honor in our New York headquarters.

And when you see the headlines about Bosnia, the Middle East, South America, Somalia -- or some other area where help is urgently needed --- you'll know you are sending doctors to <u>stop the suffering and save lives</u>.

I can tell you from my own experience, there's something unforgettable in the eyes of people who see you haven't abandoned them.

And I assure you that your help, as a Founding Sponsor of Doctors of the World, will never be forgotten.

Please don't wait until you see the next tragedy in the headlines. We're counting on your involvement right now.

I know you understand that human suffering knows no national boundaries or political allegiances.

I thank you, in advance, for showing that politics and borders won't stop human compassion.

Sincerely,

Jonathan Mann, MD, MPH
President, Doctors of the World
François-Xavier Bagnoud Professor
of Health and Human Rights
Harvard School of Public Health

P.S. Right now, Doctors of the World needs a single gift of $1,000 to purchase <u>medicine and equipment for a complete mobile emergency clinic</u> to be deployed throughout villages in Somalia. If you're able to make a gift of this amount it will help us save thousands of lives.

Certificate of Recognition

HONORING

MR. JOHN DOE

AS A

FOUNDING SPONSOR

OF

DOCTORS OF THE WORLD

■

Human suffering knows no national boundaries
or political allegiances.
We will not let politics or borders
stop human compassion.

2/16/93

DATE

JONATHAN MANN, M.D., PRESIDENT

▲ PLEASE DETACH HERE AND RETURN THE BOTTOM PORTION IN THE ENVELOPE PROVIDED

```
To:    Jonathan Mann, M.D.
       President
       Doctors of the World
       625 Broadway, 2nd Floor
       New York, NY 10012

From:  Mr. John Doe
       123 Any Street
       Any Town, AS 00000
```

01DOE

American doctors to the

Human suffering knows no national boundaries
or political allegiances.
We will not let politics or borders
stop human compassion.

2/16/93
DATE

JONATHAN MANN, M.D., PRESIDENT

▲ PLEASE DETACH HERE AND RETURN THE BOTTOM PORTION IN THE ENVELOPE PROVIDED

To: Jonathan Mann, M.D.
President
Doctors of the World
625 Broadway, 2nd Floor
New York, NY 10012

From: Mr. John Doe
123 Any Street
Any Town, AS 00000

01DOE

Yes, I'll play a leadership role in sending American doctors to the world's most troubled areas—regardless of the political obstacles.

Enclosed is my tax-deductible gift to enable Doctors of the World to answer desperate calls for help from around the world.

I understand that every dollar I send will provide 50 times its value in medical care.

☐ $200 = $10,000 value in medical care   ☐ $ _____

  ☐ My gift is $200 or more.

    ☐ Please inscribe my name on your International Roll of Honor as a Founding Sponsor.

    ☐ I wish to make my gift anonymously.

☐ I will provide medicines and equipment for a complete mobile emergency clinic to be deployed in villages throughout Somalia. Enclosed is my tax-deductible gift of $1,000. Please dedicate the clinic in the name of:

_____

Your gift to Doctors of the World is tax-deductible. Thank you.

DOCTORS OF THE WORLD   625 BROADWAY, 2nd FLOOR   NEW YORK, NEW YORK 10012

RECYCLED PAPER

16

GOING FOR BIGGER GIFTS

Persuading People to Make an Extra Commitment

The Bread for the World response device reproduced here illustrates three of the elements commonly encountered in donor upgrade appeals:

◆ *Even without reading the letter that accompanies this form, you can tell at a glance that its purpose is to* **upgrade** *John Doe's support. The copy reads, in part, "providing additional support." (Some fundraisers refer to any special gifts as "additional support," but I think that's a bad idea! The phrase is correctly applied only in circumstances such as these.) This is a special appeal to Bread for the World members, but its stated and obvious purpose is to persuade already generous members to contribute even larger sums.*

◆ *Several gift amounts are suggested, allowing Mr. Doe the opportunity to set the level most comfortable for him.*

◆ *Two giving societies are featured: the $1,000-a-year National Associates and the $2,500-a-year Founder's Society.*

How donor upgrade appeals are different from other fundraising letters

Fundraising letters of many types — including special appeals, renewals, and High-Dollar appeals — frequently feature donor upgrade options. But those options are rarely emphasized. A true upgrade letter lays out a set of reasons why the donor should give *more* — and the argument to give more is a central theme in the copy, not an afterthought. This is the primary characteristic of an upgrade letter.

For example, a special appeal might seek gifts equal to or greater than the donor's highest previous contribution (HPC) to the charity. The reply device might even offer three alternative giving levels: HPC, HPC + 25%, and HPC + 50%. But that alone wouldn't make the letter an upgrade appeal. To qualify for that characterization, the letter would need to build a case for the *increase* in support. In inflationary times, that case might be to help the organization cope with steadily rising costs — and the letter might illustrate just how quickly costs were

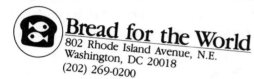

Bread for the World
802 Rhode Island Avenue, N.E.
Washington, DC 20018
(202) 269-0200

Mr. John Doe
123 Any Street
Any Town, AS

I want to take the lead in providing additional support — so Bread for the World can expand its leadership role on behalf of poor and hungry people. Enclosed is my special gift:

[   ] $1,000   [   ] $500   [   ] $250   [   ] $____

Since **Bread for the World** lobbies Congress, contributions are not tax-deductible. Tax-deductible gifts may be made to **Bread for the World Institute on Hunger & Development.**

RECYCLED PAPER 60642C

64DOE
00000000

☐ *I accept your invitation to join the National Associates and have made my annual contribution of $1,000.*

☐ *I prefer to become a National Associate by making quarterly contributions of $250. I've enclosed my first gift; please send me reminders.*

☐ *I prefer to become a member of the Founder's Society and have or will provide $2,500 in annual support.*

rising by giving concrete examples. Or the letter might spell out how much more the charity can accomplish if the donor sends a gift that's 25 percent or 50 percent larger. More commonly, however, an upgrade appeal is distinguished from a special appeal because it invites the donor to join a special group or giving category that requires significantly higher gifts. (That's the case with all the examples in this chapter.)

Three additional traits are shared by most upgrading efforts:

1. Upgrade letters customarily spotlight opportunities to join giving clubs or otherwise feature special benefits, premiums, or incentives for making the larger gifts requested. (Keep in mind that some or all of those benefits of incentives may be intangible!) In other words, there's a Marketing Concept appropriate to the request for a larger gift.

2. Upgrade efforts frequently offer two, three, or more alternative levels of support. Although this approach isn't universally used in upgrading efforts, it's common, because the purpose of such efforts is usually to secure the largest possible gift — and the writer rarely knows how much that's likely to be.

3. Personalization and high-quality paper stock are often found in upgrade appeals — to match the ambitious request.

Case Study: "People for the Environment" Monthly Sustainer Invitation

Once again I'm going to depart from form with an illustration that's not a Before and After case study. The letter and reply device appearing on pages 194 to 199 were parts of a monthly sustainer invitation package I wrote for an organization I'm calling "People for the Environment" (PFE). I've included this package as a case study in upgrading because it depicts what I believe to be the single most important way to persuade donors to give more money: by launching a monthly giving program.

But take care about using this letter as an example: For many charities that depend on small gifts from donors recruited through the mail, monthly giving or sustainer programs can bring in as much as *one-third* of their contributed income. Almost every nonprofit can benefit from a monthly giving program. But launching and managing such a program entails significant investment and continuing attention. It's not an effort to be undertaken lightly — certainly not as a short-term excuse to ask donors for larger gifts!

This package was conceived as an invitation from "Barton Snodgrass," PFE's Executive Director, to more than half of PFE's 80,000 members. Its purpose was to ask them to become Charter Members in the new "Friends of the Environment," a monthly sustainer program featuring six categories or levels of support, from $10 per month to $50 per month. Those who "cannot join at this time" were to have the option of making one-time gifts.

Eventually, every level of membership in the program would offer unique benefits or services. Initially the concrete benefits of Charter Membership at any level were to consist of just four items:

◆ Personalized certificate

◆ "Insider's newsletter" compiled by PFE staff and tentatively titled *PFE in Perspective*, which would be published at least six times per year

◆ Listing as a Charter Member in PFE in Perspective

◆ Automatic renewal of PFE membership — with freedom from regular and frequent fundraising letters (except the year-end appeal and any emergency package that might be necessary).

In addition, anyone who joined at the level of at least $20 per month would receive a complimentary copy of a highly prized coffee-table book.

Although this invitation offered only a "Bill me" option, we anticipated that those who signed up would be immediately invited to convert to the "PFE Checkfree Giving Plan," which would use Electronic Funds Transfer exclusively.

This initial sustainer invitation package was to be followed up with phone calls within a month of the maildate (at least to the most promising segments of the file). It was also to be adapted into an invitation sent to every new member shortly after a Welcome Package was sent.

Package contents

The contents of this package were to include the following four items:

1. *Outer envelope* — This was to be a size #9 (slightly smaller than a standard business envelope), non-window ("closed-face") envelope addressed by laser printer. The paper stock would be off-white (obviously recycled). Letters sent to the most loyal and generous members would bear live, first-class stamps; others would receive their letters with bulk postage. In the upper left-hand corner the PFE name, logo, and return address would be printed in color, with "Barton Snodgrass" typed above it. Lower, on the left, there was to be a bold teaser:

New Opportunity for PFE Members

2. *Letter* — The letter would be four pages long, printed in the format of standard PFE letterhead, with page one laser personalized if possible. Text was to be printed in black, with the PFE logo and page 4 signature printed in dark blue. To fit the #9 envelope, the paper stock would be 8 x 10", and it was to match the color and weight of the paper in the envelope.

3. *Reply device* ("Charter Membership Enrollment Form") — This form was to be laser personalized, measuring 8 x 10" and printed on tinted, recycled stock different from that of letter and carrier. (Instead, the form was to match the reply envelope.) It was to be printed in three colors (black text, PFE logo, green "Friends of the Environment" name and logo). The list of membership benefits would appear on a perforated, detachable panel (to reduce the size of reply device so that it would fit neatly into the reply envelope). [Note: Only *three* specific Ask amounts were to be offered to any individual member. Amounts would be assigned based on giving history.]

4. *Reply envelope* — This was to be addressed to "Personal Attention: Barton Snodgrass." In letters sent to all genuinely active donors, the reply envelope would bear live stamps (either two or three stamps or one commemorative); others would receive Business Reply Envelopes instead. The reply envelope was to be a size #6-3/4 or #7, with the paper stock matching that of reply device. In either case, the "Friends" name and logo was to be printed on the left side. ▶

CHARTER MEMBERSHIP ENROLLMENT FORM

People for the Environment
Friends of the Environment

Prepared expressly for PFE Member(s):

NAME1
NAME2
ADDRESS 1
ADDRESS 2
ADDRESS 3

YES, I am pleased to accept Barton Snodgrass's invitation to join PFE's exciting new Friends of the Environment as a Charter Member. I want to play an active, ongoing part in helping PFE sustain its leadership role over the long haul – and rapidly respond to new threats to the environment as soon as they arise.

☐ **I'm enclosing my check in payment of my first monthly contribution, and I pledge to send the same amount each month. Please bill me. I understand I may cancel this arrangement at any time.**

☐ **$50** ☐ **$25** ☐ **$20** ☐ **$15** ☐ **$12** ☐ **$10** ☐ **$_____**

_____   _____
Signature: NAME 1   Date signed

☐ **I cannot join the Friends of the Environment as a Charter Member. But here's my special contribution to PFE in the amount of:**

☐ **$HPC+50%** ☐ **$HPC** ☐ **$____**

Friends of the Environment
Charter Membership Benefits

☼ Help PFE sustain its worldwide leadership role in protecting the environment.

☼ Help PFE reduce its fundraising costs.

☼ Complimentary subscription to *The PFE Perspective*, a newsletter published at least six times per year exclusively for PFE's most loyal and involved supporters.

☼ Your name removed from the list of those who are mailed regular and frequent fundraising letters.

☼ Listing in the Charter Membership Roll in *PFE in Perspective*.

☼ Automatic renewal of your PFE membership for as long as you remain a member of the Friends of the Environment.

☼ Special certificate acknowledging your Charter Membership.

☼ You may cancel your participation at any time.

And you'll continue to receive the PFE newsletter, and enjoy all the other benefits and privileges of your PFE membership.

Six Ways to Join PFE's Friends of the Environment:

☐ **Friend** -- **$10 per month**   ☐ **Leader*** -- **$20 per month**

☐ **Colleague** -- **$12 per month**   ☐ **Patron*** -- **$25 per month**

☐ **Associate** -- **$15 per month**   ☐ **Founder*** -- **$50 per month**

* If you accept Charter Membership in the Friends of the Environment at any of these levels, we will be pleased to send you, as a token of our deep appreciation, a copy of xxxxxxxx. This magnificent, full-color volume is xxxxxx and retails for $xxxxx.

                                        DAY OF WEEK, DATE
NAME1
NAME2
ADDRESS 1
ADDRESS 2
ADDRESS 3

Dear SALU:

     I get lots of questions from committed PFE members like
you.

     I'm often asked whether there's any way an PFE member can do
more to help heal the earth. Something that a busy person
without a whole lot of money can do -- without changing jobs, or
flying to Brazil, or going into debt.

     Something that will really make a difference.

     Concerned members like you also frequently ask me what we
can do to reduce PFE's fundraising costs. Our fundraising
program is already one of the most efficient, but I share your
concern to make it even more efficient. So I, too, have asked
whether there isn't some way to send fewer fundraising letters
-- and still raise enough money to meet PFE's growing budget.

     These are questions we wrestle with all the time at PFE.

     Now, finally, we've come up with an answer to both these
important questions. It's a way for you to multiply the impact
of your PFE membership -- and help us save substantially on
fundraising costs.

     I'm writing you today because I want you to be among the
first to know about this exciting opportunity.

     The new program is called the PFE Friends of the
Environment. I invite you to get in on the ground floor.

     As a Charter Member of the Friends of the Environment,
you'll receive special, additional membership benefits and
privileges.

     More important, though, your participation in this important
new program will help sustain PFE's worldwide leadership role in
protecting wildlife and the environment.

     Here's what the Friends of the Environment is all about:

Whenever I need to raise money to support a crucial PFE program like saving the rainforests or countering threats to endangered species, I know I can count on you. PFE members are extremely generous. You've always come through in the past.

But raising money by mail takes time, so it's tough to assemble the necessary funds to respond quickly to a sudden, unexpected crisis.

For example, when [INSERT EXAMPLE OF EMERGENCY HERE], there wasn't time for me to send you a letter to ask for your financial support.

But there was no choice. I simply had to take action. I know you would've <u>insisted</u> I do!

Still, [THAT ACTION] took money. And, instead of taking your support for granted, I sure could've used a "ready-response" reserve fund.

Also, some PFE programs are long-term efforts, requiring <u>years</u> and <u>years</u> of dedicated work. But it's wasteful to write you when there's no new news.

Our work on the landmark [ENVIRONMENTAL LEGISLATION] is a perfect example. That bill included an innovative amendment -- drafted by PFE -- that will permanently [ACCOMPLISH SOMETHING VERY IMPRESSIVE].

But many <u>years</u> of work by PFE staff members preceded that crucial amendment. We had to fund their work, day in and day out, during times when public awareness of [THAT ISSUE] wasn't very high.

And that points to another important truth about our work: PFE programs sometimes just aren't very popular!

For instance, PFE played a leading role in [COMBATTING A MAJOR WORLD-WIDE ENVIRONMENTAL PROBLEM].

But when PFE scientists <u>began</u> their work on [THAT PROBLEM] years earlier, the issue was hardly known outside scientific circles. And few people -- except a handful of dedicated environmentalists such as you -- were ready to step forward with financial support.

As you can see, the crux of the matter is this: PFE needs a stable, <u>dependable</u> source of funds. Money we can count on, month

- Page 2 -

after month, through good times and bad.

We need the resources to help us <u>meet</u> <u>emergencies</u> and continue our work on a <u>broad</u> <u>range</u> of environmental issues -- without interruption.

That's why we've decided to launch the Friends of the Environment. And that's why I'm turning to you again.

To become a Charter Member in the Partnership, what I need from you today is a commitment to make a small, monthly gift to PFE -- as little as $10 per month.

Here's how the program will work:

o   As soon as I receive your check in payment of your initial monthly gift, I'll see to it that your name is removed from the list of those PFE members who are sent regular, frequent fundraising appeals.

o   You'll continue to receive the PFE newsletter. But I'll <u>also</u> see to it that you're mailed the premier issue -- and every succeeding issue -- of <u>PFE</u> <u>in</u> <u>Perspective</u>. This is a very special new "insiders-only" newsletter we'll be sending at least six times per year -- exclusively to members of our Board of Trustees and a few others.

o   Your name will appear in the Charter Membership Roll published in <u>PFE</u> <u>in</u> <u>Perspective</u>.

o   And I'll inscribe and mail you a certificate of appreciation for enrolling as a Charter Member in the Friends of the Environment.

o   Then, each month thereafter -- unless you decide to cancel -- you'll receive a reminder from us with a remittance envelope enclosed.

As you can see at a glance, the Friends of the Environment answers <u>both</u> the challenges I mentioned at the beginning of this letter:

(1)   Your <u>reliable</u>, monthly support will help PFE continue -- and expand -- our worldwide leadership role in protecting the environment.

(2)   You'll substantially <u>lower</u> <u>our</u> <u>fundraising</u> <u>costs</u> -- and reduce our consumption of paper -- by enabling us to mail

- Page 3 -

you fewer solicitations.

I hope you'll accept this opportunity today to become a Charter Member of the Friends of the Environment.

Your dependable monthly gift of $50, $25, $20, $15, $12, or even $10 will multiply the impact of your membership in PFE manyfold.

I urge you to consider those gifts an investment in your future -- and the future of your children and your children's children. They're an investment in the future of our planet.

Thank you sincerely for hearing me out.

In high hopes,

Barton Snodgrass
Executive Director

P.S. If you accept Charter Membership in the Friends of the Environment at the level of $20 per month or more, I'll be pleased to send you a copy of xxxx as a token of my appreciation. This magnificent volume....

- Page 4 -

SEEKING ANNUAL GIFTS

Building Long-Term Loyalty, One Year at a Time

he Bread for the World membership renewal device reproduced here contains five elements that are both typical and important:

◆ *This is clearly labeled a "Membership Renewal" form.*

◆ *There's even a detachable membership card.*

◆ *The form offers several different membership levels, each with its own name and corresponding gift amount.*

◆ *The organization's mission is summed up and restated. (It appears on the membership card: "A Christian citizens' movement on behalf of poor and hungry people.")*

◆ *There are blanks for John Doe to write in his occupation and other information that will be useful to Bread for the World.*

How renewal letters are different from other fundraising appeals

Annual renewal efforts are of two general types: "annual fund" appeals (most commonly found at schools and colleges) and "membership renewal series" (which aren't limited to organizations with formal membership structures but are most frequently used by them). However, both types usually share the following five characteristics:

1. There are clear and explicit references to "membership dues" or the "annual gift". In other words, it's unmistakably clear that the organization expects the donor's support, year after year.

2. The letter focuses on the process of *renewal* — repeating an action taken last year (and maybe for many years past).

3. The case is usually made in general and institutional terms rather than focusing on a particular program or special need. An annual gift, after all, represents support for the institution, not for some limited aspect of its work.

You can count on my continued involvement in this effective citizen's movement. Enclosed is my membership contribution:

☐ **$25** Individual Membership
☐ **$50** Contributing Membership
☐ **$35** Family Membership
☐ **$100** Sustaining Membership*

Occupation _____

Denomination _____

Home phone ____ / _____

Work phone ____ / _____

Mr. John Doe
123 Any Street
Any Town, AS 00000

*Sustaining Members receive sample copies of Bread for the World publications and are ~~recognized~~ in our annual report.

MEMBERSHIP RENEWAL

SEE REVERSE SIDE FOR VALUABLE INFORMATION

▼ Detach here

Bread for the World
A CHRISTIAN CITIZENS' MOVEMENT ON BEHALF OF POOR AND HUNGRY PEOPLE

_____
MEMBER'S SIGNATURE

1991 MEMBERSHIP CARD

1-8097M2A

Since Bread for the World lobbies Congress on behalf of poor and hungry people, contributions are not tax-deductible.

Bread for the World's 24-hour Legislative Update: **202-269-0494**

How to contact your member of Congress:
U.S. House of Representatives
Washington, D.C. 20515
U.S. Senate Office Building
Washington, D.C. 20510
Phone for both House and Senate:
202-224-3121

Bread for the World   **202-269-0200**
802 Rhode Island Avenue N.E.
Washington, D.C. 20018

◀ **Detach card here.**
Return larger portion with your membership gift in the envelope provided.

Thank you.

New York residents may receive a copy of the last financial report filed with the New York Department of State by writing to: New York Department of State, Office of Charities Registration, Albany, NY 12231 A copy of the official registration and financial information may be obtained from the Pennsylvania Department of State by calling toll free, within Pennsylvania, 1-800-732-0999. Registration does not imply endorsement. Virginia residents may obtain financial information from the Virginia State Division of Consumer Affairs, Department of Agricultural and Consumer Affairs, P.O. Box 1163, Richmond, VA 23209. Others may write to Bread for the World, 802 Rhode Island Avenue, N.E., Washington, DC 20018

RECYCLED PAPER

4. Renewal letters are typically short. The most important point to make in such letters is "please renew" — and that may be *all* you really need to say.

5. The element of time and its limits is always at least implicit: "this year's dues," "your expiration date," "the deadline for renewing."

Case Study: Peace Action Membership Renewal Series

Peace Action asked me to help fine-tune their membership renewal series. On pages 205 to 211 you'll find the draft text of the five-effort series in the form I received it. The final text of my edited version begins on page 212.

In each case, I'm reproducing the full set of five letters in sequence rather than alternating them, *Before* then *After* for each letter in turn. I'm doing this consciously because I want to emphasize the importance of looking at a renewal series *as a whole*. These are *not* individual fundraising letters. They're components of a continuing program to elicit annual support from a member, year after year.

At the outset, before I launch into my customary nit-picking, I want to make one very important point that's brought to light by the mere existence of this membership renewal series. Unlike so many non-profit organizations, Peace Action has actually taken one of the most critical steps they could possibly take toward the long-term financial health of their direct response fundraising efforts — operating a genuine membership development program. It's also significant that Peace Action's renewal series included five notices. Most nonprofits stop (prematurely) with two or three — and a disturbing number mail only one. So Peace Action is way ahead of the game, as it's played by most fundraisers.

With that said, my principal criticisms of the renewal series follow.

Renewals vs. appeals

These letters read too much like special appeals and not enough like renewal notices. To serve well as renewal notices, they need to be more business-like, devoting fewer words to the issues and values that dominate the draft copy — and more to the business of the *relationship* between Peace Action and its individual members. The model to follow, in general, are the subscription renewal notices we receive from magazines. When you mail a renewal series — particularly the first *two* notices — many people will respond simply because you tell them it's time to renew. But that has to be downright *obvious*. It can't be buried in copy about issues or programs. Membership dues are the business at hand in these letters.

Benefits

There's far too little emphasis on membership *benefits* in the draft letters. Every direct response appeal should focus on benefits — even if they're all intangible — but this is *doubly* true of a renewal series. (If I'd had a list of membership benefits to work from when editing this renewal series, I would have featured it in every one of the five letters.)

Benefits are central to a membership development program and must be emphasized at every opportunity. If you're constructing a comprehensive list of benefits for members (or donors) of your organization, I suggest you include *everything*: newsletters, action alerts, networking, access to local affiliates, national or regional events, whatever. Label the list something unsubtle like, "Membership Benefits" and include it as a stand-alone insert in effort #1.

In subsequent renewal efforts, you might consider including the benefits list on the response device — on the front in some cases, on the back in others. Don't hesitate to include it in *every* notice (though I'd suggest varying the typeface, size, color, and position on the response device, or some combination of these variations).

Format

The proposed format of this series was unvaried. I prefer to see renewal packages alternate envelope sizes and formats, because otherwise many members might think "I've already gotten that letter" and throw it out. If production budgets allow, you might use, for example, a #10 envelope for the first effort, then a #9, then a Monarch (#7-3/4), then another #9 and finally a #10 again.

In cases like these, the letters could be printed simultaneously with a special appeal. This would achieve economies of scale, particularly for the envelopes, which are the most expensive element in most direct mail packages. This approach should make it possible to keep production costs low enough to make varied envelope sizes practical. If that proves impractical, then choose *two* different sizes to alternate, one after another. But also be sure to use bold colors on the envelopes to help distinguish one effort from the next.

Teasers

I favor bold envelope teasers on most renewal notices. In this case, I suggested the following:

1. **MEMBERSHIP RENEWAL NOTICE**

2. **It's Time to Renew Your Membership!**

3. **Before it's too late...**

4. **LAST CHANCE!**

5. **Have You Forgotten?**

Important: please notice that these proposed teasers are consistent with the themes and approaches I've worked into each of the corresponding letters.

Survey

I, too, like the idea of a poll or survey to help boost response, as is proposed in the draft copy. Generally, I include such a survey in the third or a later notice, because I'm optimistic that the notice alone will do the trick with the first two notices. But that's a judgment call, and — barring test results to the contrary — not a significant one, so I've left the poll in the second effort, thinking it's unnecessary in the first effort and not wanting to repeat the idea.

I suggest, however, making the poll a little more credible by taking one or more of the following actions:

◆ Call it a "Membership Priorities Survey" or some such rather than a "poll." Polling suggests bigger numbers than is the case here.

◆ Consider at least one substantive question, to which the answer isn't an obvious yes or no (though not one that requires a lot of thought and thus poses potential delays).

◆ Use the laser printer on which these appeals will be printed to number and print the questions and spaces for answers, so the poll will look (and be) more up-to-the-minute.

◆ Format the device so it looks like someone's going to process and record the answers. The proposed layout looks too much like standard direct mail fare. I also suggest adding official-looking computer codes and including "instructions" on one of the margins. (Think about government documents or college entrance exam papers as possible models.)

Deadlines

Just as a laser printer can plug in a personalized name or Ask amount, it can easily insert a different deadline every day. I urge making use of this capability in the first two, personalized efforts in a renewal series such as this. Deadlines are compelling — especially for that minority of members who'll be quick to renew. I know someone has to do a little planning with a calendar to work out appropriate deadlines for efforts #1 through #3 — read my edited copy, and you'll see what I mean — but the effort involved will be worth it. Deadlines *work* in direct response!

Appreciation

In a couple of places, I've inserted thank-you language. As a general rule, it's almost *always* in order to express appreciation for past support when asking for another gift. Every solicitation ought to be a thank-you!

Name change

I used several similar devices to make passing reference to Peace Action's name change in each of the letters. But I didn't think it necessary (or desirable) to use the same language indefinitely. Such references could be dropped from the renewal series after, say, three or four months. Presumably, by that time, each member would have gotten the same message at least three other times, through newsletters, appeals, and the like. Three times should be enough. *However,* even then, I think it would be worthwhile to include a tagline on the response device (and possibly even the letterhead, too) wherever the new name and logo are run — just to be certain. I'd do that for six months. Keep in mind that this is *advertising,* like it or not. And research demonstrates that just when advertisers get bored with the repetition of the message, most consumers are just starting to notice it!

Lead quote

The draft of effort #1 begins with a quotation from Dr. Martin Luther King, Jr. Though it was powerful, I dropped it because (a) it detracts from the impact of the personalization, since it's positioned on top and (b) the quotation isn't directly related to the line of argument in the letter. If the quote is really needed to help set the right tone and establish the correct associations in the minds of members, then it could be put in big type, boxed, and placed on the reply device — preferably with a small photo of Dr. King.

Type and formatting

In membership renewal letters, many of which don't pretend to be personal notes from one person to another, I often alternate between 12-point Courier and a proportional font like Palatino to achieve variety. I reformatted these five draft letters accordingly. (In special appeals, I almost never use proportional fonts, however. They *are* almost always "personal notes.") In a typeface like Palatino, devices such as boldfacing and italics are perfectly natural. But I generally avoid them in Courier, because that typeface suggests the fiction that the letter was *typed,* an impression that's undermined by italics or boldfacing, which can't be performed easily with typewriters. Admittedly, that fiction becomes more transparent with every passing year. But, believe it or not, lots of people still assume the original copy, at least, was actually typed!

With that, we come to the end of Part Two. In the remaining chapters of Part Three, "The Letter-Writer's Toolbox," you'll find a collection of practical tools you can put to immediate use as you craft your own fundraising letters. ▶

"Our world is a neighborhood. We must learn to live together as brothers (and sisters) or we will perish as fools. For I submit, nothing will be done until people put their bodies and souls into this."
Martin Luther King, Jr.
April 3, 1968

February 20, 1993

1~?
2~?
3~?
4~?

Dear 6~,

For the second time in three years, U.S. military forces spent this season of peace on foreign soil with their lives at risk.

I know you are concerned with news reports of violence and starvation at home and around the world. Please take a moment to consider the importance of a strong peace movement in the years ahead **and if what I have to say makes sense to you, renew your support to PEACE ACTION.***

In many ways our domestic ills are a mirror image of our foreign policies. We flood the world with weapons and suffer a flood of weapons at home ... we are quick to employ the use of force to solve international problems and suffer an increasingly violent culture ... we spend billions of our tax dollars on all the security weapons can buy and suffer an insecure future.

President Clinton has begun the first hundred days of his presidency. He ushers in a new era and it begins with great hope.

But it will take hard work and not hope alone to solve these problems. You are part of the solution.

If this is to be a time of healing and rebuilding the place to start is reordering our priorities as a society. Let our priorities reflect our values. Let our priorities mirror the kind of future we hope for.

`Your membership in PEACE ACTION is one step you have taken in this direction.` `I'm sure there are other groups you belong to and actions you take in your community. That is why there is hope.`

`*formerly SANE/FREEZE: Campaign for Global Security`

With your support we will:

    * reduce the use of our tax dollars for funding the defense of western Europe and Japan and see that money is directed instead to rebuilding our economy

    * support efforts to strengthen non-proliferation of weapons of mass destruction

    * work to end the international arms trade

    * end the B-2 bomber and Star Wars programs

    We know the time is ripe for change. Through your membership in PEACE ACTION you have become an agent of hope for the future.

    Please renew today. The momentum is with us. But we have yet to win the race. **Your membership can make a difference, both for the financial support you give and the moral support it represents.**

Yours In Peace,

Peter Deccy
Membership Director

P.S. The Cold War is over, but peace has not been won. We need your continued support. If you can renew at the 9~ level this year, it will be a great help. **Thank you!**

Second Effort

February 20, 1993

Dear Member,

Your membership is about to expire and we need you!

President Clinton has begun the first hundred days of his presidency.   He has inherited a staggering debt, millions unemployed and both this country and the world riddled with violence and war.

But a powerful movement has formed to promote solutions to these challenges. And you are a part of the solution! Your continued support for PEACE ACTION* puts you on record as supporting global cooperation and a peace economy.

Your membership in PEACE ACTION amplifies the voice for sanity in the nuclear age, sanity in the way we spend our tax dollars and sanity in the way we relate to the rest of the world.

The military industrial complex is launching an all out effort to keep military spending levels at Cold War levels. At the same time, they are working feverishly to increase the sale of arms overseas. More often than not, these weapons are sent to the world's most troubled regions.

In fact the United States transfered over $300 million in weapons to Somalia during the 1980's. The practice of arms transfers continues, creating tomorrows excuse for continued Cold War levels of military spending.

Military contractors can spend millions lobbying for your tax dollars now and pass on the expense of that lobbying to the Pentagon later. We pay at both ends.

They need to be challenged, or they will stand in the way of our efforts to curb the international arms trade and stop nuclear weapons proliferation.

They need to be challenged, or they will block our country's efforts to make the transition from Cold War levels of military spending and increased investment in our economic future.

The work we do is instrumental in building a movement that is strong enough to effect change. Your membership is essential to keeping that work going.

*formerly SANE/FREEZE: Campaign for Global Security

With your support we will:
* reduce the use of our tax dollars for funding the defense of western Europe and Japan and see that money is directed instead to rebuilding our economy
* support efforts to strengthen non-proliferation of weapons of mass destruction
* work to end the international arms trade
* end the B-2 bomber and Star Wars programs

We know the time is ripe for change. Through your membership in PEACE ACTION you have become an agent of hope for the future.

Please renew today. The momentum is with us. But we have yet to win the race. **Your membership can make a difference, both for the financial support you give and the moral support it represents.**

Yours In Peace,

Peter Deccy
Membership Director

P.S. The Cold War is over, but peace has not been won. We need your continued support. If you can renew at the 9~ level this year, it will be a great help. **Thank you!**

Third Effort

February 20, 1993

Dear Member,

You are part of the solution!

We can solve the problems of a staggering national debt, millions unemployed and both this country and the world riddled with violence and war.

Your membership is very important to PEACE ACTION* and we need you to renew your membership today! Being a member of PEACE ACTION amplifies the voice for sanity in the nuclear age, sanity in the way we spend our tax dollars and sanity in the way we relate to the rest of the world.

Think about it!

* While nuclear war looks less likely today than it did five years ago,
   more and more nations are on the threshold of developing nuclear weapons.
* While the Warsaw Pact has vanished, we still spend more money defending
   Germany than they spend defending themselves.
* While our education, health care systems and our environment are in
   crisis, we are spending more on Star Wars than ever before.
* War and famine fueled by the international arms trade rages around the world.

PEACE ACTION has become the largest grassroots peace organization in American history. It is your support that got us to this point.

So please renew your membership today. Working for peace is as important today as it ever was.

In Peace

Peter Deccy
Membership Director

* formerly SANE/FREEZE: Campaign for Global Security

Fourth Effort

February 20, 1993

Dear Friend,

PEACE ACTION* is working to make real our hope for the future. An effective peace movement is essential if we are to counteract the influence of those who profit from the status quo. They have brought us the problem of staggering national debt, millions unemployed and a world riddled with violence and war. **You are part of the solution!**

Your continued support is critical during the first hundred days of the Clinton Administration. What happens in the next few months will set the pace for the next four years.

The membership of PEACE ACTION is the source of our strength. Every member is important. So please renew your membership today!

We are closer than ever to winning substantial legislation that will:

* reduce the number of nuclear weapons in the world
* reduce the military budget and increase investment in domestic needs
* give job training to workers in defense plants and provide businesses
  with funds to help them convert to civilian production
* provide funds for the clean-up of the thousands of toxic dump sites
  the military has left all over country
* work to curb the global arms trade and nuclear weapons proliferation

Membership is the engine of our organization. Many of our members are very active in their local communities. Others write their senators and congresspersons several times a year at our request. Others lend only financial support. **Every member is important.**

We need you in the struggles ahead. Please renew your membership today.

In Peace,

Peter Deccy
Membership Director

*formerly SANE/FREEZE: Campaign for Global Security

Fifth Effort

February 20, 1993

Dear Friend,

Your past support to PEACE ACTION has made us the largest grassroots peace organization in American history.

I want to ask you again to renew your membership. Your membership is important to us, both for the financial support you give and the moral support it represents.

For over five years now we have been building a powerful movement to win a shift in government spending away from expensive and unnecessary military spending to increased investment in our economic future. And that message has been well received by President Clinton and many members of Congress.

But the military/industrial complex has been busy too. They have launched a major campaign to keep military spending at Cold War levels and to offset any losses in lucrative contracts with the sale of arms to other nations. We cannot allow their greed to shatter the hope we all feel.

During the 1980's we transfered over $300 million in weapons to Somalia. Weapons sold during the Cold War are causing havoc around world. Yet, the practice of weapons transfers continues, creating tomorrows excuse for Cold War levels of militray spending.

In many ways our domestic ills are the mirror image of our foreign policies. We flood the world with weapons and suffer from a flood of weapons at home. We are quick to employ the use of force and suffer from an increasingly violent culture. We spend billions of our tax dollars on all the security weapons can buy and suffer an insecure future.

A strong, effective peace movement is necessary to hold the Clinton Administration to remain true to the promise of increased investment in our future and global cooperation.

Please renew your membership today. Our strength comes from you.
In Peace

Peter Deccy
Membership Director

*formerly SANE/FREEZE: Campaign for Global Security

First Effort

February 20, 1993

1~?
2~?
3~?
4~?
5~?

Dear 6~,

Are you part of the <u>solution</u>? Or are you part of the <u>problem</u>?

All our lives, you and I have resisted the mindless oversimplifications of the Radical Right. But <u>one</u> question isn't very complicated at all:

For the second time in three years, U.S. military forces spent the past season of peace on foreign soil. The question is, do you <u>support</u> the policy that placed our troops at risk -- or do you <u>oppose</u> it?

If you question the dangerous, interventionist policies of the Pentagon, as I do, then there's an easy and important step for you to take right now:

<u>RENEW</u> <u>YOUR</u> <u>PEACE</u> <u>ACTION</u> <u>MEMBERSHIP</u> <u>TODAY</u>.

Your membership is due to expire very soon -- but I invite you to be part of the solution by renewing <u>BEFORE</u> the [DATE HERE] deadline.

The organization you and I called SANE/Freeze has a new name now: PEACE ACTION. But the issues that led you and me to give so much of our heart and soul to PEACE ACTION have <u>not</u> changed.

And if you renew before [DATE HERE], you'll be helping in four different ways:

(1)　　You'll save money for PEACE ACTION by lowering our fundraising costs.

(2)　　You'll allow us to put your membership dues to work right away -- without delay.

(3)　　You'll help conserve resources by saving precious paper.

(4)　　And you'll be saving yourself the time and trouble of responding to additional appeals by mail.

Like me, you may look to the new Clinton Administration with great hope. But it will take a lot of <u>hard</u> <u>work</u> -- not hope alone -- to solve the age-old problem of war and peace.

And I'm betting that you're part of the solution. I know how generous you've been in the past, and I'm very grateful to you.

With your generous support, PEACE ACTION has already taken giant strides -- despite the hostility we encountered in the White House for 12 long years:

** We've built substantial grassroots support for <u>reductions</u> <u>in</u> <u>military</u> <u>spending</u> with increased funding for education, job creation and other domestic needs.

** PEACE ACTION has taken a leadership role in forging a <u>strong</u> <u>coalition</u> working to stop the global arms trade and nuclear proliferation.

** We've continued to be the nation's <u>strongest</u> <u>voice</u> for disarmament.

Now, with a more favorably disposed administration, our hopes have grown. But you and I will have to challenge the Clinton Administration to be as thoughtful and forward-looking on peace issues as it is on health care reform and civil rights.

And that's why we need an effective peace movement.

As you know, perhaps better than I, PEACE ACTION is effective because we are <u>the</u> grassroots peace organization.

We are the voices for peace in every community in the land ... in every Congressional District ... in all 50 States.

For the sake of our nation, and the future of our children and our children's children, our voice for peace must not be stilled.

Please continue to be a part of this vital work. Renew your membership <u>today</u>.

- Page 2 -

In Peace,

Peter Deccy
Membership Director

P.S. Last year, according to our records, you contributed $xx to SANE/Freeze. Will you consider renewing your membership in PEACE ACTION by increasing your gift to $xxxx? Please indicate the level of your dues support on the enclosed Membership Renewal Confirmation Form and return it to me before the [DATE HERE] Due Date. Thank you!

- Page 3 -

February 20, 1993

1~?
2~?
3~?
4~?
5~?

Dear 6~,

Your membership in PEACE ACTION (formerly SANE/FREEZE: Campaign for Global Security) will expire on [DATE HERE].

I'm writing you because I want to give you eight reasons why it's so very important that you <u>renew your membership</u> before [DATE HERE]:

(1) President Clinton has inherited a staggering debt, millions unemployed and a world riddled with violence and war. Your continued support for PEACE ACTION puts you on record as supporting <u>global</u> <u>cooperation</u> and a peace economy.

(2) The military industrial complex is launching an all-out effort to keep <u>military</u> <u>spending</u> levels at Cold War levels. Your membership in PEACE ACTION amplifies the voice for sanity in the nuclear age.

(3) <u>Military</u> <u>contractors</u> are spending millions lobbying for your tax dollars now. They need to be challenged, or they'll stand in the way of PEACE ACTION'S efforts to curb the international arms trade and stop nuclear weapons proliferation.

(4) Without your help to challenge the military contractors, they'll block our country's efforts to make the transition from Cold War levels of military spending and increased investment in our <u>economic</u> <u>future</u>.

(5) PEACE ACTION needs your continued membership support to push for cuts in spending for the

defense of <u>western</u> <u>Europe</u> <u>and</u> <u>Japan</u>. Your
membership dues help us lobby to direct that money
instead to rebuilding the U.S. economy.

(6)   Your dues help underwrite PEACE ACTION'S efforts
to strengthen <u>non-proliferation</u> of weapons of mass
destruction.

(7)   Your membership support helps our work to end the
international <u>arms</u> <u>trade</u>.

(8)   You can help PEACE ACTION put an end to the <u>B-2</u>
<u>bomber</u> <u>and</u> <u>Star</u> <u>Wars</u> programs.

Through your membership in PEACE ACTION, you've
become an agent of hope for the future, and I'm very
grateful to you.

Please renew before [DATE TODAY]. To be sure you
don't set this notice aside, write and mail your check
<u>today</u>.

Your membership can make a difference, both for
the financial support you give and the moral support it
represents.

Yours in Peace,

Peter Deccy
Membership Director

P.S. I'm enclosing an important "Peace Action
Membership Priorities Survey." Please take a
moment right now to complete it -- and return it
<u>today</u> along with your check. Thank you!

Third Effort

February 20, 1993

Dear PEACE ACTION Member,

In less than one week, your membership in PEACE ACTION will expire.

Unless you act **today**, you'll no longer be an active member of the largest grassroots peace organization in American history.

Remember, it's **you** that got PEACE ACTION to this point. Your support for SANE/FREEZE: Campaign for Global Security (our former name) was generous -- and I, for one, am very grateful to you.

As a member of PEACE ACTION, you amplify the voice for sanity in the nuclear age -- sanity in the way we spend our tax dollars, and sanity in the way we relate to the rest of the world.

- While nuclear war looks less likely today than it did five years ago, more and more nations are developing **nuclear** weapons.

- While the Warsaw Pact has vanished, the U.S. government still spends **more** money defending Germany than Germany spends defending itself!

- While our education and healthcare systems and our environment are in crisis, our government is spending **more** on Star Wars than ever before!

Please renew your PEACE ACTION membership today. Working for peace is **more** important today than ever!

In Peace,

Peter Deccy
Membership Director

P.S.   There's still time to renew your PEACE ACTION membership without interruption. Just drop the enclosed Membership Renewal Form in the mail along with your check **today**. Thank you!

Fourth Effort

February 20, 1993

Dear Soon-to-be Ex-Member of PEACE ACTION,

This is your <u>last</u> <u>chance</u> to renew your membership in PEACE ACTION.

Because you've been such a loyal member in the past, with your generous support for SANE/FREEZE: Campaign for Global Security, I'm sure it's an oversight that you haven't renewed before now.

As an active member, you help us wield great strength.　PEACE ACTION is the largest grassroots peace group in our nation's history.　With your renewed support, PEACE ACTION will redouble its effort for legislation that will:

o Reduce the number of nuclear weapons in the world.

o Lower the military budget -- and increase investment in meeting domestic needs.

o Offer job training to workers in defense plants, and provide businesses with funds to help them convert to civilian production.

o Fund the clean-up of thousands of toxic dump sites the military has left all over country.

o Curb the global arms trade and nuclear weapons proliferation.

As a member of PEACE ACTION, you are the sole source of our strength.　Your support <u>matters</u>.

Please renew your membership <u>today</u>.　Thank you!

In Peace,

Peter Deccy
Membership Director

February 20, 1993

Dear Former PEACE ACTION Member,

Your past support helped make PEACE ACTION the largest grassroots peace organization in American history.

Because you were so steadfast in your backing for SANE/FREEZE: Campaign for Global Security (our former name), I want to ask you one more time to renew your membership.

Your PEACE ACTION membership may be far more important than you think -- for three reasons:

(1)   Your dues provide <u>financial</u> <u>support</u> for the peace movement -- doubly important these days, when so many funders have gone on to more glamorous and higher-profile issues.

(2)   Our <u>strength</u> <u>in</u> <u>numbers</u> gives us clout on Capitol Hill when key military spending bills are on the table.

(3)   Your participation lends <u>moral</u> <u>support</u> to PEACE ACTION staff and other activists all across the country.

Your support for PEACE ACTION during the past five years has enabled us to build a powerful movement for new priorities. Now we're on the verge of winning a shift in government spending --<u>away</u> from expensive and unnecessary military spending and <u>toward</u> increased investment in our country's economic future.

But the military-industrial complex has been busy, too. They've launched a major campaign to keep military spending at Cold War levels.

Please don't let their greed shatter the hope we all feel!

Weapons sold during the Cold War are causing havoc around the world. (During the 1980's, the U.S. transferred over $300 million in weapons to Somalia alone!) Yet, the practice of weapons transfers continues, creating tomorrow's excuse for Cold War levels of military spending.

Only a strong, effective peace movement can hold the Clinton Administration to remain true to the promise of global cooperation and increased investment in our future.

<u>Please</u> <u>restore</u> <u>your</u> <u>membership</u> <u>today</u>. You are our strength!

In Peace,

Peter Deccy
Membership Director

PART THREE

The Letter-Writer's Toolbox

18

WHAT TO PUT ON THE OUTER ENVELOPE

The best envelope teaser ever written

Teasers suck.

Outer envelope teasers — those brassy, cute, provocative little half-statements and promises — are the bane of a copywriter's existence. I despise teasers. I can write two thousand words in the time it takes me to devise a really good teaser. More often than not, I have to settle for one that's less than ideal. Writing a teaser can drive me stark, raving *nuts!*

Yet, as the double meaning of my two-word, tongue-in-cheek lead to this chapter implies, teasers — at their best — can entice the reader to open the envelope, which nothing else may be able to bring off. A teaser that's doing its job will challenge, question, or intrigue the reader, drawing her more deeply into the "silent dialogue" that later . . . *maybe* . . . gives birth to a gift.

So teasers work. Sometimes.

However, if you've read the foregoing chapters, you're now intensely aware that fundraising letters come in a dazzling variety of shapes, sizes, flavors, and types. Like everything else in a fundraising package, the outer envelope teaser must be appropriate to its type. For example, it's hard to imagine how any of the following teasers could be used on an outer envelope for a donor acquisition package:

It's time to renew!

Special Bulletin for Members Only

Your newsletter is enclosed

All these are teasers as surely as the most outrageous come-on for a "free gift" or a petition to the president of the U.S. So are such seemingly off-handed statements as "First Class Mail" or "Official Documents."

Often, the very best teaser is no teaser at all.

Take, for example, the outer envelope pictured on page 223. That envelope, an oversized (9 x 12") closed-face carrier, was part of a High-Dollar fundraising package. As you can see, the envelope bears first class stamps and the only words in sight are those in the address and in the "corner card" (where

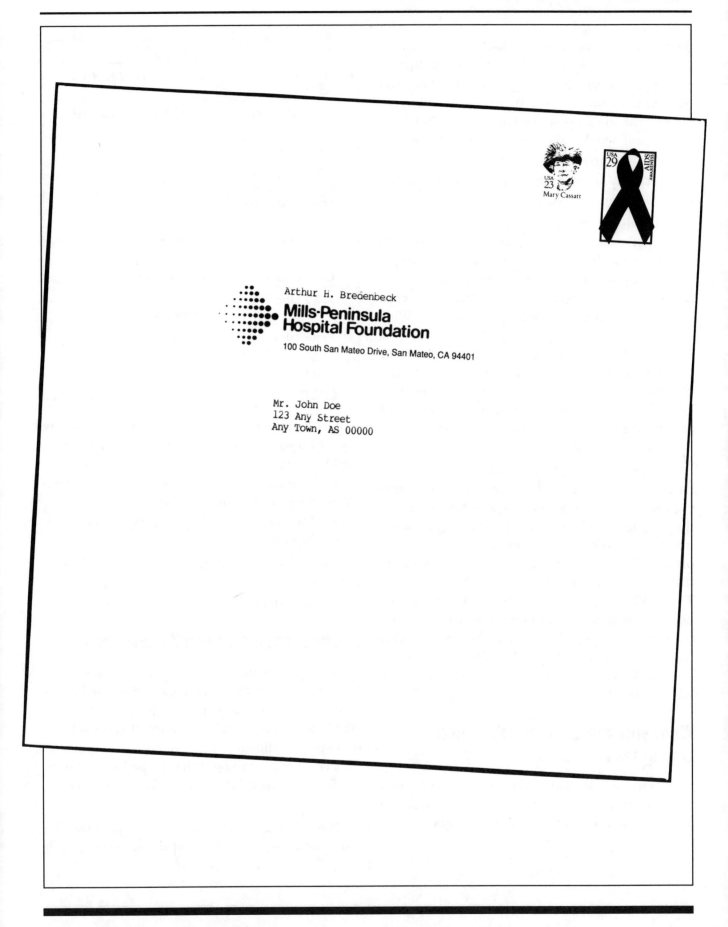

Arthur H. Bregenbeck

**Mills·Peninsula
Hospital Foundation**

100 South San Mateo Drive, San Mateo, CA 94401

Mr. John Doe
123 Any Street
Any Town, AS 00000

the return address appears). There was no teaser in the generally accepted sense of that term. But for that appeal, at that time, the *absence* of a teaser was the best possible come-on. Words calculated to call greater attention to the contents or otherwise hype the appeal would likely have *depressed* response rather than boosted it.

That's why I regard the "teaser" in the illustration as the best one ever written.

Fundraising letters are almost always crafted to mimic personal letters. So teasers may well cheapen or undermine the effect the writer hopes to achieve. In fact, extensive testing suggests that response isn't necessarily higher when you use a teaser — even when it seems eminently appropriate to do so. Why? Because, I believe, only *really good* teasers have the intended effect. Teasers that fall short of the mark probably have no effect whatsoever — or, worse, they may persuade the reader *not* to open the envelope! After all, for most people nowadays, teasers are a dead giveaway for what all too many reflexively look on as junk mail.

It's hard to make general statements about outer envelope teasers, much less lay down rules and regulations about how to write them. Instead, I'll do three things in this chapter. (1) I'll list some of the many different kinds of teasers and show an example of each. (2) I'll tell you about thirty of the teasers that have impressed me the most. And (3) I'll list Thirty All-Time Favorite Teasers from five of my peers in the practice of raising money by mail. My hope in approaching the subject this way is to tickle your imagination. Perhaps I'll help lead you to write a few all-time favorite teasers for your own fundraising letters!

What you can accomplish with a strong teaser

To increase the likelihood the reader will open your appeal, you might write a teaser to fill any one of the needs listed in the table that follows.

Function	Example
Describe the contents	*Membership Card Enclosed*
Establish urgency	*Your response needed within 10 days.*
Hint at advantages	*R.S.V.P.*
Flag the importance of the contents	*Membership Survey*
Start a story	*She was only 11 years old. She was as old as the hills.*
Offer a benefit	*Your Free Gift Enclosed*
Ask a question	*Would you spend $1 a day to save the life of a child?*
Pique curiosity	*What do these people have in common?*
Challenge the reader	*Take this simple quiz to learn your Health I.Q.*

There are both advantages and pitfalls in every one of these approaches. For example, the reader might answer a loud NO! to the question you pose, be totally unconvinced by your lame effort to establish urgency, or be miffed by the offer of a free gift. In other words, none of these approaches are guaranteed to work — *ever*.

But teasers *can* deliver. Let's take a close look now at thirty of them that really do — at least as far as I'm concerned.

Thirty of my own favorite teasers

My own all-time favorite outer envelope teaser from the fundraising field was one I didn't write. It's pictured at the top of page 225. Judge for yourself whether it inspires *you*. It certainly intrigued a lot of other people, though. That teaser has been remailed for many years running. It has helped recruit hundreds of thousands of members for Handgun Control, Inc.

The best teaser I've ever written myself was the one that appears at the bottom of page 225. It

ENCLOSED:
Your first real chance
to tell the National
Rifle Association to
go to hell!...

Recycled Paper

Nellie
Red Owl
wants a
piece of
your
mind . . .

59186
LARRY BENSKY
P.O. BOX 40247
SAN FRANCISCO, CA

***

94140

worked well, I believe, because the letter (which I *didn't* write) asked readers to do precisely what the envelope copy implied: to "give Nellie Red Owl a piece of their minds" — by jotting down a greeting or comment that could be read on the air of the Native American-run radio station that was the beneficiary of this appeal. In other words — and this is key, I believe — the teaser didn't just sucker readers into opening the envelope. It *delivered*.

Now, here are a few of my other recent favorites:

◆ From the National Republican Senatorial Committee (Washington, DC) — "rubber stamped" in red ink on an 11-1/2 x 14-1/2" brown Kraft envelope bearing six postage stamps (totaling 78¢):

PRE-PAID FEDERAL EXPRESS ENVELOPE ENCLOSED

◆ From the Smithsonian Institution (Washington, DC) — typeset in red ink on a white 6 x 9" window carrier next to a full-color illustration of a Native American ceremonial mask:

Open Carefully . . . You may unleash a powerful spirit

◆ From Worldwatch Institute (Washington, DC) — in large blue type dominating a white #10 window envelope:

"I read your State of the World every year." – Bill Clinton

Maybe you should too . . .

◆ From KQED (San Francisco, CA) — printed in blue and black ink on a 3-7/8 x 7-1/2" white window envelope

NOTICE OF ENROLLMENT:

Membership card enclosed.

Confirmation requested.

◆ From MADD (Mothers Against Drunk Driving, Irving, TX) — typeset in red ink on a white #10 window envelope next to a second window through which a real penny shows:

Because many people who sell alcohol think pennies are more important than human lives . . .

◆ From the Southern Poverty Law Center (Montgomery, AL) — typeset in bold black type in the corner card of a brown Kraft #11 window carrier:

Bill Moyers

◆ From the American Civil Liberties Union (New York, NY) — typeset in black ink on a tan #10 window envelope, with the word "Don't" underlined in bold red:

"We believe every American has the right to be different and not be punished for it." Don't open this envelope unless you agree!

◆ From Project HOPE (Millwood, VA) — a note handwritten in black ink above a headline in a broad yellow band stretching across the bottom of a 4 x 8" white window envelope:

Critical that you read this today. W.B.W.

URGENT: SOMALIA UPDATE

◆ From Common Cause (Washington, DC) — alternately typeset and laser-printed in blue, black and red ink on a white 9-1/4 x 13-1/2" personalized packet:

DO NOT FORWARD

CRITICAL INFORMATION PREPARED FOR:

[my name and address]

PETITIONS ENCLOSED FOR:

PRESIDENT GEORGE BUSH

SENATE MAJORITY LEADER GEORGE MITCHELL

HOUSE SPEAKER TOM FOLEY

IMMEDIATE RETURN REQUESTED BY: [date]

◆ From the Victory Fund (Washington, DC) — printed in blue and red on a white #10 window envelope:

OK, THE ELECTION WENT OUR WAY. NOW WHAT?

AN IMMODEST PROPOSAL ENCLOSED FOR:

[my name and address]

◆ From the Sierra Club (San Francisco, CA) — typeset in bold black and blue on a white #10 carrier:

Your Sierra Club membership EXPIRES THIS MONTH!

◆ From Last Chance for Animals (Tarzana, CA) — typeset in black and red ink above and below a photo of a pathetic puppy showing through a large second window on a white #10 envelope:

Would you go to jail to keep a puppy from being tortured?

WE ARE!

◆ From the American Association of University Women (Washington, DC), just the latest example of an old chestnut that seems to work so often — typeset in an elegant face across the top of a window on a cream-colored #10 carrier:

The Favor of a Reply is Requested . . .

◆ From the New Forests Project (Washington, DC) — typeset in white and red type within and below a broad band of dark green across the front of a two-window #10 outer (with seeds showing through the second window):

FREE SEEDS ENCLOSED

This miracle tree could mean a new life for the world's poor . . .

NOTE: If no seeds are visible, tip the envelope.

◆ From In the Life/Media Network (New York, NY) — printed in purple and gold across the front of a white #10 window envelope, alongside playful drawings and a shield-like circular emblem featuring a Mickey Mouse hat:

CHANGE THE FACE OF TELEVISION!

THIS AIN'T NO MICKEY MOUSE CLUB

◆ From St. Jude Children's Research Hospital (Memphis, TN) — handwritten in dark blue ink on the *back* of a white 3-7/8 x 7-1/2" window carrier:

Would you give $10 . . . just $10 . . . to help save a child's life?

◆ From the National Audubon Society (New York, NY) — set inside a band of red and blue on a perforated strip outlined in dashes above a personalized membership card that appears in an odd-sized window at the center of a 6 x 9" white outer:

PULL HERE FOR YOUR FREE BACKPACK (details inside)

◆ From the Sierra Club Legal Defense Fund (San Francisco, CA) — handwritten and underlined with a scrawl in dark blue ink across the face of a gray 4 x 7-1/2" window envelope:

A personal reminder

◆ From Americans for a Balanced Budget (Falls Church, VA) — handwritten above the window on a white #10 envelope:

Have you heard about Bill Clinton's NEW TAX? Details Inside . . .

◆ From Feed the Children (Oklahoma City, OK) — handwritten in red ink in the upper left-hand corner of a white #10 window outer:

What would you do with 500,000 pounds of BEANS?

◆ From the Nature Conservancy (Arlington, VA), on one of the most unusual and celebrated membership acquisition packages of recent years — printed in black ink in several different typefaces and at different angles, alongside fingers pointing to (a) a full-color portrait of a startled-looking ostrich and (b) my name and address showing through the window of a white 6 x 9" outer:

RELAX!

Both of you.

(A $10 nest egg will do it.)

(Do not fold. Bumper sticker enclosed.)

◆ From the Democratic National Committee (Washington, DC) — "typed" upper left in black and printed in dark blue on the right on what appears to be a standard bluish #10 airmail envelope (with red and blue stripes around the perimeter):

Bill Clinton

430 South Capitol Street, SE

Washington, DC 20003

VIA AIR MAIL

◆ From the Coalition to Stop Gun Violence (Washington, DC) — typeset in huge red letters on a self-contained, 11 x 15" "doormat" package beneath an official-looking address section that includes a personalized "Registered Survey Number":

IMPORTANT SURVEY ON GUN CONTROL ENCLOSED

◆ From Habitat for Humanity International (Americus, GA) — typeset above the window on a bright red 6 x 9" outer beneath a corner card reading only, "Rosalynn Carter":

Christmas Card Enclosed . . .

◆ From the American Family Association (Tupelo, MS) — printed in large blue letters across the face of a #11 white window envelope:

Here's your chance to help stop filth on television.

◆ From World Vision (Monrovia, CA) — typeset in black in the upper left-hand corner of a closed-face white 5-3/4 x 8-3/8" envelope

Enclosed: Important Information Regarding U.S. Government Grants

◆ From the Oakland Museum/Museum of California Foundation (Oakland, CA) — set in contrasting typefaces in red and green inks on the *front* of a #10 white window outer embellished with nondescript but elegant-looking designs in pale pink . . . and continued on the *back* in simple red block letters:

STEP INSIDE FOR A TASTE OF

The Good Life

YOUR FREE TICKETS FOR A PRIVATE TOUR ARE ENCLOSED

◆ From the People's Advocate, Inc. (Sacramento, CA) — printed in black above the window on a white #10 outer:

Do you want to lose the Property Tax Exemption for your home?

Another thirty all-time favorite teasers

Taste in teasers is a function of style as well as the character and circumstances of the charities that use them. To give you a broader range of examples than my own files and taste will permit, I turned for help to my colleagues in the Association of Direct Response Fundraising Counsel (ADRFCO), the trade association for companies that provide direct mail fundraising services to nonprofit organizations. Several firms responded to my call for nominees for the All-Time Favorite Fundraising Envelope Teasers.

I received eighteen nominees from Charlene Divoky (Divoky & Associates). The following are the ones that teased me the most. The nonprofit mailer's name appears below the teaser text that was printed on the front of the outer envelope:

P.S. We named the duck Harold.

Community Service Society of New York

Why don't woodpeckers get headaches?

Boston Public Library Foundation

The committee's decision is official ...
your Kind Human Award is enclosed.

Northeast Animal Shelter

Me? Sleep in a subway station?

Community Service Society of New York

Enclosed: The Life or Death Seed Catalog

U.S. Committee for UNICEF

She finally allowed herself to be rescued.

Northeast Animal Shelter

Michael P. Scholl (Direct Mail Decision Makers, Inc.) sent me twenty-five teaser candidates. Here are the ones I liked the most:

How Sister Alice became GRANDMA

Missionary Sisters of the Immaculate Conception

Father Carl . . . brutally murdered

Passionist Missions

One of the hardest letters I've ever had to write

Missionary Servant of the Most Blessed Trinity

Fr. Bob is an Alcoholic and he's going through a private hell!

Guest House

Rejoice with me . . .

Old Saint Mary's Church, San Francisco, CA

She arrived at the Grotto with tears in her eyes

Missionary Sisters of the Immaculate Conception

Here are a few of the best teasers I received from Wendy Fisher (Mailworks):

FACT: *At 91, Emily Smithtown doesn't have a friend in the world. Not even one.*

Little Brothers/Friends of the Elderly

Think kids are safer at home than on the street? Think again.

Night Ministry/Youth Shelter Network

FACT: Last year we distributed over 22 million pounds of food to hungry people.
FACT: It wasn't enough.

Greater Chicago Food Depository

Will you be killed by a handgun in the next 23 minutes?

[BACK FLAP]: Someone will be.

Illinois Citizens for Handgun Control

Come. Step with me for a minute into Emily's apartment.

Little Brothers/Friends of the Elderly

She dared to have a dream – that one day her beloved mountain gorillas would be safe.

Safe to roam their Viruna mountains in search of food . . . safe to give birth . . . rear their young . . . safe – so that their species can survive.

Dian Fossey nurtured her dream . . . she died with that dream . . .

But her beloved gorillas are still not safe.

Dian Fossey Gorilla Fund

Here, now, are some verbal letter openers from Robert E. Hoagland (L. W. Robbins Associates):

They Were the Last Words Lisa's Parents Expected to Hear . . . And They Changed Her World Forever!

Joslin Diabetes Center

What Has No Wings, Flies, and Is Called an Angel?

Arkansas Children's Hospital Foundation

"When it Comes to Courage, This Kid Is an All-Star!"

Dana-Farber Cancer Institute/The Jimmy Fund

Your Personal Emergency Relief Kit
Open to Activate

American Red Cross of Massachusetts Bay

The Cat Licked Her Face. And for a Moment, the Woman and the World Were Young Again.

Bide-a-Wee Home Association

Here are some of the teasers suggested by my colleague, Bill Rehm (Mal Warwick & Associates):

They're at it again!

California telephone customer alert

Toward Utility Rate Normalization

My son was 29 years old when he died.

Hyacinth Foundation

[HANDWRITTEN:] I need to know what <u>YOU</u> think.

Wellstone Alliance

Can you remember where you were on June 5, 1981?

Shanti Project

IMPORTANT NOTICE about your telephone bill

Please read before paying

Toward Utility Rate Normalization

ARE YOU PREPARED FOR FIRE?

Checklist enclosed

American Red Cross/Bay Area

WELCOME BACK!

Toward Utility Rate Normalization

Now, the next to the last stop on our journey through the world of fundraising letters: a little something to help you overcome writer's block. ▶

19

HOW TO OVERCOME WRITER'S BLOCK

My experience in *editing* hundreds of fundraising letters for dozens of charities has given me a unique perspective on *writing* appeals. I've learned what most fundraisers find to be the biggest writing challenges — because I see how their draft efforts most commonly fall short. Here's where the challenges are most likely to arise:

◆ *In the lead sentence of the letter* — because it's tough to get started on the right foot!

◆ *In using the word "you"* (and other techniques to establish a dialogue with the reader) — because it's so much easier for most of us to write about a charity's familiar needs rather than its donors' hard-to-pin-down benefits

◆ *In writing smooth transitions* from one point to the next — because it requires skill and experience to stitch together unrelated thoughts and keep a story flowing forward (especially if you keep splicing in more and more references to "you"!)

◆ *In ending the letter* – because, more often than not, the closing lines are an afterthought (a dangerous and often costly practice)

◆ *In writing an effective P.S.* – because the postscript in a fundraising letter bears so much heavier a load than it does in almost any other kind of letter

To help you on your way in meeting these challenges, I've pulled together crib-sheets for the problems listed above. There are two ways to use them. (a) As an amusing assortment of copywriting ideas that will reassure you because they're so many and varied. Or (b) as a crutch you can lean on if you suddenly turn unsteady and feel the pavement looming up as you start writing an especially troublesome appeal.

I had a lot of fun putting this chapter together, but I didn't do it alone. The five lists represent some of the best work of my colleagues at Mal Warwick & Associates. Significantly, ideas were suggested by staff involved in almost every phase of the creative and production process: Stephen Hitchcock, Bill

Rehm, Julie Levak, Deborah Agre, Judy Reimann, Marsha Mathews, Lissa Rosenbloom, Julie Weiden-bach, Cherie Chavez, Christina Chavez, Sheila Bell, and Ramona Allen. Julie Levak and Deborah Agre won a free lunch at the famed Chez Panisse Café for contributing more ideas to the lists than anyone else — a total of seventy-one between the two. (You see? Writing fundraising letters *can* be fun!)

Strong Leads for Fundraising Letters

1. Thank you . . . !
2. I'm writing you today . . .
3. You are among the first . . .
4. You may be surprised to learn . . .
5. Did you know that . . . ?
6. Don't you wish . . . ?
7. It's no secret that . . .
8. You've probably said to yourself . . .
9. Think about it for a moment.
10. Let's face it.
11. If you sincerely want to . . .
12. I wish you could have been with me when . . .
13. I was sure you'd want to know that . . .
14. I can't get the image out of my mind . . .
15. I still wake up in the middle of the night . . .
16. I've just returned from . . .
17. I need to hear from you this week about . . .
18. I don't want to waste words or paper . . .
19. I don't usually write such long letters . . .
20. We tried to reach you by phone . . .
21. According to our records, your membership has lapsed.
22. Will you please take a moment right now to renew your membership?
23. I want to tell you a story about . . .
24. You won't believe it.
25. As I was passing through _____ recently, I . . .
26. I've just returned from . . .
27. I want to tell you about a remarkable . . .
28. I'm writing to invite you . . .
29. I'd like to take just a few moments of your time to . . .
30. I hope you'll take a moment right now to . . .
31. Because you've been so generous . . .
32. I'm writing you this urgent letter today because . . .
33. It's been awhile since I heard from you . . .
34. I have exciting news for you!
35. I'm writing you today because _____ is/are in grave danger.
36. Have you ever wondered . . . ?
37. Do you ever feel . . . ?
38. I want to share a recent experience with you.
39. I want to give you the latest information on . . .
40. I hope you'll be as excited as I am to learn . . .
41. Have you ever wanted to be part of . . . ?
42. Have you ever said to yourself . . . ?
43. If you've always wanted to . . .
44. Haven't you wondered how you could help . . . ?
45. It's no surprise that . . .
46. It's hard to believe, but . . .
47. I know you'll be interested to know that . . .
48. I know you'll want to be a part of this . . .
49. Let's be frank.
50. I have a secret.

51. You've been chosen . . .

52. If you've seen the recent headlines, you're well aware . . .

53. Someone you know . . .

54. I'd like to say it isn't so.

Outstanding Ways to Use the Word "You" in a Fundraising Letter

1. Thank you for . . .

2. Thank you very much for . . .

3. Thank you again for . . .

4. As you know,

5. I'm writing you today . . .

6. I'm sure you'll agree that . . .

7. With your generous support,

8. Because you helped,

9. You are among the first . . .

10. You're the kind of person who . . .

11. I know that you . . .

12. Would you believe that . . . ?

13. As I wrote you recently,

14. Did you know that . . . ?

15. I don't know about you, but I . . .

16. Will you spend just pennies a day to . . . ?

17. How many times have you said to yourself . . .?

18. You're among the few I can count on to . . .

19. I was delighted to hear from you.

20. You're among our most generous supporters.

21. Now, at last, you can . . .

22. You're in for a pleasant surprise.

23. Have you ever wondered . . . ?

24. . . . may astonish you.

25. You may never forgive yourself if . . .

26. The benefits to you are substantial.

27. You can rely on . . .

28. You'll be joining the ranks of . . .

29. None of this would be possible without your generous help.

30. You owe it to yourself to explore this opportunity.

31. You've helped in the past, and your generosity . . .

32. Your membership gift . . .

33. You're one of our most generous supporters . . .

34. You've been with us for a long time, and . . .

35. As one of our newest members, you . . .

36. I want to tell you about . . .

37. It's people like you who . . .

38. I know, like me, you must feel . . .

39. You're such an important friend . . .

40. Through the years, you've been . . .

41. You've shown just how much you care . . .

42. You may be shocked . . .

43. You may be surprised . . .

44. I've noticed you haven't . . .

45. Working together, you and I . . .

46. You're one of the few people who truly understand . . .

47. You should be proud of what we've accomplished together.

48. With your special gift, _____ can . . .

49. Your gift can make the difference between . . .

50. You can help them (grow strong, live a better life) . . .

51. You helped prevent . . .

52. When _____ happened, you were there.

53. Have you ever felt like . . . ?

54. Have you ever wished you . . . "

55. Please believe me — you can . . .

56. Like me, you may . . .

57. I can tell you from my own experience . . .

58. I've seen firsthand how you . . .

59. When you join . . .

60. I'll be pleased to send you . . .

61. I need to hear from you by _____ . . .

62. I'll keep you informed . . .

63. I'll want to keep you involved . . .

64. It may seem to you . . .

65. You've helped so many people with . . . !

66. Now you can play a leadership role . . .

67. Can you believe . . . ?

68. Have you seen . . . ?

69. What would you think if . . . ?

70. Because of people like you . . .

71. You're just the kind of person who . . .

72. How can you, as a _____, . . . ?

73. You and others like you are _____'s only hope!

74. Have you ever noticed . . . ?

75. Can I rely on you to . . . ?

76. I hope you'll consider . . .

77. You're someone who . . .

78. You can rest assured that . . .

79. You may never again have an opportunity to . . .

80. You're not someone to stand by while . . .

81. Your gift really will make a difference.

82. What can you do? _____ things:

83. You, too, can be part of this _____ project.

84. I want you by my side (again) at this critical time.

85. This is all possible because of you.

86. You probably had no idea . . .

87. Find out for yourself.

88. Here's a new opportunity for you.

89. For you, free of charge.

90. Reserved for you:

Ways to Handle Awkward Copywriting Transitions

1. As I'm sure you'll understand,

2. But that's not all.

3. [Use subheads.]

4. But now, for the first time,

5. Today, more than ever,

6. Best of all,

7. Here's why:

8. Thi

   nk of it:

9. One thing's for sure:

10. The truth is,

11. To show you what I mean,

12. I'm hoping you'll agree.

13. And there's more:

14. It's that simple!

15. It's now or never.

16. There's never been a better time.

17. Am I claiming too much? I don't think so.

18. That's why I'm writing you today.

19. In addition,

20. Not only that, but . . .

21. And . . .

22. Now,

23. Next,

24. [Indent paragraph]

25. Before I tell you . . .

26. As you can see,

27. Because it's people like you who . . .

28. Because there's no time to lose.

29. But wait, that's not all.

30. Why am I so concerned? Because . . .

31. Let me explain . . .

32. In a moment I'll tell you more about _____. But first . . .

33. And, most important of all, . . .

34. That's what _____ is all about.

35. It may seem hard to believe, but . . .

36. There's so much at stake!

37. Let me tell you more.

38. That's why I'm asking you to do three things right now.

39. The recent news from _____ is shocking, but I'm sure you know . . .

40. To clarify what I mean . . .

41. Now is the time to . . .

42. But wait: there's more.

43. Just imagine:

44. Consider the consequences:

45. In other words,

46. Put yourself in their place:

47. Time is of the essence.

48. Can you think of a better way to . . . ?

49. It's sad but true:

50. I know how you feel about _____ because you _____.

51. Will you help?

52. Are you willing to take the next step to . . . ?

53. Why wait?

54. It's clear that . . .

55. Despite the lack of media attention . . .

56. I think you'll agree that . . .

57. The truth hurts.

58. I know this isn't pleasant . . .

59. As you know very well . . .

60. Act now, and we'll . . .

61. If you really think about it . . .

62. Ask yourself:

63. Now that you know . . .

Powerful Ways to End a Fundraising Letter

1. Thank you for caring so very much!

2. You may not know their names, but they'll carry thanks in their hearts for your kindness and generosity.

3. From the bottom of my heart, thank you!

4. Your investment will bear dividends for years to come.

5. I'm sure you'll be glad you did.

6. Isn't that what life is really all about?

7. So you can't lose!

8. Don't miss this unique opportunity!

9. It's up to you.

11. May I hear from you soon?

12. The future is in your hands.

13. And that can make all the difference in the world!

14. I'm counting on you!

15. In return, you'll have the satisfaction of knowing that . . .

16. Together, we will . . .

17. With your help, we'll . . .

18. The satisfaction you'll receive is indescribable.

19. Thank you for joining me in this . . .

20. I'm looking forward to hearing from you very soon.

21. Together, I know we can . . .

22. When you look back at this moment in history . . .

23. Please, if you feel the way I do, . . .

24. I can't think of a better gift to give our children and grandchildren than . . .

25. Thank you for your compassion.

26. I know you won't be disappointed.

27. Please, send your gift today.

28. And I promise to send you _____ just as soon as . . .

29. Thank you for taking the time to help.

30. I know I can count on you!

31. My warmest wishes to you.

32. You'll be so glad you decided to help!

33. You'll be proud to be part of _____!

34. The _____ are depending on you!

35. _____ won't forget you!

36. I can't thank you enough.

37. I believe you'll make the right choice.

38. Please act today!

39. This is your chance to . . .

40. With your help, _____ will have a chance to . . .

41. Please show them they're not alone!

Ways to Start a P.S. in Your Fundraising Letter

1. Thank you again for . . .

2. If you respond within the next X days, you'll receive . . .

3. If you send $X or more, you'll receive . . .

4. There's not much time.

5. The enclosed X are yours to keep — our gift to you.

6. Please use the enclosed X to . . .

7. If $X is too much for you to give at this time, will you consider a gift of $Y, or $Z?

8. We need to _____ by _____, so please send your gift today.

9. Your gift of $_____ makes it possible for . . .

10. Please don't set this letter aside.

11. Remember, if you respond by . . .

12. Please take a look at the _____ I've enclosed for you.

13. As a special benefit for the first _____ people who respond, I'll . . .

14. And remember, your gift is tax deductible.

15. I've always regarded you as one of our strongest supporters, so . . .

16. Please don't wait . . .

17. Every day that goes by . . .

18. I hope I can count on receiving your gift in the next _____ days.

19. Please, as always, feel free to contact me at (phone number) if you have any questions about . . .

20. If you decide not to join us in this crucial effort, I hope you'll take a moment to write and tell me why.

21. Just as soon as I return from _____, I'll let you know how . . .

22. I need to send that shipment of _____ in the next _____ days, so . . .

23. Don't forget: . . .

24. You've come through so many times in the past, and I hope I can count on you again now.

25. _____ need(s) your help today.

26. Did you know that . . . ?

27. If you act by _____, . . .

28. Your gift of _____ will make it possible for _____ to get _____.

29. $_____ is just _____ per day!

30. For less than a cup of coffee a day . . .

31. I promised _____ that . . . .

32. When I look into the eyes of _____

33. Unless you and I act immediately, ...

34. Please know that your gift is _____'s only hope for _____.

35. Without your help, _____ don't stand a chance.

36. Won't you please take out your checkbook now and . . .

37. I hope I can count on you to respond by _____.

38. Take a moment right now to look at the enclosed _____. I'm sure you'll feel the same as I do:

39. I hope you'll enjoy — and use — the enclosed _____.

40. Remember, to reach our goal by _____, we need . . . .

41. I can't stress enough how much your support will mean to us!

42. With your support, I can't . . .

43. It's members like you who . . .

44. There's no better time to . . .

45. Don't miss this chance to . . .

46. I'd like to hear your thoughts about . . .

47. Don't delay.

48. If your check and this letter have crossed in the mail, . . .

49. What may seem a small gift to you can . . .

50. I know it's hard to imagine _____, but . . .

51. Put yourself in _____'s place for a moment.

52. All it takes to _____ is $_____!

53. If you and I don't do something right now, . . .

54. If you won't help, who will?

55. Remember, every day that goes by without our help, . . .

56. Please find it in your heart to give. Even just a little gift will help!

57. _____ need(s) to know that someone cares.

58. Thanks to friends like you . . . ▶

20

TEN OTHER BOOKS TO HELP YOU WRITE SUCCESSFUL FUNDRAISING LETTERS

You might be surprised just how many books have been published on the subject of letterwriting. Books about letters that are effective or powerful — or tried and tested. Books of "classic" or "all-time great" letters. Books of model letters. Books about sales letters. Books about business letters. Even several books specifically devoted to fundraising letters — including several volumes of sample letters.

However, I've found very few of those books to be useful. In fact, some are dangerously misleading.

It's disappointing. The books by writers whose experience lies outside fundraising sometimes make suggestions inappropriate to this very peculiar field of ours. Some of the books written by people with extensive fundraising experience have fallen into the trap of dogmatism ("This worked for me once, so it's got to work for you."). And the collections of letters pose problems of their own, since the implication is that a letter published in a book of "good" letters is a "good" model for any fundraiser to follow.

The following list, arranged in alphabetical order by the authors' last name, includes only those books I genuinely believe you'll find useful. It's a short list.

◆ Caples, John. *Tested Advertising Methods*, 4th edition. Englewood Cliffs, NJ: Prentice-Hall, 1974. $9.95. Paperback, 318 pp. John Caples virtually invented the field of direct response copywriting. His classic 1920s ad, "They laughed when I sat down to play the piano," is so well known it's become what is probably the only certifiable cliché in the business. Although Caples wrote space advertising in the main, not fundraising letters, the principles he developed through years of exhaustive testing are as applicable today — and in the writing of fundraising letters — as they were when Caples wrote his ads.

◆ Flesch, Rudolf. *How to Write, Speak and Think More Effectively*, New York, NY: New American Library, 1963. $4.50. Paperback, 352 pp. Generations of Americans have turned to Dr. Rudolf Flesch for advice on effective writing and speaking. Much of his teaching is summed up in this wonderfully useful little volume, first copyrighted in 1946 but still readily available in paperback. Flesch's extensive and well-known findings on "readability" are threaded through the text, and it's chock full of concrete and colorful examples. This book brims over with insight and useful advice — and it's a treasure chest of fascinating information for anyone intrigued by the dynamics of human language.

◆ Huntsinger, Jerry. *Fund Raising Letters: A Comprehensive Study Guide to Raising Money by Direct Response Marketing*, 3d edition. Richmond, VA: Emerson Publishers, 1989. Priced at $155.00 ($110 for nonprofit organizations) but now out of print. This is a thick looseleaf notebook; there's no sequential page numbering. There's a whole lot of common sense in this overview of direct mail fundraising, first published in 1982. As the main title implies, this workbook emphasizes letter writing. It's worthwhile reading because it's based on Jerry's own experience writing fundraising appeals for hundreds of charities over several decades. He sold a lot of copies of this book while it was in print. Chances are, you can find one in a library (especially a Foundation Center library) or on the shelves of a friend who's been around the fundraising field for several years.

◆ Lautman, Kay Partney, and Henry Goldstein. *Dear Friend: Mastering the Art of Direct Mail Fund Raising*, 2d edition, Rockville, MD: The Taft Group, 1991. $59.95. Hardcover, 378 pp. This widely circulated manual, which covers the general topic of direct mail fundraising, is useful for the aspiring copywriter because of its heavy emphasis on the creation of the direct mail fundraising package. Pages 91 to 264 are devoted to this topic. The book is filled with examples — along with commentary that makes them truly useful.

◆ Ogilvy, David. *Ogilvy on Advertising*, New York, NY: Vintage Books, 1983. $12.95. Paperback, 224 pp. The dean of the advertising industry is a direct marketer at heart, and one of its most articulate and insightful writers. Reading Ogilvy's several useful books is one of the best possible ways for a fledgling copywriter to gain entry to the mysteries of writing fundraising letters.

◆ Strunk, William, Jr., and E. B. White. *The Elements of Style*, 3d edition, New York, NY: MacMillan Publishing, 1979. $5.95. Paperback, 92 pp. If you write anything more than grocery lists and are intent on improving the quality of your work, *read this book*. See Chapter 1 in this volume for further comments about this indispensable little classic.

◆ Trenbeth, Richard, *The Membership Mystique*. Rockville, MD: Fund-Raising Institute, 1986. $34.95. Paperback, 280 pp. This is a great resource for development professionals who want to fine-tune their membership development programs — or start one from scratch. Organizations without formal membership programs can learn a lot, too. The book is crammed with examples that reflect a sophisticated understanding of copywriting.

◆ Vögele, Siegfried. *Handbook of Direct Mail: The Dialogue Method of Direct Written Sales Communication*, Hemel Hempstead, UK: Verlag Moderne Industrie/Prentice Hall, 1992. Hardcover, 323 pp. Available from Strathmoor Press, 2550 Ninth Street, #1040, Berkeley, CA 94710 at $34.95 plus $3.50 shipping and handling and sales tax, if applicable. I never thought I'd read, much less highly recommend, a dry direct marketing textbook translated from the German. But the German professor who wrote this insightful book has been all the rage in European direct marketing circles for over a decade. Vögele is familiar to some Americans as the author of the eye-motion studies I wrote about in my earlier book *999 Tips, Trends and Guidelines for Successful Direct Mail and*

Telephone Fundraising. It's time now for Americans to start catching onto the wisdom of his Dialogue Method, which is a way of looking at direct mail that's based in large part — but goes far beyond — the professor's eye-motion research. I've commented at length on Vögele's Dialogue Method in Chapter 3.

◆ Warwick, Mal. *Revolution in the Mailbox: How Direct Mail Fundraising Is Changing the Face of American Society – And How Your Organization Can Benefit*, Strathmoor Press (1990), 2550 Ninth Street, #1040, Berkeley, CA 94710. $29.95 plus $3.00 shipping and handling. Hardcover, 313 pp. This book is my attempt to place direct mail fundraising in a larger context, spelling out the strategic potential and long-range impact of launching a direct mail fundraising program. The novice copywriter will find this book useful because it contains a great many sample fundraising letters, many of them reproduced in entirety (pp. 150-252), as well as my illustrated analysis of the components of a successful fundraising appeal (pp. 71-85).

◆ —————, with Deborah Block, Stephen Hitchcock, Ivan Levison and Joseph H. White, Jr. *999 Tips, Trends and Guidelines for Successful Direct Mail and Telephone Fundraising*, Strathmoor Press (1993), 2550 Ninth Street, #1040, Berkeley, CA 94710. $34.95 plus $3.50 shipping and handling. Paperback, 316 pp. "Writing Effective Fundraising Packages" is the title of Chapter 6 (pp. 175-205) in this general treatment of raising money by mail and telephone. Here you can benefit from hard-won advice from my collaborators, topflight writers one and all: Stephen Hitchcock, Deborah Block, and Ivan Levison.

A final word

You're unlikely to write a good fundraising appeal without understanding the dynamics of direct mail fundraising. If you're serious about this — if you want to raise more money for your organization — you'll read up on the basics. For the grounding you need, I recommend two of the books listed above: Lautman and Goldstein's *Dear Friend* and my own *Revolution in the Mailbox*. **Read those two books cover to cover, understand them, apply the lessons they teach – and you'll be off to a great start in your direct mail fundraising career.** ▶

ABOUT THE AUTHOR

Mal Warwick would be on everyone's list of the five greatest professionals in the field of direct mail and telephone fundraising.

He has founded four affiliated companies that provide a wide range of fundraising and marketing services to clients throughout North America. Mal is the author of four previous books and his monthly column on direct mail fundraising, "The Warwick File," runs in *The NonProfit Times*. His writing also appears frequently in other trade publications.

He is the author of *Revolution in the Mailbox: How Direct Mail Fundraising Is Changing the Face of American Society – And How Your Organization Can Benefit.* Published in 1990, *Revolution in the Mailbox* has been recognized as a standard in its field. Mal's second book, *You Don't Always Get What You Ask For: Using Direct Mail Tests to Raise More Money for Your Organization*, appeared in 1992. *999 Tips, Trends and Guidelines for Successful Direct Mail and Telephone Fundraising* was published in March 1993. *Technology and the Future of Fundraising* followed in January 1994. All four books, like this one, were published by Strathmoor Press (Berkeley, CA).

Strathmoor Press is also the publisher of Mal's fast-growing quarterly newsletter, *Successful Direct Mail & Telephone Fundraising*.

The author is chairman of Mal Warwick & Associates, Inc. (Berkeley, CA), which he established in 1979. The firm specializes in direct mail fundraising for nonprofit organizations.

Mal is also cofounder and chairman of The Progressive Group, Inc. (Hadley, MA), which offers telephone fundraising services. And he's the founder and president of Response Management Technologies, Inc. (Berkeley, CA), a provider of caging, cashiering, list maintenance, and data processing services.

These three affiliated companies have served more than four hundred nonprofit organizations, including some of the largest fundraisers in the nation. Mal's list of clients also includes five recent presidential candidates.

Through Changing America, Inc., Mal operates EditEXPRESS™ and has completed editorial and consulting projects for the Environmental Defense Fund, Apple Computer, Inc., Salvation Army, Jewish Community Federation of San Francisco, Ben & Jerry's Homemade Ice Cream, and Co-op America, among others.

Mal is president of the Association of Direct Response Fundraising Counsel (the national trade association of direct mail fundraising agencies), and a member of the National Society of Fund Raising Executives (NSFRE). He organized NSFRE's first-ever full-scale educational programs on direct mail fundraising at the 1992 and 1993 International Conferences on Fund-Raising.

Mal was a cofounder of Business for Social Responsibility and served on its national board and executive committee in 1993, its first year. He currently serves as a director of five nonprofit organizations. He also cofounded a community foundation, the Berkeley Community Fund, in 1992, and serves on its board and as chair of its executive committee.

Mal was a 1963 graduate of the University of Michigan, studied international affairs at Columbia University, and was a Peace Corps volunteer in Ecuador from 1965 to 1969. ▶

INDEX

HOW TO ORDER MAL WARWICK'S BOOKS

How to Write Successful Fundraising Letters is Mal Warwick's fifth book on fundraising, and the fifth to be published by Strathmoor Press. His other books are:

◆ *Technology and the Future of Fundraising: The Interactive Edition* (1994). Softcover, 144 pages. 300 copies, numbered and signed by the author. A thought-provoking look at how emerging technologies will affect the prospects for fundraising in the 21st century. This is a long-term view in a field well known for focusing on the short term. $32

◆ *999 Tips, Trends and Guidelines for Successful Direct Mail and Telephone Fundraising* (1993). With Deborah Block, Stephen Hitchcock, Ivan Levison and Joseph H. White, Jr. Second printing. Softcover, 316 pages. A well-organized, easy-to-read compilation of 119 articles, plus many tips and timesavers, from Mal's newsletters, columns, and workshops. Covers fundraising trends, donor acquisition, upgrading, annual renewals, writing effective fundraising packages, design and production techniques, High-Dollar fundraising, telephone solicitation techniques, and lots more. $29.95

◆ *You Don't Always Get What You Ask For: Using Direct Mail Tests to Raise More Money for Your Organization* (1992). Third printing. Softcover, 126 pages. A jargon-free, fun-to-read introduction to the mind-bending improbabilities and complexities of direct mail testing. Full of money-saving suggestions about what to test and what not to test. $19.95

◆ *Revolution in the Mailbox: How Direct Mail Fundraising Is Changing the Face of American Society – And How Your Organization Can Benefit* (1990). Hardcover, 312 pages. A best-selling introduction to the field of fundraising by mail. Rejects fundraising by formula, emphasizing instead a strategic approach that requires every nonprofit organization to design its own uniquely well suited direct mail fundraising program — or none at all. $29.95

All five of Mal Warwick's books are available from Strathmoor Press. So are Mal's newsletter, *Successful Direct Mail & Telephone Fundraising*™, and a limited selection of books and videos by other top fundraising professionals.

There are three easy ways to obtain details about the full list of Strathmoor Press learning tools for fundraisers:

1. Call Strathmoor Press toll-free at 1-800-21-PRESS (1-800-217-7377). Ask for our latest catalog.

2. Fax a request for our catalog to Strathmoor Press at 1-510-843-0142. Send your complete mailing address, or attach your business card.

3. Write us at the following address:

Strathmoor Press

2550 Ninth Street, Suite 1040

Berkeley, CA 94710-2516

If you wish to order books

There is a shipping and handling charge of $3.00 per title.

All Strathmoor Press products are subject to California sales tax when shipped within California.

For information about discounts on bulk orders of this book — or any Strathmoor Press product — call us at 1-510-843-8888. ▶